Product Placement
in Hollywood Films

# Product Placement in Hollywood Films

## *A History*

KERRY SEGRAVE

McFarland & Company, Inc., Publishers
*Jefferson, North Carolina, and London*

LIBRARY OF CONGRESS CATALOGUING-IN-PUBLICATION DATA

Segrave, Kerry, 1944–
    Product placement in Hollywood films : a history / Kerry
Segrave.
        p.      cm.
    Includes bibliographical references and index.

    ISBN 0-7864-1904-0 (softcover : 50# alkaline paper)

    1.  Product placement in mass media—United States—
History.   2.  Motion pictures in advertising—United States—
History.   I.  Title.
HF6146.P78S44    2004
659.1—dc22                                      2004008626

British Library cataloguing data are available

Front cover: Paul Newman (*Pocket Money,* 1972) in a
product placement shot for the fast-food chain and
root beer company A&W

Manufactured in the United States of America

*McFarland & Company, Inc., Publishers*
    *Box 611, Jefferson, North Carolina 28640*
        *www.mcfarlandpub.com*

# Table of Contents

# Preface

This book looks at the history of the union between advertising and motion pictures, from the slide ads of the 1890s to the product placements of the early 2000s (excluded are trailers for coming attractions). The earliest cinema ads were one- or two-reel (10 to 20 minutes) ad shorts. Ads as we know them today (60 seconds or less in length) and product placement (defined here as the deliberate insertion into an entertainment film script of a product, its signage, a verbal mention of a product, and so on, for a consideration) barely existed in the silent film era.

Over time enthusiasm for cinema ads waxed and waned, as did the efforts to produce and place such material. Onscreen ads never amounted to much because strong opposition always existed, much of that from within the film industry itself. For various reasons Hollywood could not dominate the onscreen ad field and went out of its way to see that no outsiders would gain much of a foothold. As a result onscreen ads remained a marginal part of the U.S. cinema experience.

On the other hand, product placement has grown dramatically in the past 25 years. Initially it was regarded as a somewhat sleazy practice, always hidden, almost never admitted. Exhibitors relentlessly opposed the practice. However, by the end of the 1970s that opposition no longer existed, and product placement became a way of life for Hollywood movies.

Research for this book was conducted at the University of British Columbia, Simon Fraser University, and Vancouver Public Library, using various hard-copy and online databases, with the backfiles of *Variety* being especially useful.

# 1

# Motion Pictures as Business Boosters

## *The Silent Era to 1926*

All the world is keen for the movies, and the audience at a picture show is fair game for the American advertiser.
—Anonymous U.S. manufacturing executive, 1918

Advertising on the screen is a very serious problem. The exhibitor must, above all things, consider the rights of his patrons.
—Exhibitors' alliance, 1919

Can the moving picture we send abroad ... be made to help our trade?
Lewis Freeman, 1920

What are the motion pictures doing for industry?
—Julius Klein, 1926

One of the earliest forms of advertising to appear on theater screens was the slide ad. Although it never held more than a minor position in cinemas it was long lived and continued to appear onscreens right up to the present. An account written in 1929 reminisced about the pioneer days when movies cost a nickel (the nickelodeon era) and advertising appeared between entertainment reels. According to the account the audiences, waiting expectantly for the next episode of *The Perils of Pauline*, "were forced to sit quietly while colored slides advertising the dry goods store, the butcher shop and the ice cream parlor were thrown upon the screen."[1]

A Chicago shoe dealer whose customers came largely from the immediate neighborhood was said to have found that his most profitable form of advertising was slides exhibited in cinemas. In 1913, two theaters in the neighborhood gave five performances a day and attracted around 20,000 people each week. Those slides, which displayed only the "latest styles," were changed several times a month and the store manager declared he could trace increased store sales directly to those slides.[2]

Four separate food markets were set to open in New York City in September 1914. One at the Queensboro Bridge had 20 wagons and 108 pushcarts while one at the Manhattan Bridge contained 30 wagons and 208 pushcarts. Advertising for those markets included posters and slide announcements on the screens of 200 cinemas that were part of the Motion Picture Exhibitors Association.[3]

Reporter Darwin Teilhet, looking back from 1931, remarked that while advertising slides were run for a while in the silent era the "better class" houses reluctantly gave up the idea because of "heated audience protest."[4]

Slide ads became even more marginalized as the plush cinema houses, or palaces, replaced the lower-class nickelodeons and as the large cinema chains formed up—usually with a policy against running any slide ads. They never entirely disappeared, but typically they were screened only in second- and third-run neighborhood venues, and only in a minority of those. National advertisers hardly ever used slides, and on the rare occasion that they did (in the past and in the present) they never used them for a national advertising campaign. At most they would make an area or a regional buy of slide ads.

Advertisements of the type most familiar to people today—commercials running 60 seconds or less, as found on television and radio, were almost entirely absent in the silent movie era. Reportedly Alka-Seltzer began using such ads around 1922, but it would be the late 1930s before the minute-ad would start to become more prevalent.[5]

That type of ad was largely absent because of the nature of the motion picture industry. Mass consumption and advertising did not really hit their full stride until after the end of World War I. Prior to that time advertising was still developing and tended to concentrate on other media such as magazines and newspapers. Movies initially attracted a lower-class audience, and it was not until the movies showed they were here to stay and could attract a mass audience from all spectrums of society that advertising devoted more of its attention to this medium. Since entertainment films were themselves mostly brief, the short, one-minute ad did not develop. Through the mid 1910s most film programs consisted of a group of one or two reels (running time was roughly 10 minutes per reel) of entertainment pictures. In the first decade of the 1900s it was very common for entertainment films to run for only six or seven minutes, for example. As time passed, of course, movies got longer. Some national manufacturers did get involved with filmed ads from very early on but those few that did enter the field made one-reel ads, no different in length from many of the entertainment features the audience was seeing.

It was all started, according to one account, back in 1894 by the man who distributed Dewar's Scotch whiskey in America. One day as he walked along Broadway in New York City he noticed all the men standing in line to get into the peep shows that were the current rage in that city. Why not, he thought, run a peep show to advertise Dewar's?[6]

Films for advertising purposes in the season of 1895-1896 were made for Maillard's Chocolates, Dewar's Scotch whiskey (this was long before Dewar's became a Schenley product), Columbia Bicycles, Piel's Beer, and Hunter's Rye Whiskey. Maillard claimed its chocolate was prepared originally for Cardinal Richelieu and its ad showed the cardinal enjoying it in liquid form as hot chocolate. A banner in the background that ran the full width of the set exclaimed, "Maillard's Fine Chocolates." Dewar's commercial featured a Scot (in a kilt, plaid socks, and so on) having a drink of the product as he stood before a background of three paintings, each of a male. As he downed his drink the three men stepped out of their respective picture frames to join him. This commercial ended with all four characters performing a Highland fling. The ad short for Columbia Bicycles depicted a cycling race with the commercial angle achieved by the display of a large banner giving the company name, product price, and location of New York dealers. When the race finished two men hurried into the center of the course with another banner that stated, "Columbia Wins." Piel's Beer's ad explained that people with constitutions unable to withstand hard liquor could drink beer with no ill effects. Mass distribution of such commercials was not possible at that time and their exhibition was limited to New York. They were shown on the roof of the Pepper Building at Herald Square, a site that was later occupied by R. H. Macy & Company. Reportedly, they were very popular with people and it was that success that led to their downfall. Crowds lined up on sidewalks to get in and overflowed into the streets, creating a serious traffic problem. City fathers stepped in to declare that disturbances of that sort had to end and, said reporter Patricia Murray, "this particular type of commercial film presentation was banned."[7]

Other major manufacturers who produced ad films in the period around 1900 included Admiral Cigarettes, Pabst's Milwaukee Beer, Lever Brothers, and the Nestlé firm. Biograph (the U.S. film-producing studio) apparently briefly dabbled in this type of commercial product and made a small number of advertising films for, among others, Shredded Wheat Biscuits and Mellin's Baby Food, around 1903.[8]

After a brief period of activity advertisers seemed to lose interest in the medium. However, more and more they embraced film for other uses—industrial films for in-house consumption. Large concerns began to create their own movies—or commission outsiders to do it for them— to train their staffs, to explain and show new products to dealers, to motivate salespeople, and so forth. Usually these films were shown in house, or on the road at dealerships, for example. Rarely did the general public have any knowledge of these movies, or access to them. Occasionally, though, especially in later years, such films might be available to clubs and organizations such as Rotary or Lions, who could borrow them at no charge to fill some time at one of their gatherings. The successful use of the modern type of industrial movie began around 1909–1911 when it was pioneered by the National Cash Register Company and International Harvester Company, among others. In those earliest sponsored films produced in those years, Ford demonstrated the manufacture of the Model T; General Electric depicted the work-saving possibilities of home and farm electrification; and the National Association of Manufacturers (NAM—the industry's main lobby group) dealt in workplace safety. NAM abandoned the production of industrial films around 1916.[9]

Located in Providence, Rhode Island, the New England Butt Company (manufacturer of braiding and cable machines) used films in 1913 to increase its profits, all part of its "scientific management"—then a hot topic in management circles. A worker was filmed at his task with every movement recorded on the film, while a clock nearby recorded the time that was required.[10]

After a lull due to World War I, interest in, and use of, the industrial film picked up sharply in the 1920s. It was given credit for many accomplishments. A salesman for a U.S. mining machine manufacturer traveled throughout South America but could make no sales. But he was a stranger, his machinery unknown, and for obvious reasons he could not travel with his product. Then he hit upon the idea of showing his products in action in a movie, which he screened for mine operators. He began to make sales. On a 1920 trip through the Southern U.S. John O'Donnell, a clothing salesman for a Philadelphia firm, carried with him and showed to potential buyers a film of models wearing the latest styles. Workers in a large U.S. manufacturing plant were shown films at the noon hour on accident prevention in the factory. People of the State of Illinois were in part sold on a statewide plan for building hard-surfaced roads by a movie produced by the Illinois Highway Improvement Association; at the following election the bond issue to fund the roadwork passed by a large majority.[11]

Under the auspices of the Bureau of Research and Information of the National Retail Dry Goods Association, in the very early 1920s, arrangements were made for the showing of industrial films in retail stores. Those films were of an educational nature and were used to give employees a chance to become familiar with the processes of manufacture of the merchandise they were selling. Subjects of those movies included cotton goods, electrical appliances, fountain pens, hats, shoes, silks, silverware, soaps, and woolen goods. Over two years those films were estimated to have been screened in 250 stores before 100,000 employees, as well as in 26 schools and local associations.[12]

That industrial films were growing in stature and importance could be seen from the fact that in 1923 NAM established a national non-commercial motion picture distribution service to supply private and public exhibitors throughout the country with industrial process, educational, and "Americanization" films, although it no longer directly made such movies itself. It was a service designed to make such films easily available "to general non-theatrical and non-commercial public exhibitors throughout the country."[13]

Industrial films were becoming just as popular in Britain. Vickers had been producing such movies of itself since prior to World War I and was said to have a "large library" of topics by 1921; it even had its own small theater on site for screening purposes. One business film it displayed there in 1921 was called *Bristol*, which told the story of the manufacture of Fry's cocoa and chocolate. According to an account, at a later date *Bristol* was to be included in the program of 700 cinemas in all parts of Great Britain.[14]

Paralleling the development of the industrial film was the increasing prevalence of and belief in the idea that the motion picture could be a powerful tool in selling American goods—not just in the home market but anywhere and everywhere abroad that American movies screened (by the end of World War I U.S. films held a majority of screen time in most nations of the world). And that powerful selling ability was unintended, incidental. The purchasing urge came to people watching not ads but entertainment movies. Viewers became hooked on home interiors, fashions, and so forth displayed in the film. It led to the idea, very popular in the 1920s, that trade followed the film.

One of the earliest articles to touch on that, in combination with advertising shorts, was published at the end of 1918 in *Scientific American*. Discussing the rapidly expanding foreign markets for U.S. products in a post–World War I world, Lynn Meekins mentioned Chile and said that a lot of magazines and illustrated weeklies there showed the North American influence. Also, one of the members of the foreign sales department of a large U.S. manufacturing company was in a small UK city. One night he happened to go to a cinema where two of the many short reels he saw were ads. One was for a shoe and boot manufacturer and the other was for an auto maker. Impressed, he declared the experience convinced him of the value of the cinema screen as an advertising medium. "I had seen slides used for advertising purposes but they were generally rather crude and didn't leave a lasting impression," he explained. Still, he saw a need for improvement: "The industrial motion pictures that had come to my notice were entirely too heavy, seeming to absorb too much of the mechanical features of the manufacturing process and lacking completely the necessary human interest to make them effective."[15]

Meekins' executive then wondered how his company (and others) could advertise to the average, say, Peruvian—a majority of whom could not read. "All the world is keen for the movies, and the audience at a picture show is fair game for the American advertiser," he concluded. "But he shouldn't take advantage of it. The people are there to be entertained, and the pictures showing his goods should be as full of life and originality as possible." This article introduced the idea that the ad film should be entertaining—that it should not be an obvious industrial film. One-minute ads (hereafter called "trailers" to distinguish them from one-reel ad shorts that, if they did not run a full 10 minutes, usually came close to that mark) were essentially non-existent in this period. Since the ad shorts had the same running time as many of the entertainment films screened on the same program, why not make the ad short look like an entertainment movie?[16]

A UK counterpart to NAM was the powerful Federation of British Industries, formed in 1916. By the end of the war it wanted to engage in much more publicity to promote and help British manufacturers to exploit foreign markets. Generally, it wanted to become involved in more international expositions and organized newspaper and periodical advertising and to develop "a fuller use of the moving picture film." The Federation had recently issued a pamphlet titled "Round the World by the Film." One reason for the attention to the film medium was the sky-rocketing attendance at cinemas, which had made moviegoing "an almost universal habit." In Great Britain film houses drew 500 million patrons a year—12 times the population. In its pamphlet the Federation concluded that through the enterprise of the American cinema trade the United States was by far the best advertised nation in the world: "Every day millions of people all over the globe have before their eyes American scenery, American heroes and heroines, American industrial and social backgrounds, offices, factories, farms and households, and American taste in all manner of articles of trade." At the time the Federation was in the process of polling its members for suggestions on how to use motion pictures to the advantage of British industry.[17]

Lewis Freeman wrote a lengthy article in 1920 more clearly focused on how the cinema had successfully advertised American goods in foreign lands. It was published in the widely circulated *Saturday Evening Post*. One example he gave was in Java, where many peasants had gathered to watch a U.S. movie but displayed little interest in the picture until there was a scene wherein the heroine used a sewing machine. Then the entire audience became interested because every household in Java had a sewing machine—although not a good electric one as shown in the film. However, in this case the peasants of course could not afford to buy such a machine. A Dutch planter in Java told Freeman he thought U.S. exporters had not taken advantage of the opportunities opened to it by the spread of American movies to the screens of the world, and the dominance of those screens. Freeman clarified that he was referring only to entertainment movies, "in which the display of some article of possible foreign export is quite incidental to the development of the plot. These are, of course, quite distinct from straight advertising and demonstration films, which both American and European manufacturers have sent abroad for a number of years to popularize and introduce certain of their articles of export."[18]

Several U.S. consuls stationed in South and East Africa told Freeman that the showing of certain comedy films set off a lively inquiry among the locals for flexible rubber hammers and daggers. In Muscat, Baghdad, Damascus, and other Middle East locales, the showing of American westerns invariably was followed by demand from Arabs for U.S. saddles. The same thing happened in Australia and Argentina; in both of those places it was "considered a mark of distinction that the saddle shall be an imported one rather than a cheap local imitation." After he gave those, and a few other, "humorous" examples, Freeman moved on to examples "with the class of people who count." A South African railway manager used an extremely compact, folding-metal combination washbasin and table on his railroad that he tracked down and ordered after seeing it in a sleeper car scene in a U.S. film. In Sudan a railroad official showed Freeman water tanks he had acquired after seeing them in an American picture. The Calcutta Tramway Corporation used passenger cars seen in an American movie (the design was copied— that is, stolen, after a second and private showing of the movie was arranged). In a barber shop in Hobart, Tasmania, the reporter found a shop full of American fittings; the barber tracked them down and ordered them after seeing them in a movie. Many lumber mills in southern Chile used a particular type of band saw in their mills, reportedly after one mill operator saw it at the cinema. Freeman gave many other examples before he declared it was hardly necessary to give any more in order "to prove the incalculable help—direct and indirect—American foreign trade has derived from the fact that well over nine-tenths of the goods shown on the movie signboards of the world are of Yankee manufacture."[19]

All of that led Freeman to wonder and to speculate whether the movie signboard could be made even more helpful in the future than it had been in the past. He noted that such advertising as had been done in that way up to that point had been "absolutely accidental—incidental to the photo play itself." There was not a single instance, he wrote, where he cold find evidence that the machine or item that led to buying behavior had been deliberately inserted into the film to give it publicity. "The intriguing speculation is—can this be done? Can the moving picture we send abroad, like every newspaper and magazine, be made to help our trade?" wondered Freeman. Of course he was speculating about product placement long before it had that name and long before it was practiced to any degree.[20]

NAM was active around this time in trying to exploit any advantage the movies offered its members. Under its auspices a conference of manufacturers, motion picture producers, and film distributors was held in 1922. That gathering was told that industrial films had become the strongest factor in developing the sale and use of American goods in foreign countries, especially non–English-speaking ones. Delivering that message was Dr. Julius Klein, chief of the Bureau of Foreign and Domestic Commerce of the U.S. Department of Commerce. He said that American goods heretofore little known in foreign countries were finding a large and ready market through the advertising afforded by industrial motion pictures.[21]

A few days later Klein discussed both the industrial film and the entertainment film in the context of trade and boosting sales. Klein declared that motion pictures were the "latest form of silent salesmen, not so much perhaps for the goods of some individual firm as for classes and kinds of goods as a whole." He added, "While the industrial film is the essential medium through which these results are being accomplished, it is nevertheless well worth while to consider first for a moment the part which the entertainment film plays along these same lines." In spite of (or perhaps because of) the fact that there was no conscious "trade propaganda" in the entertainment picture, the entertainment film, thought Klein, was "proving a considerable force in helping to arouse on the part of the buying public a desire for the many types of products most commonly shown on the screen."[22]

An "obvious" example Klein cited were the "fashion show" scenes exhibiting the latest styles on living models "but forming an integral part of the picture. It has been used in at least a dozen of the most popular films during the past year—shown to millions of women the world over." He felt such pictures were especially effective in country towns and that they played an important part in stimulating interest in clothes and thus in an indirect way were of marked assistance to the clothing industry. Exactly the same process was at work to a greater or lesser degree along many other lines, he argued. Besides women's dress, influenced by the movies were men's wear, furniture of all kinds, and a variety of other products that were "particularly aided through their use in motion picture scenes." Klein said the best evidence to support his argument—the unconscious role that the entertainment movie played in selling goods—came from abroad. According to the commercial attaché of the U.S. Department of Commerce in Rio de Janeiro, for example, the use of the California-style bungalow and the outdoor swimming pool in Brazil "was really brought about through the showing of these on the screen." Recent styles both in clothes and shoes throughout most of the Near East region were said to have been set by American movie stars. Incidents like those and many others, said Klein, had given rise to the slogan "Trade follows the film." He admitted the influence of the entertainment film as an advertising force was indirect and that it was through the industrial film that the direct suggestion was made to buy the product of one firm or group of firms.[23]

Frank Tichenor, president of the Eastern Film Corporation, observed in 1926 how pervasive the idea that trade followed the film had become. He noted that the use of American automobiles in U.S. films with wide foreign distribution had so infuriated European car makers that "they have gone to very great pains to induce exhibitors to cut film stories and even obliterate names and trademarks from some motion pictures."[24]

Another development at the same time gave further evidence of the power of motion pictures to sell—the practice of stars endorsing products off screen, in other media. By 1919 that system was well entrenched, with the studios themselves more and more in charge of the endorsement system. In earlier times a star was approached to endorse a product and negotiated the best deal he could—keeping all the proceeds for himself. As the practice grew the studios cut themselves in for their share by making it a condition in an actor's contract that no outside endorsements be undertaken without the approval of the studio. For example, in earlier times an actor might get a number of gowns for free and in return would allow the dress maker to show photos of her in those dresses, on its premises and in its advertising material. Once the studios began to dominate the endorsements, in the above example, the dress maker would find itself having to mention the star's forthcoming film in its ads. Merchandising tie-ins were also well in place by the end of World War I. For example, Charlie Chaplin drew a "considerable royalty" from lending his name to Chaplin statues, Chaplin dolls, and a host of similar items.[25]

Another method tried in the 1920s silent era to link movies and advertising was short lived and bizarre. Donald J. DeLancey, Ralph C. Thayer, and Harry Stewart had a scheme whereby exhibitors would be paid $1 per seat per year for the lease of their cinema chair seat backs for advertising purposes. Details of the plan came out in a court claim against the three men for money owed to Hal Hodes. He claimed he had signed up cinemas with a total of 225,323 seats but had not been paid the commission due him by the defendants. Their plan involved placing luminous ads on those seat backs. One reason Hodes had not been paid was that the defendants did not have national advertisers lined up, as they had alleged.[26]

By the end of the war motion pictures were getting more and more notice from manufacturers as a medium that could be used in various ways to increase the sales of their goods. The industrial feature of one reel or so became the most popular way to try and use movies. Some of those industrial movies were presented in the old way as obvious industrial films while others, to a greater or lesser extent, tried to disguise themselves as entertainment films. A high-ranking government official such as Julius Klein liked both types and had words of praise for each as potential selling tools. One of the earlier examples of the masquerading industrials was the 1913 release *The Family Jar* in which Mrs. Cheltenham had a difficult time trying to please her dyspeptic husband until she served him the Pure Food product Beech-Nut Bacon. Apparently the film showed how the bacon was prepared in compliance with all the standards of cleanliness. The producer of the film was, of course, the Beech-Nut firm, which was following the kind of advice then just starting to be found in the early journals—that an advertiser's message should be contained in "moralizing narrative stories that could be shown as shorts in theaters." This film was clearly an ad for Beech-Nut but was also clearly different in style from the early ads for Columbia Bicycles or Maillard's Chocolates.[27]

On the other hand an example of the old-style industrial picture was one produced in 1914 for the Savings Bank Section of the American Bankers' Association. Its film featured the advantages of the school savings bank for children and the savings bank and loan association for their parents. Produced at a cost of $10,000, the American Bankers' Association expected its film would eventually be exhibited to an audience of six to seven million people.[28]

Hollywood's major producers had an on-again, off-again relationship with the production of these ad films. Although in a way they were the most logical companies to produce industrial pictures—with their state-of-the-art equipment, technical expertise, and so on—they played only a minor role. As mentioned, Biograph made a few around 1903. In 1918 Universal produced *The Yanks Are Coming*, which was described as "made by the Universal people for the Wright-Dayton Co. primarily to show the accomplishments in their aeroplane plant."[29]

Hollywood film studios did make an effort in 1919 to try and convince advertising executives generally on the value of appealing to the public through the screen. At a convention of the Associated Advertising Clubs they showed a film to 17,000 ad delegates, stating that the motion picture, as a means of publicity, was something that should not be overlooked.[30]

Keeping Hollywood in the background as only a minor player was the often fierce resistance thrown up against advertising on the screens. December, 1919, saw the formation of an organization of "prominent" film exhibitors for the sole purpose of protecting U.S. exhibitors from screening news films and industrial "features" (shorts) containing advertising matter. Those exhibitors grumbled that since the inception of the picture business "millions of dollars" had been accrued by manufacturers exploiting commercial products on the screens of theatre owners while the exhibitors received not so much as a cent of that money.[31]

The Committee on Organization for Protection of the Screen (Sydney S. Cohen was named temporary chairman) placed an almost full-page ad in the trade journal *Variety* in December 1919, that was addressed to the motion picture theatre owners of America. In part the ad said, "Advertising on the screen is a very serious problem. The exhibitor must, above all things, consider the rights of his patrons. No doubt there are pictures in which the advertising and the entertainment value are inseparably bound up. No other kind of picture, under this plan, will be shown on his screen, because no picture will be offered until it has been passed by a supervising committee composed of exhibitors." In addition to pre-screening films for advertising content, this group stated that all money derived from advertising in the movies shown in each state would go to the exhibitor organization in each state for use as they saw fit. However, they gave no details on how they planned to accomplish that task. That ad was signed by more than a dozen exhibitor groups, including: the Motion Picture Exhibitors' League of New York State, Michigan Exhibitors' Association, Los Angeles Theatre Owners' Association, Northwest Exhibitors Circuit (Washington, Oregon, Montana, and Idaho), and the Illinois Exhibitors' Alliance.[32]

A few weeks later an unnamed *Variety* columnist noted that one picture concern in particular was making more and more money out of the commercial film. He defined it as the type of picture that usually shows a process of manufacture in which "the advertising nature of the showing is cleverly kept in the background though it cannot be concealed." A certain "world-famous manufacturer" was said to be making these ad shorts and then renting them to exhibitors for a "ridiculously small price." Despite the savings exhibitors, the columnist wrote, were beginning to complain about that sort of thing because if they screened that film, "They want their share of the profits."[33]

Hollywood film director Marshall Neilan issued a protest in 1920 to producers against the practice of inserting advertising in films and collecting from both ends—from the national advertiser who commissioned the making of the film and from the exhibitor that screened it. Neilan grumbled that he knew of cases where movies had been fully paid for by advertisers and then "rentals were demanded and obtained by exhibitors." A journalist gave his own example in which a large producing-distributing film concern gave a showing of a so-called safety device at one of New York's large cinemas that was "nothing less than a campaign to advertise an invention controlled by a large corporation." Reportedly, some exhibitors were getting wise to the practice and were then demanding payment for screening these ad shorts, instead of paying rentals for such items.[34]

With Hollywood virtually uninvolved in the production of industrial films, manufacturers sometimes produced them themselves or commissioned specialized producers who turned out advertising films only— that is, they did not produce any entertainment films. Either way distribution was a problem. Specialized distribution agencies rose up to fill that gap. One such was the Bureau of Commercial Economies, which claimed to have some 55 million feet of film in circulation in the world in 1921. Executive director Francis Holley described the films his company handled as ones designed to help and to teach and ones that dealt with topics such as travel, industry, agriculture, public health, and science. Speaking of the advertising value versus the publicity value of the screen Holley said that in order to have publicity value a film had to display "some degree of modesty and put the message over with adroitness and reservation. The story must be interesting, holding the audiences sympathetic and leaving a theme of thought and food for reflection as the audience quits the theater." Holley remarked that advertising men did not realize the "combative" spirit that was aroused "when an audience which has paid to be amused finds its dignity slighted and its feelings outraged by being forced to gaze for several minutes at some fool picture introducing a patent spark plug through the medium of the tea party in an alleged drama."[35]

Another example of an ad short masquerading as an entertainment film was a 1921 item produced for the Maxwell Motor Corporation (an early U.S. auto maker). An account described it as an "interesting experiment" in advertising in which the picture clearly advertised the Maxwell auto without appearing to be an ad. Reportedly the film told a "thrilling story, and the cloven hoof of advertisement is so deftly concealed that it can hardly offend anyone." That movie was available to exhibitors in the ordinary way for inclusion in their program. In the film the heroine was kidnapped by the bad guys and taken to a remote stronghold in the heart of a rocky and precipitous area. The bad guys got there on horseback (there were no roads or tracks near the hideout). Although the hero had no horse he did have a car—a Maxwell. Much of the film was taken up with the car performing miraculously as it got in and out of that rugged territory, going through rivers, thick undergrowth, and so on. "If all film advertisement is to be as clever as this, there should be very little doubt of its efficacy," concluded the account.[36]

Over in England the ad short was also making headway despite the fact the London-based Cinematograph Exhibitors' Association reportedly looked with disfavor upon any attempt to introduce advertising matter into films. "Advertising story films are already being made," said a reporter. In some cases regular UK producers and studios were involved in their production as were actors looking for extra money. Ideal Studios was then turning out an ad short to advertise a popular brand of relish. The department store Harrods was reported to be planning to make a series of such pictures, all of which "will be played by first-class artists, and the cinemas showing them will be paid more than they themselves would pay for an ordinary short feature."[37]

Frank Tichenor, president of Eastern Film Corporation, had been making films for advertising purposes, he said, since 1910. Prior to that he produced ordinary entertainment movies. In 1924 the National Fur Association (the industry's major trade group) called him in as a consultant, as the industry was then in a serious slump. He decided to make two reels (2,000 feet of film) on furs in the usual fashion format of models walking up and down modeling fur apparel. According to him, "The result was such an advertising picture as was quickly seized on by exhibitors, because of its sheer beauty and appeal to women's hearts, as an entertainment picture." Tichenor added that the demand for it "not as an advertising picture but as an exhibition picture" became so great he could barely keep up with it. Reportedly the movie played in Manhattan in one of Broadway's first-run houses for three weeks. He claimed that a big sales increase for furs from all over the country could be directly traced to that film, although he gave no details. "The picture at no point mentioned a fur store or dealer and the exhibiting theatres, therefore, were not 'advertising' anything, according to the old idea of what constitutes advertising," Tichenor argued. "Its entertainment value was so high that the exhibitors paid good prices for the privilege of showing it."[38]

Product placement (defined as the deliberate insertion into the script of an entertainment film of a product, brand name, signage, verbal mention, and so on, for consideration) was only rarely mentioned in this period. However, it did exist, albeit in a very minor way. One reason for that was the brief length of entertainment films themselves. Through World War I, roughly, most of what an audience saw at the cinema were one- and two-reel pictures. It made little sense for an advertiser to try and place a plug in one of those entertainment films when he could just as easily commission a one-reel ad short displaying his product exactly

as he wished. Although in that case, of course, the advertiser ran the risk
the exhibitors would recognize it for the disguised ad that it was and that
most would refuse to handle it. However, if that happened the advertiser
still had a couple of cards to play. He could offer his exposed ad short
to the exhibitor for nothing (saving the cinema owner the cost of renting one entertainment film). If that failed the advertiser might even offer
to pay the exhibitor to screen it. In any case, product placement probably was viewed as a very distant second choice (to the ad short) by film-
oriented advertisers of the period.

Philip A. Fuss was assistant sales manager of Knickerbocker Broadcasting Company of New York City in 1935. That year he wrote a letter
to the *New York Times* about a controversy then under discussion about
product placement. Fuss recalled three instances from his own past advertising experiences. The first took place around 1915 when he was advertising manager for the Thomas G. Plant Company in Boston; the second
occurred around 1922 when he was with the Edison Phonograph concern; the third happened in 1925 when he was with yet another company. In each case, he said, he was approached through the mail by
motion picture producers offering to feature the name of the product he
was advertising in a feature film, and asking a stated fee. Fuss, in 1935,
could not recall more specific details. Regarding the offer when he was
with Edison, Fuss received the actual script in the mail and a reading of
it indicated Edison Phonograph would be "sufficiently featured by both
name and illustration of the various models." Fuss declined all such
offers.[39]

According to a 1919 account the U.S. federal government contemplated a film-related move to foster the sealskin industry (then in an over-
supply situation) to the extent of making that fur the fashionable thing
for the following winter. They had reportedly retained a "propagandist"
to instill the desire for sealskin garments in "the feminine mind." One
effort was to be done with the aid of film stars. Ten $4,000 sealskin coats
were to be distributed among an equal number of Hollywood stars to be
worn in their movies and also to be worn by them out and about in the
streets, "to sow the seed" of desire amongst the populace. The reason
the government wanted a bigger market was the large number of seal-
skins secured through a recent, large kill off Alaska—said to have been
necessary to control the seal population. There was no evidence this idea
ever went beyond the planning stage.[40]

Carrying product placement a little farther was the so-called Irene
Castle Fashion Show that was being sold to exhibitors in 1922 in conjunction with the movie *Slim Shoulders*, in which Castle starred. Orga-
nizers of the fashion show had three complete show units on the road
playing cinemas. Each show had six models, a couple of dancers, and a

singer; the exhibitor was charged whatever could be obtained. One New Jersey exhibitor said he did not believe the fashion show was worth the asking price but thought he would have one anyway because he would receive the cooperation of his local department store. It would furnish the models and gowns and, in addition, it would buy space in the local newspapers advertising the theatre and the show. Those live models, of course, modeled the clothes that Castle wore in the picture.[41]

Although details are absent it has been reported that in the 1920s cigarette manufacturers encouraged actors and actresses to smoke in films, on the assumption that their example would influence consumers and increase smoking rates. Brands of individual cigarettes were almost never visible; this form of product placement was an example of attempting to stimulate sales for a class of goods as compared to an individual brand. If it worked then, of course, all brands stood to benefit.[42]

As the silent movie era came to an end advertising was only a very minor part of the motion picture industry. Product placement and onscreen ads as we think of ads today (running one minute or so in length and openly and obviously an advertisement) were close to nonexistent. What advertising that did exist was mainly the one-reel ad shorts (generally running from a few minutes in length up to 10 minutes). More and more those films were moving away from being direct ads to a more indirect approach as they accepted an increasing conventional wisdom that these movies should tell a story and only sell indirectly. More and more these films imitated and tried to pass themselves off as ordinary entertainment films. Such items were a very tiny part of the industrial film business with most of those movies strictly for in-house use or specialized audiences. Those ads that appeared in cinemas, in whatever form, tended to draw a hostile reaction, especially from exhibitors who were ever on the lookout for such items. Hollywood studios were little involved in the minor amount of advertising that did involve the movies. There wasn't much money in it and they did not want to antagonize the exhibitors. Also, Hollywood was busy into the 1920s rationalizing itself with the Hollywood cartel (the major production studios—Warner Bros., United Artists, MGM, Universal, 20th Century–Fox, Columbia, Paramount, RKO, and, much later, Disney), who in 1922 officially formed the Motion Picture Producers and Distributors of America (MPPDA— later the Motion Picture Association of America, MPAA [from 1945], and later still the Motion Picture Association, MPA [from 2000]).

As the motion picture industry grew by leaps and bounds more people began to look to the industry as a possible medium to exploit for commercial purposes. Through the 1920s evidence began to mount, albeit mostly anecdotal, that even ordinary entertainment films had a powerful impact on people in getting them to buy certain products and adopt certain styles, even though no direct advertising effect was intended. Films were seen as a powerful weapon to be used abroad to sell American goods and items that were featured in the movies. No less an authority than the U.S. Department of Commerce praised movies—both entertainment and advertising films—as potent weapons to be used in an expected post–World War I trade war as America battled the United Kingdom and other nations for world markets and trade domination. And America had an advantage since its movies held a majority of screen time in almost all nations of the world. Added to that background was the arrival of the talkies in 1927, with the result that films could do so much more. It all combined to set off a period of intense interest and activity in joining advertising to motion pictures—a period that lasted until around 1932.

# 2

# The Talkies Arrive,
# Commercially Speaking
## *1927–1932*

[The motion picture] is the greatest agency for promoting the sales of American-made products throughout the world.
—Will Hays, MPPDA head, 1929

[It is] a serious mistake to figure that because the radio broadcasts contain advertising it is all right for the movies to do it.
—Carl Laemmle, Universal head, 1931

Screen advertising is unfair to our audiences. An advertisement on the screen forces itself upon the spectator. He cannot escape it, yet he has paid his admittance price for entertainment alone.
—Nicholas Schenck, MGM head, 1931

As sound films debuted many accounts printed a rosy, very exaggerated picture of the effect it would have on advertising in the movies. One early 1928 account told of how manufacturers of nationally advertised commodities had already made approaches to the motion picture industry since they saw the talkies looming up as a big commercial advertising medium of the near future. Speculation in this report was that if producers of talking-movie equipment who also operated theater chains (such as Fox) accepted commercial advertising shorts, they might be in a position to receive almost as much revenue from that source as from admission receipts. Since the Depression struck not long after the arrival of the talkies, the cost to theaters of converting to sound (many had not done so by the time of the economic crash) became more onerous and it was argued by this reporter that the advertising aspect of films figured to make equipment installation profitable for cinema owners since revenue from advertising was expected to exceed $10 million a year as soon as enough theaters were sound equipped. It was even speculated that advertisers would try and line up stars to endorse their products, such as cigarettes, for those predicted advertising short films.[1]

Western Electric (a major supplier of cinema talkie equipment) also saw a great future for industrial films, commercial and educational. With regard to educational films Western predicted that people in all countries would be exposed to the great minds of the world, who would be filmed on their topic with those films being screened all over the planet. The same kinds of things were predicted with the advent of radio, television, cable TV, and so forth. Executives of the greatest U.S. industrial concerns were said to be holding meetings with Western Electric on the possible uses of talking pictures, an area the electrical concern felt to be "unlimited." This company never did get involved to any extent in the production of industrial movies.[2]

In May 1929 an account reported that William Wrigley Jr. (the chewing gum magnate) and a group of other users of national advertising on a similarly large scale were prepared to spend from $5 million to $10 million in the production of talking advertising shorts. Those items were to be distributed to exhibitors, both chains and independents, free of charge. When the interested industrialists first broached the subject to various film producers the first proposal was that the advertisers would pay fully all the costs of production if the producers would undertake to distribute the output. Each picture would carry the tag line in the credits "Presented through the courtesy of...." However, those producer-distributors (not named but presumably some or all of the Hollywood cartel members—known simply as "the majors") turned the proposal down. Then the industrialists decided not only to produce at their own cost, but also to distribute. To that end it was understood that advertising agencies handling the accounts of those manufacturers had been submitting a plan to theater chains and to independent cinema owners asking if they would exhibit talking shorts, given at no cost, carrying the tag line of the advertiser who paid for the production. Those potential advertisers wanted to go after big-name talent for their ad films since they were cognizant of the supposed potent effect of such commercials on the radio. Movies were an even more enticing medium for such ads because the customers could not turn them off. Advertisers, in estimating costs, saw a possibly greater return with talkies from a smaller investment than on radio. With radio they paid performers $2,000 or $3,000 for an hour over the air, with the number of listeners problematic (ratings and audience number polling did not then exist). It would be possible, they felt, to obtain the services of the same artist for a talking short for very little more and to have the feature produced in a day at a cost probably equaling that charged for radio airtime. And the motion picture audience figures were accurately tabulated and had been so for some time. Reportedly the inspiration for this scheme on the part of Wrigley and company was the pioneering talkie Studebaker ad (see below).[3]

"Trade follows the film" was a concept kept alive in this period, especially by Will H. Hays, head of the MPPDA, the powerful lobby group for the Hollywood cartel. In a 1929 address on the topic of "Motion Pictures and Business" before the New York Board of Trade, he declared that the motion picture "is the greatest existing agency for promoting the sales of American-made products throughout the world." Hays added that, according to the U.S. Department of Commerce, every foot of film exported brought a return of $1 in stimulated trade, an estimate he personally felt to be conservative. People seeing American products or styles in pictures demanded their local merchants stock those products for them, he stated, citing an automobile dealer in an interior town in Brazil who reported his sales of an American-made car had increased from four or five cars a month to four or five a day from motion picture exposure. Architects in Argentina were seeking a means of adapting the Hollywood bungalow housing type for use in that country, and sewing machines had been introduced into Smyrna and "baths into Macedonia" as a result of the influence of U.S. motion pictures, Hays added.[4]

In a 1930 radio address over a coast-to-coast network, as part of a business series, Hays gave his industry an even greater importance as he lauded the medium for its trade stimulus effect. The motion picture industry, he said, had assisted American business by creating a demand for the "comforts and conveniences available for all who will work and save." Both at home and abroad the movies had been responsible for an increased demand for American manufactured products and upon that increased demand depended "the future prosperity" of the United States. Hays added that movies performed a service for American business that was greater than the millions spent by the motion picture industry in its direct purchases, on its payroll, and so on. According to the cartel chief 115 million people attended the cinema weekly in the U.S., in a total of 22,000 theaters.[5]

Again the power (real or perceived) of the movies and its players to sell products could be seen in the off-screen endorsement industry. Requests to studios and to their actors to endorse items such as cigarettes and soap were said to have reached such a high level by the end of 1928 that some were refusing to do any more deals. Studios were reported to have received hundreds of letters a week with such requests, from firms big and small.[6]

After considering the matter for years the Hays office (as the Hollywood cartel's MPPDA organization was often called) issued a decree in the fall of 1931 banning all of its long-term contract people (actors tied to their studios by contracts up to seven years in length) from lending their names, photographs, and so on, to endorse the advertising of commercial products. The rationale for that decree was that the endorsement had become far too common and resulted in a drop in the box-office draw of high-caliber screen names. Also, said the decree, "In many instances the nature of such advertising is undignified and tends to discredit the motion picture industry as a whole as well as those individuals whose names are used." One exception was to allow endorsements for charitable purposes, but they had to be first approved on a case-by-case basis by the MPPDA's executive committee.[7]

Yet less than four months later it was reported the Hays office ban had not stopped the practice of endorsements. Practically all the studios were said to have stars lined up for coming exposure on radio advertising tie-ups. Lucky Strike, Lux, Coca-Cola, and others had met little resistance in getting big names from studios because of the widespread publicity offered—studios found it hard to refuse and thus ignored the decree. Recent radio appearances by stars such as Bebe Daniels, Marie Dressler, Jeanette MacDonald, Jack Oakie, and Clark Gable on General Motors radio time had also helped to weaken the Hays edict. Auto manufacturer Studebaker was then said to be visiting the studios to sign up names in connection with an advertising campaign for its cars.[8]

As national manufacturers worked on increasing advertising in cinemas they also experimented with using their ad films in other venues. In 1929 Syracuse, New York, cinema operators were unhappy with the presentation of the picture *Free All-Star Movietonemotor Show Champions*. Syracuse was the first town to get the film (free to the public) exploiting the Studebaker automobile. After Syracuse, the movie went on the road, playing a regular itinerary. In that New York State city the Studebaker showrooms had been transformed into a theatre for the film's three-day stand. Screenings were continuous every day from 11 A.M. to 11 P.M. with the film 45 minutes in length. Featured in various variety acts in Studebaker's film was an all-star cast that included Flo Ziegfeld and his Follies beauties, Knute Rockne and his Notre Dame football stars, Eva Le Gallienne, Al Jenkins, Ralph Hepburn, Ann Pennington, the Howard Sisters, and a Vogue Fashion Show. Cinema exhibitors complained about, among other things, the fact the show was permitted to purchase space in the amusement section of the daily papers (where cinema ads appeared). However, in the Sunday editions copy for the Studebaker ad film was only given space in the automobile sections, or on a run-of-the-paper basis, not in the amusement sections—perhaps as a result of the pressure brought to bear by exhibitors.[9]

Paul G. Hoffman, Studebaker vice president, observed that his firm was one of the early users of the talkies as a tool of selling. He liked the idea of using a motion picture because it hit two senses (the eye and the ear) at once. When a commercial talkie was first proposed to Studebaker, said Hoffman, there were only 1,000 cinemas out of a U.S. total of 20,000 that were wired for sound pictures. Studebaker officials felt the talkie had sufficient novelty status for countless numbers in medium-sized cities and small towns to insure healthy audiences, if they could get the film to them. Another aspect of the talkie that appealed to Hoffman was its image of modernism and to have that image associated with his product and the publicity value of being the first to use talkies for commercial purposes. Hoffman made no mention of whether or not Studebaker made any attempt to screen the film in regular theaters. Either that option was not considered or distributors refused to handle it. At first Studebaker showed the movie at auto shows. Then it was sent out to dealers (all screenings were held at dealer showrooms or, if they were not available or adequate, at a rented hall in the town). Eight separate units went on the road simultaneously and were booked in the same manner as for a legitimate road show. Each unit consisted of an advance man, an operator, a print of the film, and all the necessary equipment. Newspaper advertising, handbills, invitations, and radio announcements were arranged by the advance man, who traveled from three to five days ahead of the operator. When Hoffman was asked if he could cite definite sales results from the use of the talkie ad film the executive skirted the issue by saying "Yes and no. Selling deals too much in intangibles." According to Hoffman, during a period of 10 weeks the film was screened 1,427 times in 220 cities before an audience of over 300,000 people. From Studebaker's perspective, "The talkie is but one of the mechanisms which is available to us in our task of perfecting mass selling."[10]

A different account presented similar attendance figures—250 per showing—for the Studebaker film but implied it was low and likely much smaller than Studebaker had hoped for. Speculation here was that the daily newspaper-invited public was turned off and away by having a suspicion raised that some type of hard-sell live sales talk would be delivered in conjunction with the free film. Apparently the general public had clued in to the fact that the film they were being invited to see was all too obviously an ad. In any event, the Studebaker film was said to have been the inspiration for the aforementioned proposals and examination of the film advertising issue by William Wrigley Jr. and other industrialists.[11]

Along a similar vein, in 1931, a committee representing the sales promotion division of the National Retail Dry Goods Association announced a program for the use of talkies in department stores. The plan was to cooperate with manufacturers, whose products were sold through department stores, in the making of a series of sponsored films, each dealing with a definite line of merchandise. Those department stores accepting those ad films would receive them without charge for showing to the general public. A proposed series for the first year envisioned a total of 26 films each covering a different subject and each screened in the stores for a two-week period. Nothing came of this plan.[12]

Another unorthodox method had advertisers using the theater in a live advertising manner and in a way that was not directly connected with the film being exhibited. Such methods tried to take advantage of the fact that the movies were hugely poplar and attracted enormous crowds. Beginning in October 1929 the audience lounging room of the Brooklyn Paramount was turned into the site of an "industrial exposition" under the auspices of the Brooklyn Chamber of Commerce. Under this program, engineered by the Brooklyn Paramount publicity manager Lou Goldberg and expected to last for 52 weeks, the cinema would gain a net minimum value in newspaper advertising alone of $1,250 weekly for each of those 52 weeks, with thousands more dollars to be spent on advertising in trade papers and through other means of exploitation. The tie-up called for a different Brooklyn mercantile establishment to hold an exposition in the theatre each week. To do that, the merchant had to guarantee the cinema to spend that minimum $1,250 a week in advertising the exposition at the theatre and also advertising the picture being screened. At that time Goldberg claimed there were 12 merchants lined up for a week each, with the Chamber of Commerce charged with procuring the others, as it had done for the first dozen.[13]

The first firm to hold one of those industrial expositions was scheduled to be the Bohack Grocery Stores, which owned and operated around 500 stores in Brooklyn and Long Island. Bohack, besides the newspaper ads, promised to get out a total of 270,000 circulars, to be distributed from each of its stores, advertising both the exposition as well as the movie playing at the time. Patrons entering the cinema during Bohack's week were to receive a shopping bag with a large ticket roll that entitled them to a free sample of each of the grocery items displayed; a ticket was torn off the roll each time the patron took a sample. A patron who collected a sample of each item on display would, reportedly, receive $4 worth of free groceries. The Brooklyn Chamber of Commerce had been on friendly terms with the Publix theater chain (owned by Hollywood major Paramount) since the Brooklyn Paramount had opened. It admitted the house, which played to about 175,000 people per week, helped to keep a lot of money in Brooklyn, since it was located in the heart of the shopping district. All deals went through the Chamber of Commerce, remarked a report, with "the Publix people remaining in the background."[14]

Another Publix tie-up was between the cinema chain and the Sid Blumenthal Company, one of the largest manufacturers of velvet. It was expected to net the Publix unit, "Velvet Revue," about $300,000 worth of free advertising. Blumenthal intended to spend $100,000 in advertising the unit in newspapers and posters, including advertising of the feature film being screened. *Velvet Revue* (a live, variety-style show that played a cinema along with the film—it was still fairly common at that time for a cinema program to contain both a movie and a live show) had 35 weeks of Publix time booked, with Blumenthal advertising the unit every week in each of the different towns it played. Also, Blumenthal requested jobbers and retailers in the various towns to spend in total twice the amount (another $200,000 on their parts) Blumenthal had committed to draw attention to the unit. It was hoped by Blumenthal that the virtues of velvet would be presented to millions of people. Hopes were that the unit would play before 25 million people with the attention of another 50 million being caught by the campaign. The advertising component was fairly subtle because during the time the *Velvet Revue* played a cinema there was no credit given to the advertisers, neither by signage, nor verbally, nor onscreen in any fashion. *Velvet Revue* was an ordinary variety stage show no different from any others, with the sole exception that settings and costumes were all made entirely of velvet.[15]

One unorthodox campaign involved the patrons of around 800 cinemas in the Philadelphia area that had a weekly attendance of some five million people. In 1932 they were subjected to the start of a campaign to stimulate buying, put money into circulation, and relieve unemployment. Those patrons were "bombarded" with the campaign's slogan on the screen—"Buy now for future security"—as well as subjected to speakers at every performance. No details were given as to who financed and sponsored the campaign.[16]

Active in yet another unusual advertising and film tie-up was the Publix chain. Its 1,600 theaters were laying plans for the sale of lobby space through its circuit direct to advertisers, on the basis of $100 per cinema. Paramount-Publix was touting the lobby idea as another potential wave of the future. Helena Rubenstein, manufacturer of perfumes and other toilet articles, was said to have been the first buyer of lobby space. She was sold an eight-by-12 feet space in 20 Publix houses at the price of $100 per house per year.[17]

Another offbeat ad tie-in was announced in 1931 when it was reported that an organization called Kinogram was in the process of offering free, commercialized newsreels to cinemas (at the time virtually all cinemas ran a newsreel as part of the program—it was ad free and paid for by exhibitors, as they did for any short film they booked). Almost immediately after that announcement the Northwest Allied States exhibitor group based in Minneapolis passed a resolution opposing the advertising newsreel idea. On the other hand Kinogram claimed that every exhibitor at the Rocky Mountain Theatre Owners' Association convention held in Denver signed a contract for the Kinogram advertising newsreel; this organization backed the idea.[18]

Later in 1931 the Kinogram advertising newsreel made its debut with the 300 exhibitors who had to that point signed on to take the free newsreel for a five-year term. However, Kinogram executive C. Baynes admitted no companies had contracted to advertise on it. That first release contained a free ad for Henry Ford's cars. Earlier Baynes had claimed to have sponsors such as Listerine, the Hygeniol Powder Company, and Camel Cigarettes lined up. He now admitted the first two named companies remained unsigned while Camel Cigarettes had already publicly denied having any agreement with Kinogram. Exhibitors receiving the newsreels were told that since newsreel issues would not be released regularly until paying advertisers were found, those exhibitors had better plan to give screen time to whatever newsreel service they had been subscribing to before Kinogram arrived. Baynes denied that first newsreel release was late, claiming that all 300 cinemas (including Chicago subscribers) were then showing the newsreel. However, another report said the release of that issue had been indefinitely postponed with only one print of the newsreel then being screened in Chicago.[19]

Ad trailers (the filmed commercials running a couple of minutes in length or less, that most resemble commercials as we think of them today) surfaced for the first time in an organized fashion, to a very minor extent, in this period. Illustrating how rare such trailers had been was the 1930 account that spoke of the ad trailer: "Different than anything before proposed, talkers have invented a new type of film commercial that took its first big step" with the signing of a contact between the Publix cinema chain and the Theatre Service Corporation (TSC) for the screening of ad trailers. According to the report "The idea harks back to the neighborhoods and the old grind of former days when the stereopticon slide was used to advertise products and firms." The Paramount-Publix chain was a large one with perhaps 1,000 outlets in total. Emphasized by the report was the fact that these new ad trailers were "Not to be of shorts length. Regular commercial films run 1,000 feet or more," but the trailers were to be much shorter.[20]

Another development involving trailers took place around the same time when Herman Fowler (of Fowler Studios, Hollywood) approached the Chicago-based Illinois Independent Theatre Owners organization with his ad trailer proposition. He was to pay the exhibitors certain fees for presenting on their screens certain variety acts that would be presented under the "auspices" of various merchant advertisers. Those advertising film reels contained three three-minute acts, presented by three different advertisers. Fowler reportedly managed to obtain money (ranging from $25 to $50) from some 75 Chicago-area merchants to start this advertising service, but in the end only about 10 of those advertisers secured a theater presentation. The first ad reels were previewed by about 50 exhibitors from that organization but not one received any money from Fowler. According to the exhibitors Fowler had refused, despite demands from the cinema owners, to sign any contracts, insisting all deals be made orally. Finally, the Illinois Independent Theatre Owners group advised its members not to screen any more of the Fowler product.[21]

While the Fowler operation disappeared the TSC concept continued. By the start of 1931 it went so far as to say ad trailers were no longer an experiment, but a permanent part of the Publix chain nationally. According to this story 90 percent of the people in those cinemas approved of the ad trailers then being screened. Advertisers included Chesterfield Cigarettes, General Motors, Texaco Oil, and Lysol.[22]

During its first year of the program (ending in September 1932) Publix used TSC's "Screen Broadcasts" in its smaller houses as a "more modern way" of providing advertising opportunities for local merchants, hotels, stores, and so forth. When it renewed for a second year with TSC, Publix declared it would give extended exhibition to those ad trailers. It began to dream about tie-ups with national advertisers, envisioning a lot more money for itself. Still, all was not rosy as this TSC (the company was an independent producing and promotional concern) service had reportedly aroused the ire of newspaper publishers. Although Publix said it would give wider exhibition to the ads in the second year of its contract with TSC the chain emphasized ad trailers would not be played in any of its Broadway venues or in any other of its big, first-run houses just yet, although they allowed that might come later.[23]

To that point national advertisers signed up with TSC included Borden's Milk, Dorothy Arden cosmetics, and General Electric (distributors of Frigidaire). In all cases TSC made contact with the advertiser, whether local or national. Then TSC provided the film, and an unstated fee, to the Publix cinemas involved in the program. After renewing its contract with TSC, Publix issued instructions to its cinema managers emphasizing the necessity of cooperating with TSC representatives on local tie-ups and insisting on the screening of the ad trailers as an "integral part" of the cinema program at every regular performance. That letter stated, in part, "Publix has decided after a careful survey that TSC's Screen Broadcasts are the most attractive advertising films of their kind available from the standpoint of the audience and the theatre, and they also offer Publix the greatest possibilities of revenue." Therefore Publix had renewed its contract and was determined to do everything reasonably possible to aid TSC "to sell its services and get maximum revenue for the theatres." Those ad trailers came in reels that contained up to six or seven different ads. Each reel contained about 350 feet with each ad running around 50 feet in length (30 seconds).[24]

Trailers, though, remained virtually non-existent in the context of a union between advertising and motion pictures. To the extent that advertising could be found in movies the dominant form was the ad short—one aspect of the industrial film business. When exaggerated claims and fanciful predictions were made about the increased commercial use of movies when sound pictures first arrived, it was the ad short those accounts had in mind.

Journalist Henry W. Hough was able to report in the spring of 1929 that the public was then being entertained with "the carefully prepared and often costly creations of enterprising business and industrial leaders." Broadway's most elegant cinemas had recently presented movies of that type, sponsored by the New York Stock Exchange, the Radio Corporation of America (RCA), and the New York Edison Company, among others, and Hough predicted that most of America's moviegoers would eventually see those movies in their own local houses. Industrial films, said Hough, could be classified into four different types: educational, technical, propaganda, and selling. Most industrial films were made on 16-millimeter film (cheaper than the 35-millimeter theatrical standard), although if the advertiser intended to seek wider distribution for his industrial film he might use 35-mm film to start with. Usually those industrial firms hired outside, professional production firms to make the picture as the practice of in-house production became less and less common. One such film was *The Nation's Market Place* (produced for the New York Stock Exchange at a cost of $15,000). With a running time of 15 minutes it was estimated that item had been seen by over five million people. Another movie that had played many of those prestige houses was *Man Made Miracles*, showing how radio tubes were made in the RCA factory. Several prints of that film had Spanish subtitles added so it could be exhibited in Spain during the Barcelona Exposition as well as in various South and Central American nations. "At the present time all classes of industrial motion pictures are furnished gratis to exhibitors in this country," noted Hough, "it being understood that the exhibitor is to pay all handling charges."[25]

*Business Week* remarked in 1929 that business was going in "heavily" for talkie ad shorts and that a two-reel short (20 minutes maximum) could cost as much as $10,000 to produce; several companies then specialized in producing them. Prints of such films cost around $150 each. Also noted was that the first television commercial had already been broadcast. It was a one-reel effort starring the cartoon character Charlot the cat, who had a rip in the seat of his pants. Thread from the Spool

Cotton Company repaired the problem and thus saved Charlot from the Bastille. Prepared for the French trade it was labeled *L'Histoire de Charlot* and described as "all comedy with the sales feature painlessly presented." It was broadcast by the Jenkins Television Corporation, apparently in the fall of 1929, from W2XCR, Jersey City, New Jersey.[26]

Over in the UK a series of short films, each about seven minutes in length, had been produced by the Morgan Film Service with the object of advertising "important British firms and their products." The method employed, said a reporter, "is that of weaving a simple story, attractively presented, around the firm or the goods concerned." For example, in a film sponsored by Lloyds Bank, a young wife dreamt her savings had been stolen in the night by a thief. The very next morning she went to the bank (its safes, premises, and so on, were displayed) and opened an account with the manager. Morgan had also produced films for an insurance company, a toothpaste manufacturer, and for the chemist chain Boots. Those ad shorts were to be screened, remarked the account, "at a number of suburban cinemas as part of the normal programme."[27]

Nor had the advertiser forgotten about the masquerading short. Industrialists were, said *Variety* in 1930, out to manufacture one- and two-reel items to compete with regular entertainment features. Several large business firms had reportedly already done so with the cost settling in at a minimum of $10,000 per reel. Also, they were out to employ well-known actors to play in those ad shorts. One firm made such a film with Vincent Richards and a wholesale drug company was then negotiating with Ruth St. Dennis and Ted Shawn. While the obvious object of such films was advertising, the story observed, "The way the industrials do it the plug takes a back seat, with quality riding up front." When they made those movies the industrial firms took pains to "avoid all clear deduction as to the purpose of the film, or its source of creation, because the big firms believe that to do otherwise would strain the good will value of the film and its quality. So they use the indirect method which tempers down to a mere presentation line that bears only the name of a company executive who might, or might not, be known to the theatre audiences." As the action unfolded in one of those films, "the firm's product is given pictorial display in a tasteful way." By producing an ad short by those methods an industrial firm was reportedly able to book it into at least 50 houses of one big chain. Usually those films were rented to exhibitors for free but there were said to be cases where the exhibitor actually paid for the ad short. One manufacturer then planning a talkie short was not going to insert even a single credit line into the film. Instead, it was going to use only its trade symbol on the assumption that it was well enough known. Manufacturers figured that if they could produce a two-reel ad short for no more than $20,000 (plus an additional $3,000 for 50 prints) and if they could book it into 50 houses a week, "the firms were more than satisfied."[28]

Business reporter Peter Andrews talked about the one-reel sponsored movie, complete with a name actor: "No direct advertising is contained in the picture; it is straight entertainment." It amounted to 10 minutes of amusement "differing virtually in no way" from what the moviegoer was used to, with the exception, perhaps, of a credit line at the beginning and/or end of the film. Andrews felt the 10-minute ad short would become the next significant step of the advertising industry with such items becoming a regular part of all theater programs. In these items, "The demonstration of the product, if this take place at all, is to be insinuated so as to be unostentatious but visible in the film." One benefit he spoke of was that the viewing of the ad film, sandwiched between regular films as it was, was "practically inevitable," given the captive nature of the audience. Introducing a note of caution, Andrews said, "The moviegoer is constrained to notice whether he wishes to do so or not. Too much advertising against the will, of course, brings a turn-the-dial reaction." He worried patrons might avoid a cinema entirely if they felt it contained too much advertising. Thus, he advised that advertising matter be inserted cautiously into those ad shorts, at first only at the beginning and end of the picture, and in some cases only at the end. If the audience attitude appeared to be approving, then more advertising matter could be stirred in, "until a saturation point of advertising insertion is noted." One example of an ad short he gave was one entitled *A Jolt for General Germ* produced by Paramount studios for the cleaning agent Lysol (made by Lehn and Fink). That cartoon film was then said to be running in some 1,200 Paramount-Publix houses. It was scheduled to run until it reached a box-office count of five million, at an exhibition cost of $5,000 per million spectators. Much of that wider spread of distribution was possible because of—and driven by, thought Andrews—the rush for cinema acquisition that took place in 1929 and 1930 as the Hollywood majors strengthened their grip on the industry. In 1930 Paramount (1,200 cinemas) increased its cinema chain by about 40 percent. Behind it was Fox (750), 25 percent; Warner Bros. (700), 100 percent; and Radio-Keith-Orpheum (RKO—300) 30 percent. While those 3,000 houses accounted for just 16 percent of all U.S. cinemas, Andrews remarked they drew 40 percent of the total audience.[29]

Hollywood's majors had almost completely ignored advertising movies in all aspects, as producers and/or exhibitors, all through the silent era. That business simply wasn't big enough, or profitable enough, to interest them. Also, hostility and anger from cinema operators and from audiences tended to come to the surface whenever advertising was identified as such. But given the sudden focus on such films when the sound era arrived, and given all the attention, hype, and publicity that then attached itself to the advertising and film link-up, it was almost inevitable that the majors would try and become important players in that field. As mentioned above, Paramount's Publix theater chain was running ad trailers. By 1930 Fox, Universal, and Paramount, as well as some independent entertainment feature film producers, were all involved in industrial film production. Of course many of those industrial films were destined for only in-house use or specialized audiences such as dealerships (and the friends thereof), which has always been true for industrial movies. In the vast majority of cases there was never any intention of sending an industrial film to regular cinemas. Still, some of those items produced by the majors were ad shorts masquerading as entertainment films and destined for regular houses, if they could get them in.[30]

When Paramount set up its commercial pictures department it went after advertising accounts with the same vigor as did radio, and with the stated advantage of having a guaranteed national distribution through its Publix theater chain. A somewhat skeptical reporter said, "The Par-Publix idea behind commercial picture production on its face seems far-fetched but to insiders there seems little doubt of its workability." One reason for that confidence was that guaranteed distribution set up an studio "the same as on the radio but a circulation that is far more definite and, it is stated, cheaper." Under the Paramount program the advertiser was to produce shorts of one or two reels written by professional scenarists and gag writers. For example, an ad short for a well-known oil company might contain a single shot of an actor getting off a truck marked, say, Standard Oil. Or, if a gag of some kind was worked up around a Socony gas station it would not, in the opinion of Paramount, make that picture "a pure out-and-out ad that would hurt the theatres." A clever comic writer, argued Paramount, could always work in a shot or two of the product being plugged with the chances being "10 to 1 that the public would either not notice it as advertising or would not care." Cost of these ad films of one or two reels was said to run from $5,000 upward (acting talent not included). Paramount's plan was said to be one of the possibilities of the future "in the mixture of sound and advertising for the creation at the same time of entertainment that the public will pay for."[31]

Following Paramount's lead Warner Bros. organized its own industrial talkie division, also in 1930. Like Paramount, Warner owned its own cinema chains and was prepared to offer advertisers "guaranteed circulation." Both studios differentiated between sponsored shorts (the one- or two-reel ad films) designed to be part of the regular theater programs and the longer industrial films (solely for the in-house use of the manufacturer). In making their industrial films both producers used their regular producing and distributing personnel. For its ad shorts Warner Bros. planned to have merely an announcement of the sponsor at the beginning and the end of the film—as was then the standard practice on radio programs. Warner indicated it would use actors from its stable of contract players in some of those ad films.[32]

Business turned out to be slower than expected. Near the end of 1930 Paramount had produced only five ad shorts for its cinema chains, and only one of those was running at the time. Warner then had no ad shorts playing at its houses. The single ad film that was running was only playing at 100 of the Publix venues. Paramount charged the advertiser, a toothpaste maker, $7,500 to produce the one-reel item and then charged another $15,000 for exhibiting the item over the limited circuit, $150 per house.[33]

As 1931 began the majors appeared to be planning to charge the advertiser, the sponsor of their commercial shorts, on the basis of attendance—a quarter of a cent per patron—in addition to a flat sum of $5,000 to $10,000 to cover the cost of producing the item. Movies, it was said, were "to be ballyhooed as the only 100% medium of salesmanship." Continued emphasis was placed on the cinema's advantage of having a captive audience: "Folks who go to theatres can't shut off the projection machine like the radio nor pass up pages in a publication although they, of course, can always walk out." Still, there was a fear within the industry that the public would not pay to see advertising. Thus the ad shorts had to be skillfully done, and they had to be entertaining. "Taking advantage by foisting upon audiences blunt and ill-disguised subjects of advertising is the best way to kill it," remarked an account. "Only by finesse can the advertising stigma be erased from the public mind."[34]

At the same time Paramount was presented as the major most involved, and the one most successful, in relation to ad shorts. It was said to be the first major to have sold for distribution in its 1,600 houses 52 single-reel subjects to be played in as many weeks in 1932 (the beginning of which was still close to a year away). Paramount's estimated income of $1.6 million for the 52 ad shorts was broken down into $520,000 from production of those movies and $1,080,000 for projecting them in its houses. A standard was said to be set for others by Paramount's example, as independent exhibitors who formerly played ad reels for free (they were content with the money saved from not having to pay for an entertainment short by substituting an ad short) were beginning to demand that same one-quarter cent that Publix charged. Continuously worried about public reaction Paramount officials monitored audience response to the ad reels at all of its venues. To that point only 25 of the 52 ad shorts had actually been made: "The aim is to make each one different than its predecessor so that the same divertissement afforded by the legitimate short subject may be realized in the ad reel." No matter whether the commissioned ad required a cast of actors or was a cartoon, Paramount was then charging the advertiser one price—$10,000 per reel. A reason for that was to "insure profit" and to allow for the staff overhead "deemed necessary for quality production." Fox had also entered the industrial field (actually just before Paramount) but had in fact abandoned that department by the beginning of 1931. Although this account mentioned that fact, it tried to maintain its upbeat tone by brushing aside Fox's failure. It was explained that Fox had reorganized its company in the previous year (due to financial difficulties arising from the Depression) and had eliminated many departments just because they were in the red. As Fox's industrial division was then very new it had start-up costs but little or no income so it, of course, had to be in the red. Warner Bros. was said here to have entered the industrial field "accidentally" after it purchased the Stanley theatre circuit. One of the Stanley organization subsidiaries made mostly 16-mm commercial films.[35]

Warner Bros. Industrial Films, as of February 1931 had completed just two ad shorts—one for Liggett and Myers Tobacco and the other for the makers of Listerine. Those two contracts were estimated to have produced around $75,000 in revenue for the Hollywood major. A special staff was employed by Warner to devise sponsored ideas for clients and a special scenario staff then created an adaptation. Merchandising tie-ins were provided by another staff that was devoted to exploitation. As well, Warner made industrial films that were strictly for in-house use of the client. Of all the majors only Paramount and Warner Bros. were then involved in making the ad shorts. Universal reportedly had once been involved to some extent but, like Fox, had abandoned the field.[36]

Within a few more months Warner also abandoned the field, leaving Paramount the sole major involved. Paramount admitted screen advertising was reaching a "crisis" and that for the "general good" of the industry and to make the cartel stand unanimous Paramount would have to "voluntarily withdraw" from the field also. Disingenuously, the major blamed the outsiders—independent, non–Hollywood-related companies that made most of the ad films—for the crisis. Noting that some 8,000 independent U.S. cinemas then used advertising from those outsiders Paramount blamed them for "bringing the storm of public disapproval on the advertising part of the screen." Those ad reels from the outsiders were too openly and too crudely advertising matter. Investigators were said to have discovered advertising material in some of those freelance reels occupied as much as 200 feet (1,000 feet in a reel). Said a reporter, "All agreed that if those ads had been done as at Paramount there would be less need for the industry to worry." Some researchers were said to believe that if the actual advertising was "given a maximum of 20 feet for every reel, there would be far fewer squawks from the fans." Not long after that Paramount also abandoned the field.[37]

A few years later business writers S. Walker and Paul Sklar reported that as far as the majors' exit from ad short production and exhibition was concerned the real killer had been opposition from independent exhibitors, aided by newspapers, who had squelched the project almost at once.[38]

Despite the absence of the majors from the production of ad shorts by early in 1931, that year still remained a banner year for the concept, its biggest ever. There was also much philosophizing about the topic, and the style in which those films should be made, and the degree to which the public would accept ads in a medium in which they paid full price for their entertainment (unlike radio where, said conventional wisdom, the public was more willing to accept commercials since it was getting the entertainment for "free").

W. D. Canaday was vice president at Lehn and Fink, one of whose products was the disinfectant Lysol. One of the first commercial ad shorts produced by Paramount for screening as part of the regular programs in its chain of cinemas nationwide had been the aforementioned, *A Jolt for General Germ*—done as a cartoon. Legendary cartoonist Max Fleischer had spent three months' time and created over 8,000 drawings to make *Jolt*, with a run time of 6.5 minutes. Canaday was delighted that for the first time talking pictures had been made available as a national medium for advertising national brands, much the same way that radio was being utilized. Lehn and Fink had chosen a cartoon-style film because it was considered the most effective and entertaining method of presenting an otherwise unpleasant subject—the killing of disease germs. Fleischer was said to have made the action sufficiently clever and fast so as "to file the rough edges off the advertising," and "Its advertising purpose has been completely subordinated to the requirements for a strictly entertaining feature." A good cartoonist, said Canaday, "can make a commercial sufficiently amusing to cover blunt mention of a product."[39]

As a tie-up with *Jolt* Lehn and Fink forwarded to druggists extra window displays, counter cards, and other display material for when the commercial played their town. Some retailers, Canaday reported, had placed advertisements in their local papers announcing the film. As soon as a booking for *Jolt* was confirmed for a city, a letter went out to each dealer. In part it said, "In the most unique and compelling form conceivable, Lysol disinfectant has entered filmdom! And will be shown at every performance of the Paramount theater or theaters in your city on the dates designated on the enclosed schedule." Continuing on, the letter boasted, "The film is of the ever-popular, All-Talkie, All-Musical,

Animated-Cartoon type and the audience, your customers, will see it when they are in the most receptive mood. They are being entertained and are impressionable!" So pleased was Lehn and Fink with *Jolt* that they contracted with Paramount for additional shorts for some of their other products, such as Pebeco toothpaste, although none were going to be cartoons. Paramount also produced a cartoon reel for the Texas Company and a series called *Movie Memories* for the Liggett & Myers Tobacco Company's Chesterfield cigarettes. Comprised of old film clips from entertainment features, this ad short series was unique in that the ad short had no direct connection or tie-up to the sponsoring product. In the meantime, rival Warner Bros. had produced one commercial for a product made by the Lambert Pharmacol Company.[40]

Canaday admitted that many in the film world saw a danger that ads on the screen might antagonize the audience and provoke a backlash. One of the more widely publicized of such views came from Carl Laemmle, president of Hollywood major Universal. He declared it was "a serious mistake to figure that because the radio broadcasts contain advertising it is all right for the movies to do it." Laemmle added forcefully, "I appeal to every producer not to release sponsored motion pictures—meaning pictures which contain concealed or open advertising of someone's product! This kind of profit is a false one. It is a temporary profit at best, for in the long run it will degrade the movies and earn an ill-will which will drive millions from attending the movies." Canaday's answer was to make those shorts entertaining but he admitted that if they degenerated into poor entertainment then Laemmle was right. Once the standards were let down the least bit below the current requirements for regular short features (as they had been produced by studios such as Paramount and Warner Bros., before the advent of the sponsored film), argued Canaday, "Then the talking pictures as an advertising medium will be doomed.... People will not pay to see and hear inferior pictures of any kind, much less will they pay for inferior sponsored or advertising pictures." Again he emphasized that ad shorts had to be sufficiently interesting, amusing, and entertaining so that the public would not resent the advertising. In fact, he said, they should be even better because they had something more to overcome than the regular entertainment shorts— "the natural resentment of the theater patrons against advertising, as such on the screen."[41]

At a meeting of the motion picture group of the Advertising Club of New York in March 1931 six film ad shorts were run off to the accompaniment of explanatory remarks by company executives. One of them, Richard Strobridge, secretary of the Newell-Emmett Company, threw some cold water on the concept when he declared the limitations of the screen as an advertising medium were "very definite." The screen, he said, was dedicated to the duty of entertaining those who paid their admission at the box office: "Therefore, it can offer nothing but entertainment if it is to keep faith with the public. This fact alone places it at once in the category of secondary advertising media, for its sole purpose, that of entertainment, bars it sue for direct advertising or sales appeal." Strobridge argued he was voicing no new opinion in saying the movie screen could in no way be substituted for magazines or newspapers. In a separate and unrelated development it was reported that the motion picture committee of the American Association of Advertising Agencies had passed a resolution that expressed the need for maintaining "a high degree of quality in the production of films and avoidance of any undue emphasis upon advertising, per se, such as might intrude distastefully upon the entertainment or educational element of a picture or program."[42]

As the flurry of interest in ad films continued it was reported in April 1931 that at least 28 million people had seen the first efforts and that eight national advertisers were then said to have signed up. Chesterfield's contract called for 13 ad shorts over the course of a year— one every four weeks (that was its *Movie Memories* series). Producers were then said to be charging $10,000 to $15,000 for a one-reel ad short, but if you wanted top talent such as Will Rogers in the picture, that salary had to be added on. Advertising agencies increased that cost by a flat fee of $5,000 (advertisers usually contacted an ad agency to see about getting a film made; in turn the agency would line up one of the producers that specialized in industrial films, although a few agencies were large enough that they were starting to produce in house) to make $20,000 the probable minimum cost. To that had to be added the distribution costs (not then standardized), which tended toward $5 per every 1,000 tickets sold at a cinema. Advertising agency people saw two major drawbacks to ad shorts. First was that the amount of copy that could be used in the film "is greatly restricted, sometimes to a mere 'Sponsored by...'; a theater audience has paid for amusement, must be given high-class entertainment with a minimum of advertising." The second drawback was the "restricted distribution" offered for the ad reels. The six big chains (five of them owned by the majors) had at that time a reported 25 percent of America's houses, and drew 50 percent of the audience. They did not screen ad shorts and for advertising agency people that left a "large gap"; it was something they called "spotty" distribution.[43]

That was one of the reasons the majors' entry into the field failed. A national advertiser wanted truly national distribution, something not readily available in the cinema field. Trying to put together a national cinema system for ads on a chain-by-chain basis and adding in any necessary independents would have been too time consuming and probably impossible. Perhaps the majors could have arranged it but they and the independent cinemas (both chain and solo operators) did not work together on the issue. The majors screened ad shorts they had produced in their houses and nowhere else. The independents screened ad shorts produced by independent non-entertainment, non–Hollywood producers and those of nobody else.

Marsh K. Powers, president of the Powers-House advertising agency, thought the theory upon which the great bulk of radio advertising was based (and then being emulated in the fledgling film advertising field)—"If you amuse you will sell"—had generated endless debate but was too narrowly focused. For him the real question was, "How far can the principle of commercial sponsorship be profitably carried?"[44]

As of May 1931, reported *Variety*, slightly over 50 percent of all U.S. cinemas were projecting paid advertising in their screen programs. Within that total of around 7,800 houses, some 2,000 were big circuit theaters; the remainder were independents. Sponsoring those commercial reels were national advertisers who collectively in the previous five months had spent an estimated $3 million. "The money in the film field is proving so attractive outsiders are flocking in with all kinds of propositions to theatre men," observed the account. Grocery chain A&P had produced an ad reel for its coffee and during the week it was shown in theaters A&P was said to have sold three times as much coffee as during any other similar period.[45]

That same month journalist Darwin Teilhet did a long piece on the topic, at a time when the frenzy and hype over cinema advertising was at its peak. Teilhet first described a cinema program he attended in a small suburban theater that included a test preview of a sponsored ad film. He had learned of the preview and had been given permission to attend and report on the event.

An audience of 458 people attended that night and paid 50 cents each for two and a half hours of entertainment. Viewers saw a full-length feature, the latest sound newsreel—(which Teilhet described as actually being news that was two months old), a two-reel comedy, and a 15-minute ad short. Two employees from the advertising department of the company that produced that ad reel were also in attendance. That ad short told the story of a comparatively plain woman who was suddenly dumped by her fiancé. Deeply depressed, she had no luck in attracting another man until she turned to using perfume. Suddenly she was avidly sought after by men. At the end of the movie she was in the arms of a new lover, happy, and so on. Teilhet counted the appearances of the perfume and said the square bottle of the ad's sponsor, Seduction Fleur perfume, appeared on the screen a total of 10 times with a combined display time of 78 seconds. But no other obvious advertising material appeared in the short for the brand. Then, at the end of the film was flashed the follow-ing seven-second credit: "This film is sponsored for your entertainment by the Parfum des Fleurs Company, Paris and London, Levy and Grosstein, New York, sole importers for the United States and Canada."[46]

After the theater program ended the advertising men interviewed as many audience members as they could. On the following day they gave Teilhet their results. Of the 191 people interviewed, 54 did not even real-ize they had witnessed a sponsored film. Within that group of 54, 38 read-ily recalled the name of the perfume; seven said they had noticed a perfume but could not remember the name; only five of the 54 who were unaware they had seen advertising on the screen completely missed the shots of the perfume bottle. From the remaining group of 137 people interviewed it was found that 48 thought there was some kind of adver-tising in the film but offered no objection because they said the film was so entertaining. Twenty-nine respondents were described as indifferent to the fact they had seen advertising while 42 were said to be pleased with that addition to the program. Of the entire group of 191 respon-dents, said Teilhet, only 18 were said to have had negative or unfavor-able reactions against seeing an advertising movie. Within three days after the single appearance of this sponsored film, it was reported, the two drug stores in the neighborhood had completely sold out their stock of Seduction Fleur perfume.[47]

Teilhet pointed out the financial difficulty of the motion picture industry (the Depression effects, the huge expense of converting houses to sound, and so forth) was a major reason, and a driving force, for it to seek new revenue sources. He argued that Fox had been among the first to rediscover the advertising value of the screen in 1929 when a personal plea was made to the audience (from the screen) to invest their savings in Fox stock. It was said to have been a successful campaign. "Because of the novelty of the talking pictures or because of the opportunity for subtlety of advertising in the sound film, there was no audience objec-tion," he said. Then, in the summer of 1930, theaters on a larger scale engaged in another self-serving effort. An attempt was then being made by a number of urban and municipal groups, gasoline firms, two major automobile associations, and California banks to have daylight saving time made a state law there. Cinemas throughout America had always argued against the extra hour of evening daylight whenever it was raised, convinced it would reduce their attendance at the first evening program. Remembering the success of Fox's stock promotion efforts, the Holly-wood majors as a group decided to fight by using their own houses. "Night after night for weeks, cinema audiences throughout California sat passively watching propaganda films depicting the terrors of daylight saving," commented Teilhet. "Even a theme song was written, 'You Can

Have It—I Don't Want It—Daylight Saving Time' which was sung in animated cartoon strips and Swedish dialect comedies." Despite the fact that experts thought a daylight saving time proposition then on the ballot would pass, when the votes were tallied it had failed. "Having proved that their audiences would not object to advertising films," declared the journalist, several of the studios—Paramount, Warner, and Fox—turned to the production and exhibition of ad reels as a source of raising money. In competing against radio and magazines for the advertising dollar Teilhet mentioned the same two advantages for film that others had cited—a guaranteed circulation and a captive audience. Using the Lysol ad film exhibition cost of $5,000 per million audience as an example Teilhet pointed out that radio audience numbers were still at the guesswork stage. Leading national magazines charged a cheaper rate of $2,800 per page per one million circulation but, "While you do not have to look at publication advertising you are forced to absorb a sponsored talking film…! You are placed in a position which requires you to notice the advertising message to the bitter end "[48]

Among the ad films produced to that point, Teilhet listed Warner's first effort, an 11-minute ad, titled *Such Popularity* that featured two ex-vaudevillians (Clark and McCullough) for Liggett & Myers, maker of Chesterfield cigarettes. Independent producer Metropolitan made one for Richfield gasoline that starred well-known comedian Lloyd Hamilton doing his routine in front of a service station that prominently displayed the Richfield sign. Reportedly that effort cost $35,000, but most, using lesser known actors, ran from $800 to $15,000 in cost for a one-reel ad. Still, noted the journalist, "So far no really first-rate cinema star has sold his name to any commercial film," as Amos and Andy had done over the radio for Pepsodent toothpaste, or golfer Bobby Jones had for Listerine mouthwash, or Lowell Thomas had for the *Literary Digest* news magazine, or Will Rogers had for Squibb. Once the success of the sponsored film was definitely established, believed Teilhet, stars of the first magnitude would be ready to be presented in nationally released ad films for fees "worthy of their names." Since all those stars had endorsed products in print with their signatures he felt there was no doubt they would do so in films, if the price was right. He argued, "The sponsored movies skillfully get around the human desire to receive entertainment instead of advertising by following the radio broadcasting method of sugar-coating advertising with thick layers of amusement."[49]

In the ad reel *Such Popularity* for Chesterfield cigarettes, Teilhet believed that, except for the credit line "Sponsored by the makers of Chesterfields," it was almost impossible to tell the item was an advertising film as the continuity had nothing to do with cigarette advertising. "The advertising is more subtle; the film is supposed to promote the sale of cigarettes by building up good will in the same unobtrusive manner that radio advertising is supposed to do—and does!" In comparing the different media he observed that when a person bought a magazine or newspaper he only paid a fraction of the cost and that by paying for a large part of the cost of a publication the advertisers actually paid the customer to read their announcements. Similarly, in radio the entire expense of entertaining the listener, after he had bought his set, was assumed by the advertisers. But the customer had to pay in full to see the ad film on a cinema program and, he wondered, "the moving picture producers can see nothing ethically wrong in selling you two and a half hours of entertainment and then turning around and reselling ten to fifteen minutes of that identical time to advertisers!" Teilhet concluded that whether the ad film would be successful depended entirely on the audience. That is, they could greet it with a passive acceptance or with angry protests. He was opposed to them and felt they should not be on the cinema screens.[50]

As the frenzy over ad films hit its peak in the early spring of 1931, when it seemed destined for rapid growth and expansion, the forces that almost completely destroyed it (for a time) had already surfaced. And the audience was not involved to any extent. Rather it was the motion picture industry itself—the majors and many cinema operators—that caused the withering away of ad films, with a vigorous assist from the newspaper industry.

In late February 1931 Fox Theatres announced it had banned all commercial films from its entire circuit. That move was presented as a principled stand against all the types of screen advertising "as undesirable in practice of theatrical entertainment." The situation of sponsored films was said to be then precarious because all the publicity and hype associated with it and its great promise had attracted all kinds of independent producers to the field—they aimed for exhibition of their output in cinema chains unaffiliated with the majors and in independent houses. Fox's argument (said to be endorsed by Paramount and Warner) was that ad films were okay under careful supervision when their circulation was limited but when circulation became too widespread, then "injury" to the screen could follow. Supposedly the majors worried about a lack of quality in all those ad shorts produced by outsiders, compared to the ones produced by themselves. And that could turn off the audience. Although Fox was said to believe that such a "perverse" situation in screen entertainment might not come soon, "It is taking the stand that it's never too early to be prepared and figures to stand pat on 100% entertainment with no commercial angles."[51]

Another article at the same time also argued that screen advertising was providing a problem for the film industry; executives with the majors saw it as developing "in such hectic and haphazard fashion" that it would boomerang to the detriment of the industry "and be counted out for all time, unless policed along uniform lines of operation and exhibition." Independent producers of screen ads, it was claimed by the majors, were forcing the screen ad issue to a crisis "which will result in the big producers [majors] organizing for the general protection of the industry." Such a step was then said to be under consideration. It called for the majors to discontinue all production of ad shorts and to concentrate on their distribution. To ensure the desired uniformity of quality the plan provided that one company be formed (by the majors) to produce ad shorts for all companies and for release among cinema circuits, both producer-owned and independent ones. With a single, and separate, organization, the majors argued, many "serious handicaps to the advancement of screen advertising could be overcome: all cinemas, not just those controlled by the majors, would be available for ad money, and public reaction as a whole could be studied more thoroughly." Apparently anticipating an obvious criticism of this plan a reporter stated, "That the move discussed now in big producer circles is not in the nature of a grab of all ad revenue but more of a precautionary measure to insure permanence to the advertising field is witnessed in several ways." However, he did not list any of them except to say that with a single production studio all ad shorts would be tailored from the perspective and judgment of the industry as a whole.[52]

Universal chief Carl Laemmle in a general release to other producers and exhibitors delivered another attack against film advertising, or as he described it, "prostitution of the screen." Although Universal had once been involved in producing those ad shorts it had not done so for some time. Laemmle declared there was no comparison between advertising in books and on the radio and film ads. It was different, he said, because the millions who were moviegoers paid at the box office for entertainment. "Believe me, if you jam advertising down their throats and pack their eyes and ears with it you will build up a resentment that will in time damn your business."[53]

A couple of weeks later the Hollywood cartel was said to be hard at work investigating every angle of screen advertising. Three main issues were being investigated: a) the real reaction of the paying public; b) the position that daily newspapers were taking—increasingly vocal in their opposition as they believed it took ad revenue away from them; and c) how the Hollywood majors viewed the future of screen advertising. Warner and Paramount were reported to be in favor of screen advertising; Fox and Universal were opposed to it, and RKO had not yet taken a stand. Differences also could be found in exhibitor organizations, with the Motion Picture Theatre Owners of America on record as opposed while Allied Exhibitors favored the practice. Paramount was then still producing and running the ad shorts and was very cautious in monitoring what effect those ads had on audiences. Cinema managers were required to monitor every audience for every performance that contained an ad short. If a single exception during a day's showing was registered by a patron, those managers were required to record it and to include it in a separate report to the home office. Weekly reports from managers to the home office of Paramount-Publix were said to have "brought expressions of satisfaction" with the ads as high as 99 percent and no lower than 90 percent. Yet the chain pulled the ad short for Lysol out of its houses before the scheduled end of its run. No reason was given.[54]

Still, in the early spring of 1931 the Fox-Friendly theaters of Kansas City, Missouri, were featuring in their publicity the fact that all advertising other than the announcements of coming attractions had been discontinued from their screens.[55]

In Denver at the annual convention of the Rocky Mountain Theatre Owners' Association the organization went on record to say that cinemas showing advertising films should be paid. Also, they resolved that whenever advertising was contained "in a feature or short," the contract with exhibitors should provide that exhibitors had the privilege of canceling.[56]

The Loew theater chain (the exhibition arm of Hollywood major MGM) operated hundreds of houses in the U.S. and abroad and would continue to refuse commercial screen advertising, said Loew's, Inc. president Nicholas M. Schenck in May 1931. He denounced screen ads as being unfair to motion picture audiences. As president also of MGM Schenck added that his studio would also not produce any ad shorts. And that he was making an effort to convince other producers and cinema chain owners that screen advertising was a "menace" to the picture industry and should be barred. Schenck explained he was also opposed to the practice because it constituted competition with newspaper advertising. According to him he had been repeatedly queried by the press, the public, and his own cinema executives on his attitude toward screen ads and why that potentially large revenue source should be ignored. In reply Schenck said he was against the commercialization of the cinema "because screen advertising is unfair to our audiences. An advertisement on the screen forces itself upon the spectator. He cannot escape it, yet he had paid his admittance price for entertainment alone." He worried the temptation was there to make the advertising aspect more and more obtrusive and thus more and more annoying to the audience. Emphasizing that MGM was very active in trying to persuade other producers and exhibitors to take a stand similar to that of his firm he asserted, "We are continuing these efforts to free the screen from anything but entertainment. We are hopeful that the entire industry will take a stand against screen advertising and not attempt to force our theatres into that field."[57]

Newspapers were unanimously against cinema advertising. A West Virginia newspaper publishers' association went on record against the practice. Also on record as opposed was the American Newspaper Publishers' Association, which argued that the public did not want advertising in the theaters but then added somewhat lamely that the ads should be left there and to "let the people decide." This organization (the main trade body for newspapers) had also fought long, hard, and vigorously against radio advertising. A report 18 months later, when screen ads had more or less vanished, gave the papers a great deal of credit by stating, "It was generally agreed that newspaper resentment had killed off commercial film in theatres" a year and a half earlier.[58]

Newspaper opposition, and audience hostility, were certainly factors in the demise of screen ads at this time but a more important factor was the response of the Hollywood cartel. They had a strong desire to eliminate all screen ads because of a fear of what the union of advertisers and producers (non–Hollywood majors) might possibly produce. They worried a next logical step would be for the partners to move from producing the one- or two-reel ad shorts into full-length feature films, thereby undercutting the cartel's position. That format was then being established in radio whereby the sponsor paid for and created his own program directly (hiring talent, supervising the script, and so forth). It would remain a dominant form of sponsorship in radio and even into the early years of television before the networks re-established their authority and created the programs (or bought them from independents) and then sold time on them to advertisers. Under the earlier system networks found themselves sometimes reduced to selling nothing more than transmission time to advertisers who bypassed the network completely to deal directly with the talent.

When Fox announced its "principled" stand against cinema ads in February 1931, a rumor was in circulation that a producing firm that specialized in ad shorts was said to be ready to take "the next step" and produce commercial features. Just a week later another account reported the rumor that it was "common knowledge" that an independent producer (of entertainment features) was producing and preparing to release 10 features, each of which would involve paid advertising to some degree. Nor was it believed that the producer was going to inform exhibitors about the true nature of these items.[59]

Shortly thereafter the producer rumored to have 10 features on its schedule, financed by advertisers, was identified as World Wide. So intense did those rumors become that Earl W. Hammons, head of both World Wide and producer Educational, came out on record to all exhibitor queries that there was no advertising money represented in a single feature or short subject coming from his firms. Hammons noted the "uniform contract" (the cartel-sanctioned contract used by distributors and exhibitors to cover screening provisions) prohibited the sale of movies containing advertising unless the same was so specified. Going further Hammons declared he was opposed to any kind of advertising on the screen. That same article reported that another large producer (unidentified except that it was not affiliated with Hammons) was "known to have effected a hook-up with a northern industry in a feature [not a short] which it released several months ago."[60]

Then the head of a large cinema chain (who was not named) declared he was worried that Hollywood was on the verge of seeing a new "poverty row" (a reference to a number of non-cartel independent producers such as Monogram and Republic who made entertainment films mostly on the cheap) arise "where overnight producers will be solely engaged in making commercial features." That report went on to worry that commercialized features might be offered for free to cinemas. "The situation is considered most serious for the industry," stated the account. "Independents [cinema owners] are figured easy prey for any kind of free stuff under present economic conditions."[61]

A further speculative article appeared in May 1931 that argued sponsored features would be particularly acceptable as the second half of double-feature programs. Envisioned were features in which the advertising plugs were indirect, "being confined to a quick mention of a certain product or subtly displaying labels in a picture that otherwise is a regular program feature." It was anticipated that such features would be screened in second- and third-run cinemas throughout the U.S., not in any first-run theaters. According to this report the first such sponsored feature had already been made in Alaska with the plugs being for, and the film financing from, a fur company. The second such feature was then said to be in the process of being cast, with the budget supplied by a tire company and being large enough to permit a location trip to India. In the case of this feature, everything possible was being done to make it acceptable for general release—the story was by a "recognized" author and the cast was to contain "names" while "The company putting up the dough will be satisfied for its part to have a few signs in exterior scenes advertising its tires."[62]

Before much could happen with the idea of sponsored features, though, the ad shorts began to disappear. Early in June 1931 it was reported that Paramount-Publix was refunding money to screen advertisers and that in the case of some of the commercial material the producer was trying to "knock off" the brand name and advertising bits in the hope of being able to release the revised items as regular short subjects. No reason was given for this action. It was estimated that up to $50,000 was being returned to advertisers, all of whom had been required to pay production costs for their ad shorts in advance.[63]

*Business Week* declared in a July 1931 account that ad shorts were being "abandoned" by producers before the medium was a year old, although that abandonment was being done with no fanfare and with no specific announcement. As to the reasons for this abandonment it was said not to be due to audience rejection or hostility. "On the contrary, most people expressed approval" toward the ad shorts. Nor was it because the amount of advertising contained in the films was large enough to have become "a nuisance, just as it has on the radio ... so far, cautious producers had maintained audience goodwill." The real reason was that "the newspapers—and the popular press—and not the public, have forced the producers to abandon the plan." Seeing it as a serious threat to their income and worried the ad presence in films might get as bad as radio the newspapers, said *Business Week*, were determined to nip it in the bud. During the 20-odd years of film industry growth the press had devoted large amounts of its space to discuss movies—such as reviews, gossip columns, star profiles, articles on how pictures were produced, and so on. These were all news-type pieces and, of course, did not cost the film industry so much as one cent. "Theater men realize the value of this free publicity," continued the report. "It often draws better than their own advertising in the newspapers." Publishers threatened to cut all this material from their pages. As a result, asserted the business magazine "There was little argument. Sponsored shorts are to be abandoned.... Advertising films may return in the future, but for the present they are a dead issue."[64]

Will Hays stepped in to set policy in 1932, as head of the MPPDA cartel of Hollywood majors. He placed a ban on screen advertising that was vague enough to include formats such as ad shorts and product placements. However, its vagueness left room for a certain amount of interpretation—not to mention the exceptions allowed within the ban, such as allowing a member company to accept paid ads for the screens of its own cinemas. And, of course, trailers for coming attractions were exempt. Still, it was explained that the Hays ruling "was made with the objective of protecting theatres from product containing advertising matter."[65]

Product placement remained a very minor part of screen advertising overall. However, it was a little more in evidence than in the silent era. It was a long way from being first choice for a national advertiser since they were even more preoccupied with ad shorts, which were going through their publicity frenzy, or even with the idea of perhaps financing an entire feature-length film—which, of course, was product placement carried to the extreme.

When the *New York Times* editorialized in the summer of 1929 about the disappearance from the screen of the old slide ads, squeezed out by movie management, it went on to note that those advertisers had managed to sneak back onto the screen. "Articles to be advertised are offered as props for films in the making. Automobile manufacturers graciously offer the free use of high-priced cars to studios," observed the editor. "Expensive furnishings for a set are willingly supplied by the makers, and even donated as permanent studio property. For kitchen scenes the manufacturers of nationally advertised food products willingly fill cupboard shelves." Agents trying to get publicity for jewelry or clothing were said to approach movie stars directly. If they would agree to wear a certain item in their movies, it was given to them. In cases where an object was "hard to plant" in a film, the agent, said the editor, would even "offer monetary consideration."[66]

In RKO's *Danger Lights* (1930), a new-model RCA-Victor phonograph was displayed prominently in close-up for 30 seconds in the party scene. As a cross promotion Victor gave a free phonograph and 10 records to each RKO house that played the movie, while RCA dealers hyped the show with displays in their stores. Although no money reportedly changed hands in that placement deal, the practice came close to violating the MPPDA policy that discouraged direct advertising in films. Citing examples such as that, as well as verbal mentions of cigarette brands along with highly visible billboards placed in film backgrounds, the MPPDA went beyond discouraging direct advertising to ordering a ban on all brand-name references for products in cartel-produced and controlled movies. The MPPDA explained it took such action because the practice amounted to free advertising and competed with their own effort to initiate paid advertising in the form of ad shorts. Another reason for imposing that ban was the growing intolerance of the audience to screen ads. Those shorts were said to be frequently greeted by catcalls by viewers; one such ad short exhibited at the Strand cinema in New York prompted at least 30 people to walk out. Such responses led the cartel to soon extend the brand-name ban in its entertainment film to a ban on all screen ads (including the shorts) in the cinemas controlled by its members. Worried about audience hostility to screen ads and the effect of radio on movie attendance (radio had grown rapidly from 1928 onward with the inception of the first network, CBS, but had also been rapidly transformed into a sponsor-subsidized media) the motion picture industry's bans on screen ads were attempts to publicly show it provided, theoretically, advertising-free entertainment. It was all part of the film industry's effort to differentiate itself from radio by adopting an aura of quality and sponsor-free amusement.[67]

Ban or no ban, product placement still popped up once in a while in the majors' output. MGM's 1931 release *Easiest Way* was said to carry publicity for seven national advertisers—"probably the biggest plug even accorded from the screen," said one observer. A sequence in that picture was set in an advertising agency with artists' drawings of Old Gold cigarettes, Coca-Cola, Phoenix Hosiery, Mallinson Silks, Cadillac, Parker Pen, and Santa Fe Railroad easily visible. Also included in the film was a scene showing the Old Gold blindfold cigarette taste test. Exhibitors booking *Easiest Way* were notified by MGM to obtain stills of scenes with the "open advertising" because, explained Metro, those ads "were purposely included in the picture so that exhibitors would have plenty of exploitation material with which to boost box office receipts." According to the report, "While pictures have from time to time given a free ad to nationally known companies or products, never before has any single feature combined so much as *Easiest Way*."[68]

A different account a few weeks later said the tendency to incorporate advertising in some feature films, by methods just sufficient to get over a trademark, was officially denied by the cartel as a substitute for the ad shorts, then just starting to fall on hard times. Hollywood producers explained that were they being paid for the exhibition of a trade name they would have to make that fact known to exhibitors in their contractual dealings with them. In the case of one industry, where a hookup was admitted, said a journalist, "Denial was made that any money changed hands; that the exploitation was part of the story and that the industry getting the benefit merely co-operated by way of return." Hollywood had long tried to make the narrow distinction that if no money directly changed hands in a product placement arrangement then no violation of any kind had taken place. Other considerations (free props, airline flights, and so forth) were never deemed to count in Hollywood's view, no matter how valuable they may have been, just as long as no hard cash was involved. Happily enough, the cartel's lobby arm usually conveniently saw fit to order bans, or "discourage" practices only if they were "paid" practices, leaving vague or undefined the status of things such as product placement if the arrangement did not involve any cash transfer.[69]

Independent exhibitors were said to be prepared, in the spring of 1931, to battle producers on "the issue of hidden advertising in feature productions." While the investigating independents had not yet detected any features openly containing advertising they felt several came very close to the line. Concealed advertising, those exhibitors declared, was "obnoxious" to them and those who felt that way—that those who wanted to maintain a program of 100 percent entertainment should not, even unwittingly, be subjected to screening features containing paid advertising matter.[70]

Two months later newspapers were protesting to the studios against the exploitation of commercial products in features, claiming this was depriving them of some of the money they would have received from ads. In response to that complaint the studios told the papers they were not receiving any money but were willing to give a plug to anything that in turn would plug the movies. That is, they were not averse to displaying products in their movies for which an advertising tie-in could be arranged. Reportedly one advertising agency that handled space in a number of East Coast newspapers was turned down on a contract by a drinking water company that, it said, paid $30,000 to one Hollywood major to have the water displayed in a scene. Also part of that scene was dialog that had one of the characters insisting on having that particular brand of water in his home at all times.[71]

*Variety* reported in June 1931 that the acceptance of cash from national advertisers for merchandise plugs in features from the majors was "not altogether remote." Several of the majors were then said to be considering the idea, because of the financial hard times associated with the Depression. Said one studio executive, "We are unconsciously advertising these national products now whether or not we want to. Why not get paid for it?" He added that "These advertisers support the radio and could almost be relied upon to support the picture business, if necessary." Referring to the fact that no interior of a store nor scarcely any exterior street scene could be shot without showing some signs and/or products, this plan therefore, went the story, contemplated including advertising "in such a way that the audience would not be conscious of the plug." Impetus for this change of direction on the part of the majors was said to have come from the outside. Several so-called service companies in the East had lined up national manufacturers and were charging them for trying to put their signs and products into the movies. One such company was reported to have submitted lists to the majors of over 200 companies that wanted to see their products break into films that way. Seeing such a large list of presumably eager advertisers was the catalyst for the majors to start contemplating paid product placement.[72]

Next, a month later, the angle on attempts by advertisers to get their products onscreen was the stocking in Hollywood of several warehouses with every conceivable type of commodity and a "well conducted campaign by agents to get that merchandise into the hands of producers for free use in pictures." Two agents in Hollywood each represented large numbers of national advertisers. They had catalogued every item in their warehouses and submitted the lists regularly to studios to keep them up-to-date with changes in stock. "They follow picture production schedules religiously and submit idea whenever they think these commodities can fit into scenes," said the reporter. "So far the plan has been the means of saving many thousands of dollars to the studios, but it is getting tough for the prop companies who rent articles." An example given was the free loan of $24,000 worth of office furniture to one of the majors with the loaning company being satisfied that its styles in that type of furniture would distinguish it to those that might be interested—no brand name, of course, existed to be shown. Nevertheless that furniture company did ask for, and receive, a still photo showing the furniture being used in the film. Several thousand dollars of canned goods were also warehoused in Hollywood, stored solely with the hope that eventually they would reach the shelves of a store scene in a movie.[73]

However, by the end of 1932 all of the hype and publicity and hope and expectations for a strong partnership between films and advertising had come to an end. Ad trailers had remained close to non-existent throughout the period as their time had not yet come. Product placement was somewhat more visible than in the past but slid away as the cartel took steps to limit the practice and all screen advertising. Ad shorts received the greatest attention but fell into disfavor for a variety of reasons. Audience resentment and hostility to screen ads, in any format, worried the producers as did opposition from newspapers, and as did a vigorous opposition from a good number of exhibitors. Some in the industry, at all levels, favored screen advertising because of the extra revenue, but a larger number argued the potential price to be paid—reduced attendance, newspaper retaliation—was too great a price to pay. Screen advertising, they thought, was a short-sighted strategy. All of these factors were involved in the various cartel bans to limit screen advertising. That several majors tried to get involved in the production, distribution and exhibition of the material in 1930–1931 indicated that the majors' bans were not highly principled stands designed to protect the paying audience's right to 100 percent entertainment but rather an expedient response in the face of opposition.

Another factor was a worry among the majors that independent producers of ad shorts might move on to produce feature-length films, paid for by advertisers, and thus threaten to undercut the Hollywood cartel's complete control of the industry. If the ad short business grew vigorous that prospect became more likely. There were already a lot of independents producing those ad shorts efficiently, and they did not charge the bloated fees Hollywood did (as it always had done within the inefficiencies and excess costs of a cartel system). If Hollywood could not control and dominate the screen advertising field, as it did with entertainment films—and it looked like it could not—then Hollywood would make sure the field never grew or amounted to much. And it did not, at this time. With the majors controlling the bulk of the most important first-run cinemas, and not showing ad shorts from the independents, it meant that a national advertiser could not get national circulation with an ad short (in the way he could get national circulation from popular magazines, or even from the radio) and so they lost interest to a great extent. All the while the majors and the exhibitors, who could not agree on how the screen advertising field should be structured and how its income was to be split, cloaked their differences under the guise they were defending the audience from commercialization, self-righteously pointing to the radio, and ensuring their customers got 100 percent entertainment. So, as 1932 ended, the screen ad issue was very quiet. But it would not stay that way for long.

# 3

# War on Free Shows, Stars Sell Cars, Business Finds Its Voice

## *1933–1944*

Tendencies toward the extension of advertising to the entertainment program itself invite public ill-will for the industry. This is especially true whether the effort be by direct presentation of outright advertising films or by some indirect effort to present advertising under the guise of entertainment.

—Will Hays, 1938

[Screen ads] will eventually lower theatre attendance and cast all motion pictures into disrepute. Any exhibitor showing a film not designed for either entertainment or education or both is cheating his patrons.

—S. Charles Einfeld, Warner Bros., 1939

During this period ad trailers, ad shorts, and product placement had a more equal position within the screen advertising field as each vied with the others, and assorted other opposition, to become the most important aspect of the field. However, in light of the low position to which screen ads had fallen by the end of 1932, one of the first things attempted by a national advertiser was to use a novel format—to oppose the cinema rather than to partner with it. On Saturday, December 1, 1934, in New Haven, Connecticut, Standard Oil of New Jersey opened its live Guy Lombardo advertising road show. Headed by that very famous bandleader, the show was booked for a month of one-night stands in the major cities of 15 eastern states. All performances were to be free to the public. Standard Oil was paying Lombardo $10,000 a week for the commercial show; the band's regular salary for a stage booking was $7,500 a week. At that first performance the 2,000-seat rented hall (not a cinema) was packed, with several hundreds turned away. In response, "War has been declared by show business against the commercial free show," said a report. Film men were irate. Acting as a spokesman for the Hollywood cartel Harry S. Warner stated it was imperative the show be called off because it would hurt the motion picture industry. Also worrying was that a precedent had been set; the idea might escalate. If Standard Oil did not cancel this free show immediately, Warner darkly warned, reprisals would be prepared. Specifics were not given but speculation was that the industry would respond as a whole—that cinema screens across the nation could be used and that all members of the film industry could be asked to boycott Standard (Esso was the brand) and purchase their gas and oil from others.[1]

In its review of the show *Variety* gave it much praise, calling it "a two-hour lineup of high-priced talent." More acts were involved in this stage revue than just Lombardo and his band. A full house was achieved despite an almost complete lack of advance publicity. No newspaper ads were placed and since they got no advertising revenue from it, the newspapers did not mention the show at all in any of their columns or news features. The only publicity for the program was a touring sound truck that made the rounds of the main streets of New Haven a few hours before the curtain rose. One of the acts in the show briefly mentioned Esso gasoline. Other than that the review reported the show contained no other plugs for Standard Oil except for a silver Esso drop in the stage setting and the fact that the ushers for the show wore Esso ribbons.[2]

Concerted action by the Hollywood cartel resulted in the premature closing, on December 10, in Springfield, Massachusetts, of the Standard Oil free show, after a compromise was reached. Under the terms of the agreement the combined majors' cinema circuits were obliged to take over and play the oil show, intact, for the balance of the original free-route contract. Reportedly the troupe had been guaranteed 12 weeks' work by Standard. When it played those cinemas it was specified that it had to carry the same name it had as a free show: "Guy Lombardo—Esso Marketers Revue." Other than that no other commercial mentions or inferences were to be made. In its cinema bookings the show would not be free. Circuits that agreed to contribute time at their chains were: RKO, Loew's (MGM), Warner Bros., Paramount, and Skouras (Fox). Only five of Hollywood's eight majors owned cinemas (Columbia, Universal, and United Artists were the exceptions). Exact financial arrangements were then unknown except that Esso had contracted to pay a total of $15,000 a week with $5,000 of that being the total for all the supporting acts who were also said to be receiving more than their usual rate, as was the Lombardo aggregation. Worries that the idea might escalate were apparently well founded for it was reported, "During the past week other gas and oil companies were making overtures to show sources for other exploitation shows in competition to Esso." Of the half dozen Esso free shows that were held, all drew full houses. All took place in symphony halls, arenas, and so forth, not cinemas. Originally Esso had tried to rent closed (due to the Depression) Paramount cinemas for its shows but was turned down flat. During the film industry's brief campaign against Standard Oil, Allied Theatres of Massachusetts (230 houses) sent protest wires to everyone they could think of, from President Franklin D. Roosevelt to the Chamber of Commerce to the Board of Trade to Standard Oil itself. Allied threatened to take its fuel oil business (one million gallons a year) elsewhere. Newspapers generally refused to give the show any publicity or mention whatsoever. Hype was limited to the sound truck and to world of mouth. One Boston performance had a full house of 3,300 with at least 1,000 turned away.[3]

A couple of weeks later reports from cinemas then playing the Esso show "indicate that advertising plugs for the oil company's products are being liberally sprinkled through the performance despite the circuits and Essos agreement that trade mention is to be confined to the billing." When it played a cinema in Syracuse (where a double bill cost 40-cents) one feature was dropped to accommodate the show and the price was set at 50 cents. At Schenectady, New York, the price was increased 15 cents to 55 cents while in Albany the price increase was 35 cents, above the regular 40-cent top for films.[4]

Free shows commercially sponsored as competition for cinemas, and others, then died out as a concept, but only until the fall of 1935 when the idea surfaced again. That time some 10 to 12 big industrial firms—including Standard Oil of New Jersey, General Motors, Schenley Distillers (whiskey), and the Atlantic and Pacific (A&P) grocery chain—were said to be contemplating showcasing their products in that fashion. One difference this time was that these shows would be intended for company dealers and employees exclusively. Nevertheless, there was a worry that some of these shows might be opened to the general public. Esso was said to be planning on sending out the Guy Lombardo band (which it sponsored on the radio) on a free "block parties" tour. Standard Oil planned to tie-in with local services by donating blocks of tickets to firemen, policemen, the American Legion, and other organizations. Those people could then sell the tickets, if they wished, to raise money for local charities. Singer Kate Smith was then doing a show for A&P that had already played Boston and Detroit. Monitoring the situation closely was the cartel. Reports to the Hays office on the Smith show indicated that, indeed, only A&P employees attended, and by invitation only. Kate Smith's show consisted of 30 minutes of entertainment (her singing) and 30 minutes of company sales material. Based on that the cartel dismissed the show as no threat.[5]

Another brief wave of interest in advertiser-financed free shows surfaced in 1940 when the makers of Chesterfield cigarettes rented a cinema in the Brandt theater chain (a New York circuit), but patrons at the free show made a mess and damaged the house. Chain head Harry Brandt said he would not rent one of his houses in similar circumstances again. One aspect of the affair that embarrassed Brandt was the opposition to free shows by many members of the Independent Theatre Owners Association, of which he was president. In fact that group had recently adopted a resolution, introduced by Brandt himself, against any more such free shows. Although the industry knew it would not be hurt by a one-off show like this one it continued to worry that a precedent might be set. Five years after the fact Esso was still on Hollywood's mind.[6]

Around the same time Izzy Rappaport, who operated Baltimore's Hippodrome (one of the few consistent stage show houses then left in the U.S.), was playing the Glenn Miller band, with a salary guarantee of $8,500 for the week against a 50-50 split of the gross. Miller was also doing three free broadcasts for his Chesterfield sponsor over CBS at the 3,500-seat Lyric Hall, tickets for which were distributed free. While the Lyric was a concert hall it also had a screen that could accommodate the Chesterfield 40-minute commercial film *Tobaccoland*, which was "being given away with the Miller orchestra."[7]

A related promotion took place in a number of small towns in 1935. Merchants in larger towns often made pitches to people living in smaller surrounding towns to drive to the larger centers to do their shopping, leaving small town merchants with declining sales. In response the merchants in the small town of Blue Mountain, Mississippi, came up with a free show idea. They got together and rented a cinema in their town for a specific day for a flat fee (including the films to be screened that day). Next the merchants gave out free cinema tickets to their customers in the hope that it would induce more people to shop locally. That idea was said to have spread to other small communities in the state and into Alabama. In a variation, at Bay Minette, Alabama, the exhibitor sold the merchants a batch of tickets at a special price. Then the merchants gave out the tickets to their purchasing customers.[8]

Later that same year a new film series called *Fashion Magazine* made its debut. It featured what were described as "short dramatized scenes" about Oshkosh suitcases, Underwood typewriters, Simmons mattresses, Kathleen Mary Quinlan cosmetics, and other products. At the end the film closed with a "fashion show of Paris gowns." Bypassing the regular movie houses the *Fashion Magazine* was touted as having a theater chain of its own, by the advertising man who conceived the idea, Samuel Tauber. He claimed he had negotiated with department stores across the U.S. and they had agreed to screen the films in their stores several times a day. A new edition of *Fashion Magazine* was scheduled to be released each month. Each film ran 20–30 minutes in length, devoting two to three minutes to each product. Subscribing stores would pay a rate that depended on their city's population, with $300 a month expected to be the top price (that sum included rental of the 16-mm film, the projector and sound equipment, and an eight-by-10-feet screen). Advertisers also paid, of course, a rate based on the number of stores screening the film. Nothing more was heard about this scheme.[9]

Newsreels came in for criticism in 1940 because of a supposed growing tendency of newsreels to give free plugs to commercial firms. Exhibitors argued that since they paid for a newsreel they had a right to expect it to be devoted strictly to news. Theater operators did not object if the mention of a company was pertinent to the news value of the subject but they complained that some newsreels were moving into the category of advertising films.[10]

Endorsements continued to cause a certain amount of difficulties for the motion picture industry as the cartel tried to control it. By 1935 it was reported that the Hays office ban on any more endorsements was completely gone. Companies, studios, and actors were all ignoring the edict and lining up endorsements. "With the exception of Garbo and Marlene Dietrich, almost every star in Hollywood has some sort of a commercial angle," noted one observer. Lever Brothers Lux soap had every actress in motion pictures signed up to endorse its soap, "with four or five exceptions." Warner Bros. had tied up the stars on its last 10 pictures with Buick automobiles.[11]

A beer ad in the *New Yorker* magazine upset the Hays office in 1940. The star of the ad was Ed Sullivan (newspaper columnist and stage show emcee), who proclaimed "My beer is the dry beer." Seconding that motion were actors (pictured in the ad) Arthur Treacher, Marjorie Weaver, Betty Jaynes, and Bela Lugosi. Those four were members of Sullivan's troupe when he conducted his stage tour a few months earlier. The cartel's MPPDA group, through the Hays office, had always frowned on the idea of screen personalities being used as "stooges" for alcohol promotion. In this case the four actors were let off lightly and not punished but, said an account, "it must not happen again, warned the advertising purity squad."[12]

Merchandising tie-ins continued to grow and to become an even more integral part of Hollywood and the picture business. Within a week after the opening of *Gone with the Wind* in Atlanta (it opened slowly, city by city, to keep the hype going for a longer period) retail sales of tie-in merchandise amounted to $636,250. The biggest thing about that film, thought one observer, "is that it is the first picture that shows promise of selling in substantial volume such standard merchandise as furniture, bedspreads, and drapery (chiefly reproductions or adaptations of originals used in the picture) as well as novelties like dolls, cocktail sets, children's paint books, and costume jewelry—already thoroughly exploited by Walt Disney and his animated cartoon characters." Other *GWTW* items included "Scarlett" nail polish, dresses, men's ties, jewelry, and belts. Altogether 37 manufacturers—only one from each product area— had been licensed by the film's producer MGM, with 25 more having made application. The cheapest item was a locket that sold for 25 cents; the most expensive was a dress retailing for $89.95. In a similar vein, Disney's *Snow White* sold $18 million worth of merchandise related to that film in 18 months.[13]

Near the end of 1939 Paramount set up its own commercial licensing department to effect deals for commercial tie-ins with its movies. Impetus was to cover the characters from its *Gulliver's Travels* release. MGM also had its own licensing department. Paramount had to that date negotiated contracts with 63 commercial firms, against Walt Disney's 72 separate companies in connection with its *Pinocchio*. Disney did not then have its own licensing department but went through a firm led by Kay Kamen.[14]

The idea that trade followed the film was heralded again by business writer Harry Plummer in an automobile trade journal in 1938. He argued the auto industry benefited from the steadily growing association of U.S. motor vehicles and movies, not only at home in America but also overseas. "Today one of the liveliest of auxiliary sales forces for the car, truck, and tractor producer is the photoplay, into which every type, class, and make of vehicle makes its way," said Plummer, "and sometimes, indeed, is featured in a role secondary only to that of the most glamorous star." A car in a movie, he felt, could reveal at a glance many aspects of a character, such as his financial status. Plummer declared "Oftimes, sales or rentals of a car or truck directly result from the showing of a film in which a particular model, shooting across the screen in a dramatic sequence, happens to catch the fancy of a spectator thousands of miles from the production plant or major distribution centers of that individual make." He said that on many occasions he had seen patrons from around the globe emerge from a Hollywood movie sold on a particular make of car that they went on to purchase from their local dealer, "the direct result of the involuntary selling ally, the film."[15]

In Plummer's view U.S. business received a big benefit from the American movies as an auxiliary sales force and especially so in the export markets of the world. Motor boats, electric refrigerators, all manner of other electrical goods, radio sets, sewing machines, office equipment, millinery, women's dresses and men's clothing, toilet accessories, and just about all other merchandise turned out in U.S. shops and factories were "impulsed in their saleability abroad, as well as at home, by Hollywood's product."[16]

Industrial films—the ones for in-house use—continued to grow and to flourish as one aspect of the picture industry. One 1935 account claimed a growth rate of 100 percent in the production of industrial films over the course of a few years. Most were said to be shot in 35-mm and then reduced down to 16-mm since most business firms had hardware designed for that size film. Average length of these items was three to six reels and they were strictly for use by industrial companies in their branches or for special shows conducted by their salesmen. "Few if any," said the report, "are for display in regular picture houses."[17]

Business reporter William Ganz observed that year that during the previous three years 81 national firms had made use of industrial films they produced for themselves or had commissioned; 48 of those companies had used them continuously over the three-year period. During 1934, said Ganz, 22,635 organizations in 9,826 communities across America inquired—through clearinghouses that distributed industrial films—about showing them. An example he cited for the use of industrial films revolved around the recent technological arrival of beer in cans. The American Can Company made a movie to enable their salesmen to convince the brewing industry of the soundness of the idea. A&P produced a four-reel industrial film to educate its store managers and clerks to talk coffee with their customers. Ganz identified six main uses for industrial films: 1) consumer showings to non-theatrical audiences; 2) sales training purposes in large firms; 3) trade showings to retailers and jobbers; 4) educational and vocational showings in schools and colleges; 5) point-of-sales showings in department stores; and 6) "occasional theatrical showings in neighborhood motion picture houses" (neighborhood houses were those that were not downtown and did not screen first-run features, only second-run or later.)[18]

One other main use not mentioned by Ganz was probably overlooked because it was just appearing when Ganz wrote his piece. That was to use industrial films to sell business itself—to sell the U.S. economic system. It was a type of advertising that was designed to convince Americans that, in the words of the old cliché, "What's good for General Motors is good for the U.S.A." It was left to business reporters S. H. Walker and Paul Sklar to mention, in 1938, a type of advertising that came to sometimes be called "institutional advertising." For example, Acme Widgets could take out an ad to sell Acme Widgets; it could take out an ad to sell widgets in general (hyping a class rather than an individual brand); it could take out an ad to make its name look good (by, for instance, sponsoring a march for a charity); or it could take out an ad designed to extol the virtues of a capitalist system that made it so rich that it could take out an ad designed to extol…. Those last two types of ads were institutional or advocacy advertising. According to Walker and

Sklar, during the Depression the American people turned against the men who managed American business (presumably referring to the social unrest of the 1930s, marches, demonstrations, demands for the implementation of welfare safety-net provisions, and so forth). "As business men saw it, certain of the prerogatives that management had always possessed were threatened with usurpation." As a result various business organizations began working to establish "friendly relations with the public." Management conceived that task as one of "selling business to the public," wrote the pair, which, in effect to them meant selling a certain general philosophy. "This philosophy is based on an interpretation of Adam Smith's classical economies, and it is sufficiently extensive to guide our every public action, social, political, and economic," they explained. "Furthermore, it supports the conclusion that 'American business cannot be separated from America,' which means that business management cannot be supposed to have interests differing basically from labor's, the consumer's, or the general public's." For the first time, beginning around 1933, said Walker and Sklar, business began to function as a political unit, attempting to direct and control public opinion just as political partisans always had done. Business began to make new and special use of magazine and newspaper advertising, radio, editorial publicity, and industrial films.[19]

Also in 1938, a memorandum on commercial movies prepared at the J. Walter Thompson advertising agency addressed the current and potential applications of film to business sales and institutional problems. Memo authors Wallace Boren and Fred H. Fidler concluded the screen's influence on the American standard of living—on style, recreation, decoration, and so on—seemed destined for a much broader use of "intra-organizational and public propaganda." Acknowledged by the memo's authors was the "need for an interpretive humanization of business" to the public. They recommended film to the nation's industrialists as a way to accomplish that task and "for whom Fireside Chats [a reference to President Franklin D. Roosevelt's favorite and perhaps most effective method of "bonding" with the public] over the radio are not a practical medium."[20]

During the early 1930s, said historian William Bird, public relations and advertising specialists had begun to argue that the pro-business publicity typically spread by the National Association of Manufacturers (NAM—the main lobby group for manufacturers), the U.S. Chamber of Commerce, and others had become ineffective and clichéd in containing or beating back the anti-corporate liberalism of the New Deal. They urged business to adopt the successful commercial formulas of the newest and most popular mass media. And so America's largest industrial corporations entered the entertainment business, to an extent, as the most effective way of asserting their social and political leadership. When that approach was used by industry it meant it abandoned the old industrial film method of demonstrations of manufacturing processes for the dramatization of the personal meaning of enterprise. Advertisers hoped that by using such a method they could "re-establish a political climate conducive to the autonomous expansion of corporate enterprise."[21]

As an example of the different methods used in these institutional industrial films Bird pointed out the type of film produced around 1930 by Western Electric's subsidiary, Modern Talking Pictures (a major producer then of industrial films). Modern aggressively pushed the supposed immediacy and intimacy of its typical "screen talk" film, boasting that it "Makes personal appearances in 10 cities at once." Usually such a film featured a tuxedo-clad executive delivering an after-dinner talk to, presumably, his guests—the audience (he was alone in the film). Though little evidence remained to suggest what effect screen talks had upon popular audiences during the Depression, said Bird, the little that did suggested that, like business radio talks, the sponsored screen talk failed as it delivered "a transparent and personally meaningless defense of business interests and activities." In comparison stood a 1934 sponsored film produced for the Ford car company that attacked the Roosevelt administration's proposal for an inheritance tax with a narrator talking over a compilation of factory scenes broken up by animated charts and graphs. According to famed author Upton Sinclair, who saw the film one evening in a small cinema in Pasadena, California, it moved quickly to how such a tax's effect would filter down and hurt Ford workers. Remarked Sinclair sarcastically, "Of course, we can understand that was the crux of the whole thing: that was what the makers of the movie were really concerned about—the welfare of the workers at the Ford factory! Oh, yeah!"[22]

Advertising specialists (and not Hollywood) brought dramatic, documentary effects to bear on the mounting institutional problem of the corporation as the 1930s progressed. Bitter strikes hit the auto and steel industries in 1936-1937. Only months after General Motors settled with the United Autoworkers it released the film *From Dawn to Sunset* (1937), which depicted an army of interdependent auto workers and salaried personnel awakening to a montage of alarm clocks, well-dressed children, and pleasant suburban streets that led to the gates of Chevrolet plants across America. And how the GM payroll drove the local economies of its 12 plant cities. That same year NAM resumed the production and distribution of industrial films, something it had abandoned in 1916. *Men and Machines* (1937) was one of two shorts NAM packaged as a series, called *Let's Go America,* which set out "to explode the old Frankenstein picture of the machine ruining man" (by causing unemployment). The plot of that movie pitted the time-tested wisdom of Dad against the unproven theories of young Ted. In the film's opening, well-known author Lowell Thomas narrated the story of an old retired machine-shop foreman, Dad. His son Carl had a young friend, Ted, who believed machines were ruining the country. When Ted told Dad his theory Dad set him straight by going into "the facts." *Men and Machines* just happened, coincidently, to have scenes that were full of modern consumer goods—a veritable cornucopia. NAM publicists suggested to cinema owners who booked this film that they should contact stores selling automobiles and modern consumer goods such as vacuum cleaners, refrigerators, kitchen equipment, and so forth, and ask them to display window cards tying the movie in with the articles they were selling. The window cards read "If you work ... or want to work, see this dramatic talking picture."[23]

United States Steel's *Men Make Steel* (1937) documented the production of steel from iron ore. While its Technicolor and symphonic score won it critical acclaim and theatrical release, it was done in the old industrial film style. Thus, in 1940 it was modernized with a new prologue added to the original film's demonstration of steel making that introduced the drama of steel consumption. In that prologue a newly married couple pondered over the furnishings and equipment of their new home while the narrator told of steel's contributions to present-day living and "the big part quality steel plays in the comfort, pleasure and service of daily life." As this shift in industrial film emphasis took place, said Bird, they "took on the domestic stagecraft of theatrically released feature films."[24]

One of the more famous in this genre was shown extensively at the New York World's Fair, of 1939-1940. For that occasion Westinghouse produced *The Middleton Family at the New York World's Fair* (five reels, in Technicolor), using soap-opera techniques to sell a progressive image for industry in general and its products. It was a comedy-drama about a family ostensibly on a visit to the Fair (although viewers, perhaps expecting to see a tour of that Fair, were probably disappointed when the family never got out of the Westinghouse pavilion). Husband Tom was a self-reliant, successful, small-town businessman; wife Jane marveled at Westinghouse's appliance display and needled Tom to buy her a dishwasher; daughter Babs was a college student who lived in New York with her grandmother; son Bud was resigned to the inevitability of unemployment and relief after high school, as were many of his friends. Babs had two suitors; Jim Treadway who just happened to be a guide at the Westinghouse exhibit, and Nicholas Makaroff, vaguely leftist and bohemian he liked bow ties and abstract art. Makaroff sneered at the Westinghouse "temple of capitalism." Accompanying Babs, Bud and Makaroff through the exhibit Treadway demolished his rival's pointed questions about automation and unemployment. Later Babs dumped Makaroff, but only after Granny spotted that a piece of jewelry he gave her was a fake—just cheap costume jewelry (he had said it was a valuable family heirloom passed down from generation to generation). Thus, the film's climax presented Babs's estrangement from him not as an ideological matter but as a betrayal by insincerity and deceit, because Babs was incapable of making the connection between ideology and meaning. Concluded Bird, "The material circumstances and props of the Middletons' home life exude a cheery optimism and constitute the stage upon which ideological issues play as a matter of personal convenience and well being. The home, in short, measures the meaning of the system." Scenes set at the grandmother's house showed it crammed with all the modern appliances and products.[25]

From the early 1940s onward NAM dealt exclusively in this method, whereby little plays were employed to dramatize what its publicists considered recognizable human situations—a young pilot contemplating the joys of home life; an elderly immigrant celebrating the opportunities in America; the son of a newspaper editor, who, like the flier and the immigrant, offered a plea to preserve progress impervious to political change. Titles released included *American Anniversary* (NAM, 1943) and *Postmark U.S.A.* (NAM, 1943). All of them, of course, were attempts to sell Americans on the joys and virtues of the capitalist system in general and in particular the extraordinary virtues of American business and industry as it functioned within U.S. capitalism.[26]

After an apparent absence of several years ad trailers started to resurface around 1936. One example of a regional use of trailers that year took place when radio stations KJBS (San Francisco) and KQW (San Jose) publicized their programs through the use of ad trailers on the screens of 21 cinemas in Northern California cities; the theaters likewise called attention to their feature films through the use of spot ads throughout the week on the two radio stations. Those screen trailers were said to be viewed by 200,000 people per week.[27]

Around the same time it was reported that national concern Carter's Little Liver Pills (described as a prolific user "of quickie blurbs" on radio stations across the U.S.) had made six one-minute ads for use in cinemas. Each was said to tell a little story and averaged three actors per story. Advertisers were said to be prepared to compensate cinemas on the basis of tickets sold, and other national advertisers were said to be interested. An account noted of the entry of Carter's into the ad trailer field, "This appears to be the most concerted attempt to place advertising on picture screens since the Chesterfield and similar series of five years ago."[28]

Lucky Strike cigarettes was another national firm thinking about going in for screen ad trailers. By early in 1937 it had reportedly made several one-minute trailers, using feature film actors, for testing. Before placing the ads with cinemas, however, Lucky Strike planned to ask its advertising agency, Lord & Thomas, to make a survey of the motion picture field to determine how many spots would take such ad trailers and what the charge would be. If the outlook was judged to be favorable Lucky Strike declared it would use "major" screen stars for any future trailers it might produce.[29]

One of the problems associated with ad trailers (and ad shorts for that matter)—distribution—was responded to in 1937 by the formation of two relatively large distribution companies. General Screen Advertising, Inc. (GSA) was formed by several screen advertising distributors that claimed to have several thousand movie houses, combined, under exclusive contract for advertising rights. The largest and most important single firm in that organization was the Alexander Film Company. A similar service was offered by the Screen Broadcasts (SB) group, consisting of several associated companies that produced, distributed, and serviced ad films. The rate schedule for either group was based on the number of people reached, for example, $3 per 1,000 attendance for a film 100 to 150 feet long (60 to 90 seconds). National advertisers using ad trailers of a minute or so in length were said to be increasing and then included Chevrolet cars, Bond bread, and Wesson oil. Apparently the Lucky Strike campaign had received the go-ahead, for it was reported that their ad trailers, in which "major-minor" Hollywood stars would explain their preference for the cigarette, had been released by Lord & Thomas through GSA. Other accounts with GSA were Florsheim shoes, Carter's Little Liver Pills, Alka-Seltzer, Westinghouse, General Electric, and Norge appliances. The Alexander Film Company was said to specialize in 60 and 90 second film ads and produced and distributed for about 40 advertisers of national standing including RCA Manufacturing, Zenith Radio, Philco Radio and Television, and Studebaker automobiles. A "conservative" estimate from a large producer of industrial films put the amount spent in his field at $10 million in 1936—others put the figure at $15 million. In any case, though, that represented money spent on all industrial films—the vast majority of which were only used in house.[30]

According to one report in early 1938 the only kind of screen advertising that could be said to have consistently gained regular audience consent was the ad trailer, described as "frank, straight out" advertising that was only on the screen for a minute or 90 seconds. "No attempt is made to sugar-coat or mislead the theatre patron; hence, he sometimes tolerates it," was the conclusion drawn.[31]

Later that year the spread of sponsored films and outright advertising subjects on the screens, described as largely confined to two-minute trailers, was said to have reached such proportions that various factions in the film and newspaper fields were considering plans to curb it. Favoring the continued spread of ad trailers into cinemas were advertising agencies and sponsored film producers who saw the screen as a new advertising medium. Some agency executives had accepted membership in the newly formed National Advisory Council for Screen Advertising, a body set up by the Alexander Film Company. As well, as evidence of increasing interest in the field was that five national advertising agencies had by then set up film departments while another dozen were considering the same thing. An estimate given here was that ad trailers were regularly screened by some 6,000 houses. Lucky Strike, Feenamint, and Eveready had recently employed them. It was considered almost a certainty that this reported influx of ad material would be combated by the Hays office and other film industry organizations. Less than two years earlier Will Hays had reiterated that cinemas should be reserved exclusively for entertainment. At the time he contended that the motion picture was not a proper medium for advertising, "whether this be by direct presentation of outright advertising films or by some indirect effort to present advertising films under the guise of entertainment."[32]

Within a couple weeks of the above article being published Thomas Pryor did a piece for the *New York Times* on the same topic—the increase in theater ads over the previous couple of years. He remarked that ad trailers were widely used as "straight pictorial ads" and usually ran from 30 60 seconds. According to a survey Pryor cited, as of early in 1938 more than 10,000 of the U.S. total of 16,000 houses used the ad trailers as a regular part of the program. They were said to be shown in practically every type of cinema except the deluxe first-run houses in key cities like New York, Chicago, Philadelphia, and so on. In those trailers, said Pryor, the product advertised "is undisguised and no pretense is made that the film is entertainment or has any educational value. Ninety per cent of the advertising is of local merchants and institutions ... and no deception is practiced or attempted on the audience." For each ad trailer the venue was paid from $2.50 to $25 a week, depending on the size of the house and its average weekly attendance. Those 10,000 cinemas using the trailers were spread over 3,554 cities and towns located in every state and had a total weekly attendance of 20 million.[33]

*Business Week* weighed in with its own huge article (12 pages) on how business was using movies to sell itself and its products. It was so long it was labeled a special report (with extra copies available for purchase as offprints) and appeared in May 1939. Cost to produce the ad trailers ranged from $500 to $2,500, although Lucky Strike once doubled that top cost for each of a series of ads in which Hollywood actors appeared. According to this report a problem with ad trailers (or "minute movies," as they were called in print for a time) was that they were so "obviously selling." Indeed, that touched on a prime disadvantage of the movie as a direct-sales aid, as far as cinema screenings were concerned, commented the reporter: "Radio programs are free and there is comparatively little complaint about advertising. But the public pays admission to movie theaters, and doesn't expect or welcome advertising. Hence, in theaters, the advertising message must be so short, as in a minute movie, or so disguised, as in a longer institution production, that the dose will go down easily." Commonest of the straight advertising films were the minute movies, explained the report, roughly comparable to page ads in magazines, "which everyone has seen at one time or another in his neighborhood theater." Ad trailers had been little used until this time, it was reported, because of difficulties in obtaining "certified distribution" expected by national advertisers. Those difficulties had been largely solved, or at least greatly alleviated, by the formation of General Screen Advertising (GSA) and Screen Broadcasts (SB), the two recently formed groups that brought some semblance of a national production and distribution system to the field. "Thus the advertiser can go to either Screen Broadcasts or General Screen Advertising and get complete service for the execution and national distribution of minute movies." Advertisers could run a campaign nationally, or in a single area, or in just one or two markets at a time.[34]

GSA claimed to be able to deliver 35 million circulation per week, according to the *Business Week* report, or any part thereof, through some 8,000 houses it had links with. Both GSA and SB charged advertisers the same rates for cinema exhibition of the ad trailers: for 50-to-60-feet-long trailers, $2.50 per 1,000 admissions ($5 weekly minimum): 61 feet to 90 feet, $3 ($6); 91 feet to 120 feet, $3.75 ($7.50). The most common length used was 60 seconds. A full-page ad in the *Saturday Evening Post* (a circulation of three million-plus copies per week) cost $8,000. In comparison, the cost of reaching three million moviegoers with a 60-second ad would be $7,500, with the production cost of the trailer amounting to several times that of the magazine ad. Also favoring the magazine was that it could point to some amount of "pass-along" readership that could have by itself even exceeded its audited circulation. Nor could the cinema offer the kind of audience selectivity that magazines could—that is, dramatically different demographics for different magazines. Another problem, one of the commonest complaints against minute movies, was that many of the "best" theaters did not screen them. "Of the 17,000-odd houses in the country, better than 50% accept advertising shorts," said the account, "but critics say that a disproportionate percentage of these are small-town or neighborhood theaters."[35]

At the time of the *Business Week* report Chevrolet and Alka-Seltzer ranked among the biggest users of ad trailers. Alka-Seltzer produced about 15 different minute movies in a typical year. Straight advertising trailers were regarded herein as effective in stimulating sales but had the shortcoming of having a comparatively low saturation—meaning audiences would not tolerate too many. In a few communities, reportedly, the audience had set up "booing clubs" to greet the ad trailers. Additional exhibitors to take the ads were harder and harder to sign up. Those who continually refused to accept the trailers were wary of antagonizing customers for the comparatively small revenue derived from screening minute movies.[36]

Fred Fidler, director of the J. Walter Thompson advertising agency Motion Picture Department, said, in October 1940 that more than 10,000 cinemas (out of 17,003 wired for sound at the start of that year) would accept "short advertising playlets" running 40–80 seconds—the so-called minute movies. Those theaters had over 50 percent of the total weekly U.S. cinema attendance and sold about 43 million tickets per week. Excluding local ads, the national medium's potential volume at the prevailing rates (on the basis of a maximum of three ad trailers per weekly program) would, figured Fidler, be more than $20 million per year, but, "It has not yet realized 10 per cent of that potential."[37]

Among the largest users of minute movies, reported Fidler, were: Chevrolet, Proctor & Gamble, Kellogg, Shell, Standard Oil of New Jersey, Singer, Lever Brothers, Alka-Seltzer, Ford, Kraft, Pillsbury Flour, General Electric, Westinghouse, Frigidaire, Camel, Beich Candy, Hubinger Starch, and Eveready Battery. Current national exhibition rates per thousand circulation were then $3 for a 60-second ad, and $3.75 for one of 80 seconds. A premium of up to $1.75 per 1,000 was charged for some Class A chain theaters (first-run outlets). Fidler remarked that first- and second-run neighborhood houses were the venues preferred by most advertisers and because some 20 million of that "cream" circulation (out of the 43 million) was then available to trailers, "the fact that most downtown deluxe houses are not available in metropolitan areas does not handicap the medium nationally." Continuing with his optimistic, but inaccurate, words Fidler went on to say, "Many marketers of mass-market commodities are equally interested in Class C and D theaters in low-income areas. These make up the balance of the 43,000,000 total available circulation." However, also admitted by Fidler was that the circulation of minute movies "is not yet fully audited." Circulation in most cinemas was said to be estimated on the basis of a formula that multiplied the number of seats by a factor of six to eight. Conservative enough, Fidler thought, since most cinemas ran their programs 14–21 times a week, if they ran the ads at every performance. Apparently that was not yet assured, "largely because theater exhibitors have not yet been educated to a faithful performance of contracts. As a result they may eliminate the advertising playlet at certain performances if program time is shortened by delays of any kind or if over-time for the projectionist is imminent." The idea that circulation was not yet "fully audited" was an odd idea since keeping track of the number of tickets sold was a very simple thing to do for cinemas—all ticket rolls were sequentially numbered, and so on. However, what was happening then was that a lot of exhibitors (whose film rental to the distributor was usually a percentage of his gross) attempted to cheat the system and the Hollywood majors by underreporting their attendance counts and receipts.[38]

Industrial film sales volume for 1940 was estimated at $20 million (the total amount received that year to produce such films, including those destined for in-house use only); $7.5 million of that came from standard theatrical channels. Of the advertising material then making its way into cinemas, 75 percent of it was estimated to be minute movies going to 10,000 houses with the other 25 percent being ad shorts (one reel, eight to 10 minutes in length) going to around 4,500 venues. During 1940 an audited circulation method was introduced—an actual physical count was involved—and at the end of 1940 over 500 houses with a total weekly attendance of 2,850,000 were reported to be able to offer audited circulation.[39]

Minute movies were also said to have a large export audience in South Africa and South America. Research on the cinema audience was becoming more and more thorough and sophisticated, said business reporter Dwight Wardell. Data on the size of the audience, geographic location of theaters, and percentage of audiences in upper-and lower-income groups were becoming available, in response to the needs and desires of advertisers. Yet Wardell admitted that a relatively simple thing such as providing audited circulation was only available for about five percent of the houses willing to accept minute movies.[40]

Late in 1941 Canada Dry Ginger Ale began a national advertising campaign of minute movies. Consisting of 14 different trailers, the ads were studded with Hollywood stars such as Pat O'Brien and Edward Arnold. Canada Dry's newspaper, magazine, and radio advertising all featured the film-star copy theme. Until then, declared *Business Week*, advertisers who had trailers made for regular cinemas had been "generally inclined to keep mum about their efforts; consequently, the medium has been shy of much-needed publicity. Canada Dry not only acknowledges its use of the medium; it's inferentially bragging about it, and that's a real break for the commercial movie business." *Business Week* said that 12,000 houses (66 percent of the total) then accepted minute movies whereas in 1935 only 6,500 outlets were available, and, "A lot of good theaters are on the list, not merely the 'shooting galleries'—cheap houses, often showing only wild west fare." According to this business publication there were three broad rules for choosing products for ad trailer plugging: 1) they must be products that lend themselves to demonstration (fridges, cars, and new products like soap powder); 2) they must be products with a glamour appeal (cosmetics, for example); and 3) they must be products hard to dramatize in ordinary advertising (staple items such as salt). With regard to the maximum number of trailers cinemas allowed to play per program it was reported, "A three-film rule is now half-heartedly enforced."[41]

One example of audience hostility to the ad trailers could be found in the aforementioned booing clubs that were occasionally formed. On the night of August 4, 1937, at Little Rock, Arkansas's biggest cinema, 30 members of the newly organized Society for the Booing of Commercial Advertisements in Motion Picture Theatres made their debut by booing lustily as commercials appeared on the screen.[42]

Quickly the phenomenon spread and at the end of that month Tifton, Georgia, cinema owner R. E. Martin filed a suit asking for $10,000 in damages and a restraining order. On August 30 Superior Court Judge R. Eve signed a temporary restraining order against the Tifton Booing Club that ordered them to refrain from booing commercials flashed on the screen at the Tifton Theatre. That suit named as defendants seven reported members of the club and the *Tifton Gazette* newspaper. Allegedly the newspaper published an advertisement signed by members of the Booing Club and that advertisement was injurious to the theater. That ad urged moviegoers to boo the ad films. Members of the booing society claimed they were forced to sit through "long runs" of advertising films while waiting to see the movies they paid their money to see. Tifton's booing group got moral support from the Little Rock group. Then suddenly on September 2, attorneys for the Tifton Theatre dropped the suit against all parties. No reason for that action was reported.[43]

Ad shorts had seemed to have almost disappeared by the end of 1932 under the combined weight of newspaper opposition, the Hays office edict against them, and exhibitor and audience hostility. However, they surfaced again, at least to a limited degree, as soon as 1933. One ad short produced in 1933 was a commercial for General Electric that featured Hollywood luminaries Bette Davis and Dick Powell.[44] *Variety* then declared (prematurely) that the ban on screen advertising "is definitely lifted." Cited as the main reason was Hollywood's relentless search for extra revenue in the Depression—in the face of declining attendances and income. It was estimated that advertising could mean an extra $18 million or more annually for exhibitors. The Loew (MGM) cinema circuit announced it would introduce ad shorts to its programs, but only at its morning shows. Following that, film executives declared there was a market for "shorts that do not 'shout' advertising and which can be rated as entertaining." That was an attitude, remarked the trade journal, that was contradictory to that of only one year earlier. But then, "Pressure was brought to bear upon the industry by American newspaper publishers." Some in the industry believed this so-called return to ad shorts would be permanent "if the product projected is not exaggerated."[45]

Several months after that *Variety* ran another piece to say that advertising was coming back to the screen with a "bang," despite "the edict of the American Newspaper Publishers Assn., which caused all the major picture companies and first run theatres to divorce themselves from it." Still, it was admitted that the majors were not then involved in ad shorts either as producers or exhibitors although up to 2,600 houses were said to be running ad shorts. Hollywood's cartel members were still reluctant to reenter the screen ad field for fear of reviving the war with newspapers. Houses screening the ad shorts were admitted to all be second-run venues, or "lesser grades."[46]

Headway was also being made by ad shorts in the UK. At a 1934 dinner held in London by the Imperial Industries Club the subject was "The Film in Industry and Commerce." Speaker Miles Mander declared that the British public would not suffer advertising films, which were then such a feature in Continental Europe, "But if suitable films were produced in an interesting manner they would prove a great advantage to trade."[47]

Yet, just five years later the situation had changed dramatically. In a speech at the Regent Advertising Club (London) Harold Saward of the advertising agency Saward, Baker, and Company declared that ad films had been accepted by the general public. By way of evidence he said that ad films had been exhibited in 4,200 of the 5,309 cinemas located in Great Britain and Ireland. However, he added that he thought there was "much room for improvement in most advertising films."[48]

General Electric led the way in the production of extravagant ad shorts. In 1935 it premiered its Technicolor production *Three Women* with Hollywood star Johnny Mack Brown and GE household appliances, said *Business Week*. Produced by Sound Pictures, Inc., *Three Women* was said not to be just a technical recitation of the sales arguments for GE's electric kitchen, but also "it's a full-fledged movie, complete with love plot and sufficient human interest." GE hoped to attract 15 million people to see it—not an idle hope, based on the success the company had with two previous ad shorts, *Just Around the Corner* with Bette Davis and Warren William and *What Are You Going to Do Tonight?* starring Walter O'Keefe. Other national advertisers then making ad shorts included: Ford, General Motors, Packard, and Chrysler auto makers; Southern Pacific, Illinois Central, and Chesapeake & Ohio railroads; Aetna and

Metropolitan insurance companies; Goodrich, and Firestone tire companies; Fleischmann's yeast; Wesson Oil; Coca-Cola; American Telephone & Telegraph; Ethyl Dow Chemical; Elgin Watch; E. R. Squibb & Sons; Gulf, and Sinclair refining companies; Westinghouse; Parker Pen; and the Florsheim Shoe Company.[49]

Some of the movies produced by those firms were given screenings outside of regular cinemas, if the latter could not be arranged, or as an adjunct to regular houses. One such was the B. F. Goodrich Tire and Rubber Company's *Love, Honor, and Obey (the Law)*. It ended up being shown for free in rented halls in small communities and turned into a contest with prizes awarded to audience members who correctly listed all 23 traffic violations depicted in the movie. In Marysville, Ohio (population 3,639), the Goodrich show (it contained other free features and ran to two hours) drew a crowd of 1,700 with more than 500 turned away. Cost for the whole affair to the local Goodrich tire dealer was said to be just $76.50. When GSA handled the distribution of ad shorts their charge to the advertiser was reported to be $4.50 for every 150 feet of film per 1,000 circulation. Production cost of the one-reel ad shorts ranged from $5,000 to $15,000 depending on the status of the writer, director, and actors. General Electric was said to be about the only advertiser that used big-name Hollywood stars. This account estimated that in 1934 advertisers spent some $5 million on industrial films, excluding those produced solely for sales training.[50]

A more sobering assessment of the ad short field was delivered in an article published early in 1938. After noting the growth taking place in the industrial film industry the account declared that "it is dubious if the industrials incorporating some entertainment ever will amount to much in the regular film house though hundreds of small theatres now run them for a small payment; mostly under contracts." Reasons advanced for that conclusion, aside from the obvious way the audience resented the camouflaged ad in the shorts, and that the Hays office continued to oppose screen advertising included that exhibitors regularly received complaints from patrons annoyed by ad shorts on the program. They objected because they had paid their admission and they resented any attempts to try and fool them by slipping advertising material into what was presented as just another entertainment picture.[51]

Caravel Distributing unveiled, in March 1938, its one-reel color cartoon comedy adventure *Boy Meets Dog* and claimed it would open in major cities in the following months and that it had been booked with many circuits, although none were named. Based on Gene Byrnes's syndicated comic strip the 10-minute short was made for the Ipana toothpaste account of the Bristol-Myers Company. Director of the ad short was Walter Lantz, creator of Oswald the Rabbit, while Frank Churchill, composer of music for *Snow White*, did the musical numbers. One account described the ad short as 90 percent entertainment, with only about 30 seconds "outright advertising of product."[52]

Another account observed that well-organized advertising plans had been made for the film—that is, to advertise the advertising short. Promotional plans by Bristol-Myers included broadsides to druggists, drugstore displays, and local contests designed to tie-in with the film. While this account acknowledged the same 30 seconds of outright advertising, it also mentioned that, in addition, songs in the films contained references to the virtues of tooth brushing.[53]

Around the time of the Ipana debut Thomas Pryor reported in the *New York Times* that screen advertising had grown sufficiently during the previous three years "to cause the Hollywood producers to strike out against the practice as an 'abuse' of the primary functions of the screen which are to provide entertainment and to promote culture." Reportedly, some exhibitors still booked them without charging a fee, presumably content with saving on the cost of renting a one-reel entertainment short, although most exhibitors by this time were receiving a fee for running ad shorts. As in all other accounts the only houses that did screen them were ones in small towns and second-run or lower in larger cities. Pryor added that the circulation of one- and two-reel ad shorts was still "sporadic" in comparison with the distribution of the ad trailer. Advertising matter was played down as much as practicable in ad shorts because, wrote Pryor, "theatres will only show them when convinced of getting a good short free." Nevertheless, he added, audience reaction to the ad short was reported as "not very good." While it was found that audiences did not seem to take particular offense to the advertising they said the ad shorts, with few exceptions, were dull and uninteresting.[54]

Six months later a reporter explained that opposition from both Hollywood producers and large cinema houses in the leading cities (chains owned by cartel members and independent circuits) to ad shorts indicated that form of advertising had reached its peak and would gradually decline. In some cities it was said that organized protests by local newspapers against those shorts had led cinema operators to drop them. Consumer reaction to them was herein said to be mixed, with some accepted due to their minimum of advertising and others drawing boos.[55]

Stepping into the issue once again was the Hays office. In February 1939 the MPPDA cartel organization placed a new plan in effect for supervising screen advertising by classifying it as such through an advertising code seal. Under the plan all sponsored films would be designated with the caption "This is an Advertising Subject" before it was issued. The Hays office charged $5 per reel as a handling fee for the ad material and had the right to reject the film in its entirety if the subject matter was deemed unworthy of a place on a major theatre screen. Holly-wood-controlled cinemas (then about 2,500 in number) could thus only show ad films that had been so designated. An important exception to the rule was that the new edict applied only to films over 200 feet in length (about two minutes) which, of course, left out all the minute movies. Presumably they were left out because they were obvious advertising and recognized as such by all whereas the ad shorts were often camouflaged, not obviously being advertising. Not that the new edict made any difference. Hollywood-controlled houses were little involved in screening ad films (trailers or shorts) when Hays came out with the new edict, and they remained so. Independent houses outside the direct control of the majors continued as before with their marginal flirtations with screening ad films (both trailers and shorts). But Hays's edict was important in the sense it established a tough public stance to placate opposition groups, such as newspapers, and to show that the majors opposed screen advertising and were working against the practice.[56]

Patron hostility to ad shorts was carried to an extreme in 1940 when John Miller sued the Alexander theatre in suburban Glendale, California, for $10,000, charging the house with conspiracy to defraud by showing a film "not up to the universal conception of pure, wholesome entertainment." The picture in question was produced for the National Association of Manufacturers (NAM) and was characterized by Miller as a "propaganda piece." Miller argued in his lawsuit that he was obliged to "sit through and suffer the tortures of witnessing a film called *Your Town*." Continuing, he alleged he was "lured" into the venue by a promise he would witness entertainment, but as a result of seeing *Your Town* he "developed a lasting cardiac condition caused by increased blood pressure from his indignation at the film." Apparently the short denounced unionism, although Miller said he was never a union member.[57]

In his 1940 assessment of the commercial film field Fred Fidler said that theatrical distribution of ad shorts was much more limited than it was for trailers and haphazard if more advertising matter beyond a "courtesy credit" to the sponsor was included. He felt there were perhaps 5,000 cinemas that would accept one-reel travelogue-style films from sponsors such as Sun Valley or airline or railroad companies. Somewhat fewer houses, he continued, would accept general scientific or institutional films such as those from General Electric or the NAM series, or the longer U.S. Steel and Westinghouse releases. As far as Fidler was concerned, business and industry had begun to recognize and utilize the "potency" of the screen for the "purposeful influencing of opinion, habits and conduct." They took their cue from the entertainment screen's incidental effect on the public's fashions, dances, and fads "and from the realization that millions of people have gained from the screen their clearest if not the most accurate concept of history, geography, crime, fashion, and assorted strata of business and society behaviorism."[58]

Opposition to ad films came from various sources, with the Hollywood cartel's trade group, MPPDA, as active as any. As head of the MPPDA, Will Hays issued an industry annual report in March 1938, in which he proudly pointed to a U.S. motion picture attendance of 85 million per week. He said he was pleased to report that American movies "continue to be free from any but the highest possible entertainment purpose." As a matter of industry policy, Hays reiterated an objection to any general use of the screen for advertising purposes. While he admitted the propriety of the small-town exhibitors' use of ad trailers carrying local advertising matter he argued that even that concession should be on a "reasonable" scale. "Tendencies toward the extension of advertising to the entertainment program itself invite public ill-will for the industry," asserted Hays. "This is especially true whether the effort be by direct presentation of outright advertising films or by some indirect effort to present advertising under the guise of entertainment."[59]

Just one month later Hays said again, "Studios are thoroughly awake to the possible result of a reported effort to use motion picture screens for sponsored films, primarily for advertising purposes." Organized industry continued to be "firm" against the extension of advertising to the entertainment program, he re-stated. Hays and the majors felt ad films were harmful for three reasons: 1) because they cut into the amount of playing time of "legitimate" producers of entertainment material; 2) because they aroused resentment against both the theatre and the majors in the mind of the public; and 3) because they might cause "reflex action" against an advertiser if the public resented the intrusion on the regular program.[60]

On the heels of the Hays statements a pledge that ad films would not be played in any cinema controlled by Warner Bros. was made by Joseph Bernhard, general manager of its theater circuit, at an annual sales convention. He declared that it was unfair to subject the paying public to advertising matter on the screen, adding, "Warner Bros. consider the daily newspaper primarily the place for paid advertising." Bernhard argued the industry and its growth had created a "public obligation for Warner Bros. and, "We intend to fulfill that obligation, so far as our responsibility extends, by protecting the public against a commercial invasion of its chief means of diversion—an invasion that seems to us utterly unwarranted and a menace to the entire industry."[61]

S. Charles Einfeld, advertising and publicity head of Warner Bros., added his thoughts when he declared that "the commercial advertising film is rapidly becoming the industry's greatest evil." Einfeld added that independent cinemas, by supporting the "rapidly spreading" policy of showing ad films, were contributing to a practice "which will eventually lower theatre attendance and cast all motion pictures into disrepute. Any exhibitor showing a film not designed for either entertainment or education or both is cheating his patrons and such remissness will be punished with a consequent decline at the box office."[62]

At the 52nd annual convention of the American Newspaper Publishers Association there was much discussion about competition from other media and what to do about it. It was revealed that 33 U.S. daily papers barred all radio publicity from their papers, including the listings of radio programs. Other newspapers printed the radio program listings but gave the radio no other publicity at all. Frank E. Tripp, general manager of the Gannett newspapers, urged the papers to do something about the diversion of ad revenue to film producers and cinemas through the use of open or covert advertising in films. In his speech Tripp mentioned a six-year survey he had conducted that, he said, revealed that of the 16,500 theaters in America, 7,200 (42 percent) "mostly small and intermediate houses, showing to 28 per cent of the movie patronage, were running advertising openly in trailers (exclusive of trailers for coming attractions) or concealed in films purporting to be purely entertainment." Discussion at the convention brought out a sentiment to deny newspaper publicity to such films.[63]

Tripp's survey convinced the newspaper executives that in the year before, 1937, some $5 million was diverted to screen advertising from other media. He also told the convention that Paramount had completed a deal with one commercial film company to distribute the latter's product in its 1,200 cinemas. RKO and Fox would probably follow suit, he warned, while MGM, he admitted, was still adamant in its refusal to permit ad films on its screens.[64]

Those allegations from Tripp produced a quick response from Paramount. The major declared it had never made any agreement to handle commercials, as charged, nor did it intend to sign any such deals. Paramount added that, in any event, the use of less than full-reel commercials rested with its theatre partners. Quite a few played ad trailers, for example. That was in cinemas affiliated with Paramount, but not directly owned by the studio. Some theaters tied themselves up by taking all the product from a particular major—through block-booking agreements—and thus were under a strong influence from that major, but not actually owned outright.[65]

One of Hollywood's worst fears about ad shorts—that advertisers might take the next step and finance feature films—came true in this period, if only to a very limited degree. *Vogues of 1938* was the first dramatic feature that was really nothing more than a fashion commercial. Made by Walter Wanger Productions in Hollywood, it displayed to the audience more than 100 new fall costumes, hats, and accessories. Department store R. H. Macy & Company was, according to executive vice president Paul Hollister, "a sort of god-father to the idea." Prominent rayon wear and fabric manufacturers were also said to have had their "part" in preparing the film. When it opened August 19 at Radio City Music Hall in New York, Macy's offered reproductions of the merchandise seen in the film.[66]

Another such film was *Highway Patrol* (1938) that, according to reporter Thomas Pryor, was produced by the B. F. Goodrich tire company. Both of those films were listed in the multi-volume *The Motion Picture Guide* (Jay Robert Nash and Stanley Ralph Ross, Chicago; Cinebooks, 1986), along with a capsule review, and treated as though they were regular movies.[67]

Still in 1938 a rumor circulated that other industrial concerns, specifically Ford and General Motors, were pondering the idea of making six-reel features in which only the opening announcements would contain advertising. Those industrialists considering the idea were said to be offering name actors more money than they then received while independent exhibitors were reportedly disposed toward them because those features might be offered to them for nothing—a free feature for the second half of the double bill. However, nothing more came from the idea of advertisers making feature films if for no other reason than the intervention of World War II.[68]

Product placement became far more of an issue as the practice became more prevalent. Or if it was not more prevalent then it received more media attention. A 1935 account in the trade journal *Printers' Ink* dealt with the issue in depth. According to this account, in the movie *Strangers All* a bit of incidental stage business involved the handling of a pack of cigarettes in such a way as to show the Lucky Strike brand. A specific brand of mineral water also appeared in that movie. And in *No More Ladies* where one scene depicted a raid on an icebox, it was not just an electric refrigerator that the actor opened, it was a Frigidaire. "Photography and time give the spectator every opportunity to take in small details that are characteristic of this particular make," said the account. In *I'm a Father,* which materially introduced cigars as a property item, it "seemingly goes out of its way to make it clear that While Owl is the brand preferred." Somewhat different was the "subtle" use of advertising in *Keeper of the Bees.* There was no direct mention or shot of a specific product but the lead character was in poor health and received a long, detailed talk on the health benefits of orange juice. Said the reporter, "While there is nothing done in the picture to make an audience brand-conscious, the film is, nevertheless, doing a job for the citrus industry."[69]

To this *Printers' Ink* reporter there was a noticeable trend not just to show products by brand in entertainment feature films but to mention them as well. Actor Donald Cook went into a nightclub in *Gigolette* and did not order something general, but instead said to the barman, "Bring me some Clicquot." Wondering if all this was a deliberate attempt by the film industry to slip nationally advertised products into entertainment films, the reporter asked an unnamed observer for his opinion. The man said he had also noticed an accumulation of such plugs—a Laurel and Hardy comedy film gave Wonder Bread a certain prominence while also ensuring that a pail of lard used in a scene in the same film had the brand name Cudahy readable; in another picture he had "no trouble" recognizing Chesterfield cigarettes. That observer believed it was likely that some producers were trying to subtly cultivate a public acceptance for the incidental featuring of branded products on the screen. Thus, these instances were all in the nature of trial balloons put out to see if the public would or would not complain. Believing that no money had changed hands to that point with regard to any placements, the observer felt that was the case only because producers were waiting for audiences to show acceptance, or at least not complain, and then, "Isn't it only a step for producers to sell these opportunities to advertisers?" However, the reporter was told by an executive with one of the majors that the industry was not contemplating "any move which would risk the furor created several years ago when efforts were made to present films sponsored by advertisers. At that time the public was quick to express its resentment. The attempts also met with strong antagonism on the part of the newspapers."[70]

When a property man went on a film set, concluded *Printers' Ink*, nothing was done that was not intentional, "And those experienced with Hollywood construe it as no accident when an advertiser product is allowed to get into a picture." In one case an advertiser was said to have received an offer from a Hollywood major to incorporate mention of the advertiser's product in the script—for a price of $500. The offer was not accepted.[71]

Several letters to the editor were sent to *Printers' Ink* in response to their product placement article. One was from David Hillman of the Hillman-Shane Advertising Agency (Los Angeles). Hillman said the appearance of nationally advertised products in movies did not come from the desire of producers to sound out the public but came from one person in Hollywood who had built up a "thriving business" based upon his ability to have products of his clients incorporated into pictures. Having a wide acquaintance among directors, script writers, and property men in Hollywood that person was able to obtain copies of scripts before production began. Reading them over he often found a spot in one of the scenes for a product of one of his clients, and was often able to have it incorporated because of his contacts. Reportedly he had over 60 national advertisers included among his clients.[72]

A second letter was sent by Joan Gelb, president of Clairol (maker of Clairol shampoo). She said that in the recent Fox release *Doubting Thomas* there was a beauty shop scene in which one of their large signs appeared prominently on the wall while another sign appeared on the counter. "These two signs are in plain view for a long enough time so that several people mentioned them to us although we did not know they were appearing in that picture," explained Gelb. Clairol tried to get stills of the scene to use in their own publicity but Fox denied permission because, said Gelb, "As we understand it, the moving picture industry in trying to do away with commercial tie-ups of this kind." Yet another letter was received, from J. J. Pritchard, who wrote in about *Call of the Wild* with Gold Medal Flour sacks used for window curtains in a miner's cabin. Film executives told Pritchard it was often easier and cheaper to

*Test Pilot* (1938, Spencer Tracy, seated, Myrna Loy, Clark Gable, behind Tracy). This film was cited as containing product placement with Tracy verbally calling for Coca-Cola. However, the bottle visible on the table in this shot appears to say "Sarsaparilla," not a real brand and an example of how Hollywood usually avoided the appearance of brand names in its films at this time (either having them not visible at all or by using fake brand-names).

get what they needed in the way of props from a nearby store than it was to create a fictitious package brand for each need.[73]

Exhibitors asserted, in 1937, that there was a growing practice of producers to insert "commercial shots" into their movies and they were irritated. A meeting of an exhibitors' organization in Milwaukee condemned that "seemingly unintentional commercialism" of movies. Although the operators agreed they had no proof that the commercial inserts were deliberate on the part of the studios or that they were paid by advertisers receiving the plugs, nevertheless, they insisted they resented the commercial aspect. "What's more important, picture-goers have openly squawked," they said. Separately, a group of New England independent exhibitors passed a resolution condemning a scene in *Wake Up and Live* as advertising through an arrangement with General Motors. Producers of that film, Fox, demanded a retraction of the allegation. Lawyers for the studio threatened to take legal action against Independent Exhibitors, Inc., if a retraction was not forthcoming. The scene complained of showed Broadway in New York with advertising signs, including a GM ad. In a letter to the exhibitor group, Fox noted the organization's resolution that urged members to eliminate the advertising sign "by a slight misframe" was a violation of the standard distributor-exhibitor contract that forbade altering any part of a print.[74]

At the beginning of 1938 it was reported that the names of the agents of a "huge industrial lobby" maintained in Hollywood for the purpose of receiving free film plugs "worth millions of $ for its manufacturer-clients' products," through product placement, were being sought by the MPPDA in an undercover operation then underway. "Six to eight high-salaried Hollywood agents of the lobby, operating under orders from New York headquarters, are reported to be tossing out a fortune annually in entertainment and gifts to studio execs and workers," explained the account. Attention of the Hays office was said to have been drawn to the situation when a large eastern industrial corporation, not included in the industrial lobby, complained that its competitors were being given plugs in the movies, although his own firm ranked first in the nation in that product line. One agent was said to have spent more than $25,000 to plant products in the movies. After checking recent pictures the Hays office investigators were reported to have "uncovered several examples of definite plants." Nothing more was heard of that investigation.[75]

Evidence that not much product placement was happening, at least in the area of automobiles, came from the fact that Hollywood had a number of automobile rental brokers whose customers were almost completely limited to the film studios. One broker specialized in Model T Fords; another had a fleet of every type of truck; yet another specialized in foreign cars. Studios found it cheaper to pay rentals ranging from $15 to $75 per day per car than to maintain their own fleets. Automotive writer Harry Plummer remarked that "Once upon a time the studios borrowed cars from Hollywood dealers or sales agencies, who were glad to get the free advertising. But not anymore." Russell Pierce, head of the Paramount property department, explained that was so because "Any time we get anything for nothing, we pay for it ten times over in a round-about way. And if we get one little scratch on a new car, the firm that lent it expects us to buy a new buggy."[76]

Thomas Pryor reported in 1938 that recently a Hollywood major had uncovered a Hollywood agency that was doing business by contract with well-known national advertisers to secure the placement of their products or logos in movies at a cost of $150 for each visual display and $100 for each verbal mention. Checking back after the discovery it was reported to have been found that product placement had been accomplished, "apparently without knowledge of studio executives, in fourteen previous pictures."[77]

W. Roberts, a business journalist writing in *Dun's Review* in February 1939, remarked that recently a man approached actor Wallace Beery on the set between takes and asked him to roll a cigarette from a certain bag of five-cent tobacco while the next scene was being shot. The actor declined. Then the man hinted at a substantial reward in cash, but Beery continued to decline. However, said Roberts, if he had agreed, then that tobacco would have received a powerful publicity boost—from a mass impression on millions of viewers of the name and trademark of the tobacco and from an enthusiasm for the product on the part of admirers of Wallace Beery. When Roberts wrote his account the practice of product placement was suddenly out in the open and acknowledged by the cartel. William R. Ferguson, MGM publicity executive, told Roberts his company put limits on his placement practices; for example, no promotion of liquor was allowed. MGM tie-ups were said to be with "solid" firms such as the makers of Maxwell House coffee and its 80 allied products, and in the auto field with the Chevrolet and De Soto people. No money changed hands, explained Roberts, but an arrangement existed "by means of which the two interests boost each other." Movie stars were loaned to the popular Maxwell House radio program and "Subtly the coffee or other product is called to the attention of picture fans.... It is a potent combination." Roberts added that "Sheer commercialism, however, is not tolerated in the cinema, for this would defeat its own ends."[78]

Ferguson said he received on average 100 requests a week from advertisers, large and small, asking for tie-ups. The worst of the lot were rejected immediately by him with the rest sent from his New York office to Hollywood, "where they are carefully weighed to decide whether the article to be promoted has intrinsic merit, whether it would strike a jarring note in the story to be screened, and whether it would militate against the dignity of the star and the featured players." Remarked Ferguson, "The form taken by the promotion must in itself be sound entertainment, or we will have nothing to do with it."[79]

Roberts gave his own examples of the power of the motion picture as a selling medium, even at an accidental level when that selling was wholly inadvertent. He pointed out how certain styles first introduced by Hollywood had carried over to the real world with, for example, a strong and sudden demand for the zipper-front housecoat right after its film appearance caused it to become a hot fashion item. A certain male star popularized the turtleneck sweater, "formerly worn only by prizefighters," with a craze created for the garment. Another star was said to have restored the knitted tie to popularity. Twenty-five years earlier (around 1914) Mary Pickford caused many young females to adopt her hairstyle. One of the most famous examples of the power of films to sell

*It Happened One Night* (1934, Clark Gable, Claudette Colbert). This was the much-cited example showing the power of movies and their stars to sell (or not sell—undershirts in this case) consumer goods and fashion styles to the public. In this scene Gable was preparing to go to bed in a cabin in a tourist court. When he took off his shirt he revealed that he wore no undershirt. As a result, the legend said, sales of men's undershirts plummeted drastically and never fully recovered.

(actually a reverse example) and one that has been cited many, many times over the years concerned Clark Gable in *It Happened One Night* (1934). During the course of the picture he was in a tourist cabin getting ready for bed. When he took off his shirt he revealed that he wore no undershirt. Thereafter, demand for men's undershirts was said to have decreased notably. In that same movie much of the action revolved around a bus trip from Florida to New York. Over the first six months after the picture's release there was a reported 42-percent increase in the patronage of bus companies.[80]

Later, in 1939, *Business Week* presented its own detailed report on the status of product placement. When Spencer Tracy called for "two Coca-Colas, please" in the movie *Test Pilot*, the sequence gained realism and, said the article, "The big advertiser gets a terrific plug." In *First Lady* Kay Francis stated, "Ford always makes good cars"; in *Always Goodbye* Barbara Stanwyck changed her steamer ticket so she could sail "on the *Normandie*"; in *Confessions of a Nazi Spy* Western Union got a four-minute sequence in which their method of transferring a message was dramatically portrayed; in *Fools For Scandal* Ralph Bellamy delivered many positive lines for life insurance; in *The First Hundred Years* Virginia Bruce and Robert Montgomery lovingly demonstrated a home electric organ. Advertisers were getting free and valuable publicity in picture after picture, asserted the story. Fueling the increase in product placement were the following factors: 1) movies wanted to be as real as life; 2) reality was heightened by the use of genuine props such as cars, radios, furniture, and just about all the gadgets a script might call for; and 3) props cost money and since most producers had budget trouble a free prop was frequently welcome.[81]

Active promotion of a product in the movies required direct contact with the producers, either by the advertiser or through an agency, explained *Business Week*. Two of the main ones were the Walter E. Klein Agency, and the Stanley-Murphy Service Agency, both based in Hollywood. They contacted manufacturers for properties and got a "small fee" for handling a product. They made no guarantees of getting a product into the movies but "simply by offering properties, equipment, and technical advice to the producers, succeed in getting considerable representation." A number of manufacturers were said to work directly with the producers' property departments. One office equipment firm made a practice of sending several of its newest models to Hollywood every year with the result "it has enjoyed almost a monopoly in office scenes." A big oil company furnished the studios with property gas pumps. One auto maker made his cars available "and has even gone so far as to present a few movie executives with cars from time to time." That practice brought a complaint from the Hays office, noted the reporter and, he added, it "is by no means typical of the usual procedure; veteran movie men insist that gratuities aren't necessary to win a favorable product mention or use."[82]

*Business Week* wondered about the value of a product placement in a film. One advertising executive observed first that a magazine reaching an audience of 80 million in the U.S. each week (that was the film attendance number at the time) could probably get $50,000 a page for advertising space. He then went on to say that a good movie plug "would be cheap at the same price." With regard to the power of films to sell, another advertising executive declared, "I believe the movies are responsible for about half the cigarette sales that are made today ... not individual brands, but cigarettes in general." He added that "Every time a bird like Charles Boyer lights a cigarette, I wish I were sitting in the smoking section. And do you think there would be as many women smokers as there are today if the female movie stars hadn't taken it up? Not on your life!"[83]

C. Nelson Schrader, of the C. F. Hooper firm (the Hooper ratings) did a survey on automobile representation in the movies—100 films from 10 major studios. He found Ford vehicles were shown in action 41 times, and mentioned verbally or had their signs shown three times. For other makes the numbers were as follows, respectively: Buick, 26, 0; Packard, 19, 1; Chevrolet, 10, 6; Cadillac, 14, 0; Rolls Royce, 5, 2; Cord, 4, 0; Plymouth, 3, 0; Chrysler, 3, 0; Dodge, 2, 0; Lincoln, 2, 0; Lincoln Zephyr and La Salle and Pontiac, and Terraplane, 1, 0.[84]

Schrader provided a reporting service to inform advertisers as to the extent to which products were mentioned onscreen as well as to try to evaluate the impression left on the moviegoer's mind. When he did a survey of 140 feature films he discovered that alcoholic beverages were referred to in one way or another in 137 of them, describing 113 as favorable mentions and the other 24 as unfavorable. Heading the compilation was champagne, mentioned 24 times, all favorable. He mentioned the movie *Love Affair* because of a scene in which Charles Boyer ordered pink champagne for Irene Dunne. Because of that, and another mention in another picture, Schrader said a profound effect could be seen in the sales of the beverage, claiming that sales of the colored beverage tripled after release of those films. According to Schrader some brand mentions occurred by chance while others were deliberate and arranged. He cited *Second Honeymoon, Big Broadcast of 1938*, and *When Love Is Young* as instances where actual brands showed in films. Worried about such a disclosure (Hollywood tried to present itself as pure, wholesome, and so on) the Hays office declared that the MPPDA producer firms "exert every means possible to keep out anything amounting to free advertising in features but that sometimes such trailers creep into completed picture versions."[85]

*Skylark* (1941, Claudette Colbert, others unidentified). Colbert wore jewelry supplied by the De Beers jewelry company as part of its product placement campaign in the early 1940s, which successfully placed material in several movies.

During the 1930s and 1940s the diamond firm De Beers increased the role of diamonds in Hollywood films. De Beers publicity efforts led a film's title to be changed from *Diamonds Are Dangerous* to *Adventure in Diamonds* (1940). The De Beers campaign also managed to introduce a scene about selecting a diamond clip and bracelet for Claudette Colbert in *Skylark* (1941) and helped get Merle Oberon to wear $40,000 worth of diamond jewelry in *That Uncertain Feeling* (1941).[86]

Screen advertising enjoyed a flurry of interest and activity in this period. In the last few years of the 1930s the use of ad trailers, ad shorts, and product placement seemed to be more prevalent than in past periods—although screen ads were still very much in a minority position. For the first time product placement was mentioned openly. Hollywood's cartel members still avoided all contact with screen ads as producers, distributors, or exhibitors, at least at an official level. The MPPDA made all the right noises about defending the screen from all ad material. It did that, of course, to placate critics. Underneath it all, though, the majors were getting involved in product placement—it was the easiest type of screen advertising to get away with. That is, when a product appeared on the screen it was often difficult to tell if it was a deliberate plant for consideration, an accident, or left in by a director because he thought it suited the scene, with no prearrangement involved. But then war intervened and little was heard of the issue. Further developments would have to await a return to peace.

# 4

# Everything Follows the Film
## *1945–1949*

The people pay to get into theatres and won't go for any hint of commercialism in the screen medium.
—Frederic Ullman Jr., RKO president, 1947

Never before in the history of the motion picture has window shopping been possible at a movie theater—until now.
—Sportswear maker Koret of California, 1947

Indiana [theater] indies frothing against beer plugs in 5 recent features.
—*Variety*, 1948

With the return of peacetime the idea that motion pictures were a potent selling force was once again trumpeted, extending to even more phases of life. Hollywood was particularly enamored of itself. A reporter reminisced in 1946 that ever since the screen became a "potent force" in setting styles of dress, promoting a demand for many kinds of articles and creating a desire for higher standards of living in general, there had been a popular saying "Trade follows the film." In recent years, though, he added, "The screen has become one of the most effective media for influencing all phases of modern life, so that today the axiom could very well read, 'Everything follows the film.'" According to this reporter, Warner Bros. president Harry M. Warner, speaking at the fifth annual Nobel anniversary dinner in New York at the end of 1945, declared the motion picture to be the closest thing to a universal language we were likely to get in our time and that the motion picture "can help create the conditions of international goodwill that are the essential foundations of lasting peace." At that dinner Warner was introduced by U.S. Senator J. William Fulbright, who stated that the "future of all the countries of the world may be shaped by the policies set forth by this man." And, of course, the other major producers also.[1]

Next the reporter gave examples of the prominence, influence, and power of films. Around 1,000 films were turned out by the U.S. Army Pictorial Service in its peak year of 1944—most of which were training films. Hollywood sent its own features to the troops, said to be integral to building and maintaining morale. An increased use of film by business was also described. General Motors then had a catalog of more than 50 films, "most of them carrying no direct advertising message, but providing entertainment and enlightenment of some kind." Somewhat bizarrely, the account declared Hollywood films to be educational: "Biographies of great historical figures, particularly, and picture versions of classic books have done a lot to win over the educational field to the possibilities of the screen as a teaching medium." Also noted was the making of religious films, strictly for showing in churches and other places of worship and that, of course, it remained true that trade followed the film. Movie stars were still besieged for endorsement deals and the motion picture fan magazines—15 of them at the time—were read by over 35 million people every month. On top of that, more than 70 million people got daily news and gossip about Hollywood films and personalities from their newspapers.[2]

Darryl F. Zanuck, 20th Century–Fox's executive producer, declared you could sell almost anything but politics or religion by way of motion pictures "Let us show a new refrigerator, or some new gadget like an easy can-opener, or talk about pink champagne which the vintners formerly couldn't give away, and you know how the public becomes a commercial pushover," he observed. Zanuck noted that it also worked in reverse, claiming that Clark Gable's presence in *It Happened One Night* without an undershirt "well nigh put the men's undershirt industry out of business." As evidence that films could not sell politics Zanuck pointed to the $2 million loss Fox suffered with *Wilson* (a biography of former president Woodrow Wilson). Zanuck argued that if films could sell religion then movies such as *Song of Bernadette, Going My Way,* and *Bells of St. Mary's* should have produced a lot more Catholic converts.[3]

U.S. Department of Commerce film chief Nathan D. Golden argued in 1945 that industrial and commercial films would be one of the most important stimulants to the maintenance of a high level of production and full employment in the coming few years. Golden proposed that manufacturers in general consider the use of a series of five films that he outlined as follows: 1) a training film for shop employees; 2) a film to teach sales forces about their products and selling methods; 3) a film for instructing retailers about the product and about the best selling methods; 4) a film explaining the appropriate service and repair methods for the merchandise; and 5) "a film designed to show consumers the merits of the product and create desire for it." Pointing out that American entertainment pictures had long been recognized as excellent salesmen of

American goods, Golden argued the industrial film could take advantage of the goodwill created by the entertainment film in foreign markets. The industrial film, he said, would serve to exert direct selling pressure. Going further Golden suggested dubbing of those industrial films for use abroad and that arrangements might soon be completed for the showing of commercial films in U.S. embassy projection rooms throughout the world. He added that British salesmen were going out armed with "excellent" selling films and that U.S. companies would be ill advised to ignore the "potent advantage" those items gave the British in the competition for world markets.[4]

Around the same time, on its own initiative, big business was reported to be contemplating widespread use of 16-mm films in an "educational and propaganda" campaign. Business wanted to make up for lost time and felt such a program was then of "utmost necessity." That was because industry figured it had to "take measures to counteract a series of liberal films seen by every GI in the Army." The Army indoctrination and orientation films produced with the Office of War Information and other government agencies were described as having often been made "with a liberal viewpoint which doesn't see things with the same slant" as did big industry. Or, as a source close to big business put it, the government-produced films, seen by more than 12 million men, "do not carry the slant that industry would have liked. If such liberal propaganda would be allowed to take its course, even more 'liberal' measures which would cost Big Business vast amounts of coin would inevitably result. Industry must counter with films projecting its own viewpoint." Noted by the report was that the idea of using industrial films for propaganda purposes was not new; the National Association of Manufacturers (NAM) had been in the field for some nine years. Utility companies had produced films for school consumption to combat public ownership and the TVA. However, concluded the account, "Present plans exceed anything hitherto done in that field."[5]

Historian William Bird wrote that in the years following the Second World War the leaders of NAM, the Chamber of Commerce of the United States, and allied industry groups including the American Association of Advertising Agencies, the Association of National Advertisers, and the Advertising Council redoubled their efforts toward "the integration of public consciousness and free enterprise ideology." In the years following the Second World War, he stated, "the new vocabulary of business leadership became inseparably bound up with a broadcast and screen grammar of entertainment and integration." However, the focus shifted to television as that medium got underway, with the ad short slowly disappearing from the film program, as all short subjects did. That cutting of the film program was a cost-saving measure in the face of a sharply declining attendance, caused by television. Dramatic anthology television series sponsored by major corporations such as the "General Electric Theater," "Du Pont's Cavalcade of America," the "U.S. Steel Hour," and others, declared Bird, "met their sponsors' requirements for a popular format of tightly controlled information and entertainment with which to prosecute their public relations among a wide and indifferent public."[6]

Average weekly cinema admissions in 1946 were 80.5 million; in 1947 the number was 78.2 million; in 1948 it was 69.2 million. After that it got worse, as the effects of television were really felt. Motion pictures were in trouble before the small screen was a serious factor in American life; its full-scale arrival only speeded up an already underway decline in attendance.[7]

Endorsements and merchandise tie-ins continued to be an integral part of Hollywood's marketing strategy, even when product placement was not involved. It was testament to the supposed power of stars to sell products. Royal Crown Cola (RC) announced, in 1946, the launch of a huge movie tie-in campaign featuring Bing Crosby (the number one box-office star in 1945) and his upcoming movie *Road to Utopia*. Kicking off the campaign was a full-page ad in *Life* magazine with a picture of Bing holding a bottle of RC and exclaiming, "You bet RC tastes best!" Also part of the campaign were 3,500 billboards, one-minute radio spots on over 200 stations, newspaper ads on the amusement pages of newspapers in all the major cities, plus other publicity efforts. Also, during February, March, and April, some 450 Royal Crown dealers—serving over 300,000 retail outlets—received a complete assortment of Bing Crosby display pieces including large framed cards, window posters, and lamp cord pulls. From there the 450 bottlers took over the promotion; linking it with the local showing of *Utopia*. Their promotion included newspaper ads, one-minute spot announcements over the local radio station, and stickers on the store display cards stating when and where the movie would be screened. Local cinemas were expected to cooperate in the campaign by allowing the bottler to put a product display in the lobby of the theater. Over time RC used in the neighborhood of 100 Hollywood stars in its tie-in campaigns, though most were nowhere near as elaborate as the one involving Crosby.[8]

Child movie star Margaret O'Brien was once all the rage with a merchandise tie-in campaign aimed at a target market of 14 million girls aged four to 12 for coats, suits, dresses, hats, shoes, accessories, and so forth. MGM had organized a group of 23 of the leading manufacturers of children's apparel and accessories into the Margaret O'Brien fashion group. Paramount's release *Frenchman's Creek* tied in with fashion and cosmetics firms such as Dorothy Gray. Although that film was a period costume drama, the items—clothes, jewelry, shoes, gloves, and so forth—displayed in the film, said a reporter, "lent themselves to a modern fashion adaptation." Remarked Bert Carpenter, promotion manager for Dorothy Gray, "Paramount gave private screenings to hundreds of department store executives who visited New York. We toured the original wardrobe of the picture approximately 100,000 miles over the United States and Canada and it was exhibited to thousands of people."[9]

Ad trailers continued to have a presence in the immediate post-war era but it was not too different from what it had been in the late 1930s. One unusual presentation of ad trailers came in 1945 with the formation of an organization called Telecast, Inc. Designed to feed radio newscasts to cinemas, Telecast was then experimenting with broadcasts in several New York neighborhood cinemas and one on Broadway (the Rivoli) to gauge audience reaction. Telecast simply fed a radio newscast into the theater with the audience looking at a blank screen while the radio

*Frenchman's Creek* (1944, Joan Fontaine, Nigel Bruce). This film had tie-ins with cosmetic and fashion companies. Even though it was a period film the items of clothing, jewelry, shoes, and so forth were given a "modern fashion adaptation."

announcer read the news report, which lasted about three minutes. Before and after each news show, a 15-second commercial was aired. Although Coca-Cola had not signed up for any commercials under this program, for the sake of an experiment Telecast obtained some Coca-Cola copy and used it to test audience reaction. An advertising executive from a major agency was asked to sit in at the Rivoli and give his assessment. He remarked that on the whole, audiences were "passive" during the commercials. According to its plans, Telecast was considering having the commercials screened in either still or animated form on that blank screen during the newscast. However, cinema managers thought that would be self-defeating since it would distract from the announcer's news. Nothing more was heard about Telecast.[10]

With the war over for less than a year, minute movies were said to be used "to good advantage" in foreign countries by American manufacturers who recognized their value in helping to recapture the markets lost because of the conflict. The motion picture department of the J. Walter Thompson advertising agency, headed by Robert Gillham, was then producing many of those ad trailers for U.S. industrialists at Thompson-owned studios in England and Australia. Those ad trailers got good play in regular cinemas abroad, said Gillham, since there was "much less aversion" to them on the screen than there had been in the United States. Clients for Thompson's overseas ad trailers included Kellogg, Lever Brothers, and American Home Products. As well, the Thompson agency had produced a series of 10-minute one-reel ad shorts for *Reader's Digest*, dubbed in Spanish for Cuban audiences and was then preparing another series for distribution throughout Latin America.[11]

On the home front, George Gladden, an executive with J. Walter Thompson, said his agency was then dickering with several of the Hollywood majors to produce commercial and industrial films. However, he thought the profits from industrial films were too low to interest the cartel members, compared to what they could make from theatrical films. Average price for a two-reel ad short was $25,000 to $40,000, said Gladden. Subtract from that the $20,000 production cost and overhead of $5,000, and the profit (20 percent) was about $5,000. If the majors were then dickering and considering the possibility of producing such items Gladden thought they did not really mean it and expressed an interest in that direction only to protect themselves. "They want to make sure that they're not losing out on a good thing." Gladden added that the number of cinemas available for commercials had remained static during the war years with 9,000 to 10,000 houses then accepting minute movies while some 3,500 venues would screen one-reel ad shorts for a price.[12]

More optimistic was Reginald Evans, vice president of General

Screen Advertising. He declared that motion pictures as an advertising medium had grown from 5,400 outlets in 1934 to 12,000 houses in 1946 with an audience of 45 million per week. Still, he admitted the field of minute movies had not been "fully exploited" but said advertisers were showing a "mounting interest" in that field. The cost of screening ad trailers in cinemas was then said to be $3.50 per 1,000 moviegoers.[13]

Even more optimistic was an account published at the end of 1946 that claimed cinemas had an income that year of $10.5 million, a 40-percent increase over 1945. According to that report one unidentified Iowa town became so annoyed over a rash of 30-second ads for commercial products that appeared on local screens that it passed an ordinance banning them altogether. Some 12,000 houses then accepted ads and "made themselves up to $1,000 in extra change for the year." However, it was admitted that most of the cinemas running the ad trailers were subsequent-run neighborhood houses, with very few first-run houses or large circuits then taking the material. Distributors of the minute movies commented that exhibitor opinion was split over the feasibility of using them. One distributor executive said, "Some of the theatre men think they're box-office poison and won't touch them with the proverbial pole." The Iowa furor took place, said the report, because of poor management: "A smart salesman won't let a theatre play more than four advertising films at a time." In explaining the supposed increase in the use of ad trailers in cinemas, besides the obvious one of a return to a peacetime consumption economy, the main factor was said to be GI psychology. That is, GIs had learned so much through films during the war that they were sold on the medium above any other.[14]

Ad shorts enjoyed their last real flurry of interest in the late 1940s before they, and shorts of all types, faded away. Harry Donahue of Monogram Pictures had a circuit of 245 department stores hooked up to play his fashion reels late in 1945.[15]

Stanley Neal, president of Associated Filmmakers (makers of industrial shorts) thought that with more and more business concerns turning to motion pictures as a new advertising medium it was possible that advertisers might soon buy time in cinemas in much the same manner as they then bought radio time for their commercials. Neal predicted, bringing an old Hollywood fear back to the surface, that full-length features would be industry sponsored in the near future and that they would show up on the nation's screens. An ever-increasing recognition of the "tremendous power" of sponsored films was paving the way for that, he argued. "Popular pictures, presented by commercial firms in the same manner that radio now presents its shows with no advertising other than the sponsorship, will be a customary thing," he explained. "With the caliber of today's commercial film on the upgrade, made possible by the awareness and wealth of industry, the tremendous production costs necessary to present our films will become absorbed by big industrial firms interested in doing an institutional type of advertising." With his ad shorts the exhibitor did not pay and Neal believed his predicted feature-length films would be distributed the same way.[16]

Several of Associated's ad shorts, said Neal, such as *Quicker Than You Think* (a cooking picture sponsored by Armour & Company), had been reviewed by newspaper critics. Another of their shorts, *Every Two Seconds*, was said to be the only ad short ever booked by the large, first-run circuit Interstate, a Paramount affiliate. Like most others in the field Neal stressed the advertising message in these pictures had to be secondary to the entertainment value. What he said he had in mind for those proposed industry-sponsored features were those like MGM's *Weekend at the Waldorf* and Paramount's *Stork Club*, which he thought displayed a type of institutional advertising and both of which provided some "excellent plugs" for the title names. With those thoughts in mind, said Neal, his company planned to take the ad film out of its "stepchild" position and move it to a "place of prominence."[17]

A few months later the idea was again raised that advertisers might some day buy screen time in the nations' cinemas to publicize their products. It came at a time when advertisers were spending to get their ad films on television. WNBT, NBC's television outlet in New York, was then selling time to advertisers for the screening of the commercially-sponsored films at the station's regular rate of $300 per 30 minutes ($200 of that was for the use of the studio; $100 was for the transmitter charges). Since the television audience in New York was then limited to not more than 10,000–15,000 people it was an expensive ad medium. Advertising agency executives pointed out that the NBC charge for a half hour was often as much or more than the average small town theatre grossed in a day, which made cinemas look inviting. Although the idea of buying screen time in cinemas had "often" been broached by the top ad agencies and their clients it "has always been nixed by exhibs as something the paying customers wouldn't go for." WNBT's practice would much later become very common known, of course, as infomercials.[18]

William W. Riethof, head of the motion picture department at the Lester Wolff, Inc. ad agency admitted in 1946, "Great inertia must still be overcome" before ad shorts "come into the prominence they merit" in the advertising sphere.[19]

Richard de Rochemont (a producer of ad shorts) was one who thought ad shorts had a rosy future. He pointed out that the public had become so accustomed from radio to taking their entertainment with a "heavy dose of commercialism" thrown in that moviegoers no longer seemed to resent the inclusion of ad shorts on commercial screens.

Scoffing at that idea was Frederic Ullman Jr., president of RKO-Pathe. The mere fact that most exhibitors had consistently voiced opposition to the idea in the past, he said, "despite the payola some of the sponsors use as bait, is enough to outlaw the suggestion." Ullman said the public did resent ad shorts on the screen. The public did not pay for its radio entertainment and could always shut a program off, whereas "The people pay to get into theatres and won't go for any hint of commercialism in the screen medium." For that reason, "plus the fact that exhibs squawk if any commercialism is included in the shorts for which they must pay rentals," ad shorts did not have a good future. According to this account, some 6,000 U.S. cinemas ran ad trailers on the screens (much lower than other estimates) with an unknown (but much smaller) number exhibiting ad shorts.[20]

On the other hand, some exhibitors did favor using the ad films. Charles P. Skouras, head of the National Theatres circuit, announced he was planning on increasing the revenue of his chain by screening more ad shorts. Skouras and his aides had been approaching big industrial companies and urging them to utilize the cinema as a prime medium in which to push their products. At the same time Skouras said he was willing to help them and gave them advice so those ad shorts would not be too crudely commercial or poorly put together. That pitch for more ad shorts came following the playing of the one-reel *Land of Tobacco* in a large number of the chain's houses; it publicized Liggett & Myers Chesterfield cigarettes. Skouras stressed that he did not want ad shorts that would "outrage patrons by their poor quality or blatant commercialism."[21]

Whatever interest that exhibitors did display toward using ad films received a setback in 1948 from action taken by the Motion Picture Association of America's (MPAA—as the Hollywood cartel had renamed itself in 1945) board. It decreed that commercial movies more than 200 feet in length had to carry the words "This Is An Advertisement" in the introductory frames of every print. While the independent theaters, which had been playing the sponsored movies for years, were not bound by the MPAA edicts and while they were not expected to pay much attention to the MPAA action it was said that, nevertheless, the edict "will mean a heavy blow so far as major-affiliated circuits are concerned and many other large chains and houses which abide by the MPAA rules." Noted was that the National Theatres chain was leading the way in the experiment of playing ad shorts. It was the action of Skouras, and other exhibitors taking similar steps, that brought the whole matter to the attention of the MPAA board. During that discussion by the board someone recalled that a similar influx of commercial films about 10 years earlier had resulted in a resolution requiring such items to be labeled and to be passed by the MPAA's Advertising Code Administration. The reasoning behind the cartel's public resurrection of that old edict was that "with the industry already suffering from bad public relations (long involved as a defendant in an anti-trust case brought by the government the U.S. Supreme Court would soon declare Hollywood to be, in fact, a monopoly and would order sweeping changes) it would be foolish to provide more ammunition for the critics by attempting to foist sponsored films on ticket-buyers under the guise of entertainment." Another reason was that Hollywood worried that newspapers, radio, and other media that depended on advertising for their existence would resent cinemas "poaching on their bailiwick and add further grist to the 'sock Hollywood' mill." That the edict was passed 10 years earlier and resurrected in 1948—as perhaps nothing more than a public relations measure to show that Hollywood was doing the right thing—could be seen in the fact the cartel apparently forgot that such an edict was on the books. It took some amount of debate in 1948 before someone remembered the ruling from the past.[22]

With styles worn by stars in Hollywood movies long having influenced the world of fashion and choices of consumers, it was a logical place for Hollywood's worst nightmare to come true as a commercially-sponsored feature-length film was made. A California apparel manufacturer, Koret (a maker of female sportswear) of California, Inc., San Francisco, set out to make a more direct connection between the visit to a cinema and the purchase of a new outfit. "Every link in a merchandising chain reaction has been carefully forged to show returns to the store, theater, and advertising in the town booked for a showing of a specially produced film highlighting Koret garments," noted an account. Called a brand new method of merchandising, it was said to be the first time a large manufacturer had costumed a motion picture and manufactured the same items of apparel for sale to consumers. Koret, in conjunction with the Monogram Studios, produced a regular full-length film of "the lighter entertainment type, affording plenty of opportunity to show sportswear in action." The apparel company designed the garments worn in the picture and mass produced the same designs to retail through regular dealers everywhere. Those dealers used store displays and other advertising tie-ins linked to the showing of the picture in a local theater. *Vacation Days* was the name of the movie.[23]

Prior to the release of *Vacation Days* in 1947, a test picture (the first to "bring screen fashions to the American woman at prices within her reach") called *High School Hero* had come out in September, 1946. Results from the test film *High School Hero* were said to have made all concerned happy with the box office receipts reported to be "very good and merchants and movie goers both were reported enthusiastic."[24] *Vaca-*

*tion Days* was to be handled on a much more ambitious scale than the test picture, with a plot centering around a group of high school students spending the summer holidays on a Western cattle ranch—a mystery-thriller with a love interest. Stars of the film were Freddie Stewart and June Preisser. Humor and musical numbers were said to broaden the film's appeal to include all ages of moviegoers. A credit line, "Wardrobe by Stephanie Koret," was given "prominence" but to the audience "the only other connection with commerce is that women (and men, too) learn through associated promotions that they may go out and buy the styles they have just seen." Promotional items for retailers included a sign that said, "Never before in the history of the motion picture has window shopping been possible at a movie theater—until now."[25]

A piece Koret sent to the dealers only described the movie as "loaded from beginning to end with sportswear designed for the high school, college, and business girl." Dealers were told by Koret that the movie afforded them two advantages: "1. Your merchandise shares the limelight with the glamour of Hollywood and a famous designer; 2. your customer is pre-sold at the theater. She will be in a buying mood when she enters your shop. For these reasons *Vacation Days* is a natural for lively promotion and sparkling publicity."

*Vacation Days* (1947, actors unidentified). This full-length feature film was financed by a manufacturer—Koret of California, maker of women's sportswear. It was one of a small number of full-length movies financed by manufacturers. That concept of manufacturer-financed films greatly worried the Hollywood majors.

Product placement continued to occur, but fairly infrequently and always done surreptitiously. Nobody openly admitted to practicing product placement. Early in 1946 a hush-hush note was circulated among the foreign managers of the Hollywood majors by the MPAA. That note was about a disclosure by the J. Arthur Rank organization (Britain's largest film producer) to use its movies to plug British industrial products through product placement. Supposedly it was all part of a post World War II battle between the U.S. and the UK for world film dominance, and the business advantages that were believed to follow in the wake of such dominance. The note was circulated, declared a report, "as a tipoff to American companies which may lead to formulation of a policy of greater cooperation with U.S. industry by the studios in identifying American brand names and otherwise promoting commercial and industrial products." J. Arthur Rank had recently given an interview in Britain in which he endorsed the old sentiment that trade followed the film and that a great many of the estimated 90,000 cinemas in the world could become "shop windows for Britain." Prior to that Rank had said, also in Britain, that his studio was cooperating with the Board of Trade and the Council of Industrial Design to insure that his films portrayed only the best and latest of British products. According to the U.S. reporter, Hollywood producers had always been careful not to emphasize particular manufactured wares because the mere sight of them was a "mighty plug." On the other hand, he observed, American exhibitors had "constantly squawked at brand name identification under the suspicion that producers who mentioned Coca-Cola or Buick cars, etc., were profiting from both ends."[26]

One of the best-known examples cited of a movie from this period containing product placement was the 1945 release *Mildred Pierce* wherein actor Joan Crawford was seen to drink Jack Daniel's whiskey. Another was *Angel on My Shoulder* (United Artists, 1946) in which Anne Baxter and Paul Muni were shown beside a new portable RCA radio. RCA planned a nation-wide promotion of the new radio to coincide with the film's release."[27]

Exhibitors did indeed complain when they felt they were subjected to films containing product placement. Through the pages of one of its bulletins to members the Associated Theatre Owners of Indiana (ATOI) warned Hollywood producers in 1946 that product advertisement as exemplified in the recent release *Whistle Stop* could boomerang. ATOI observed that the exhibitor "receives nothing" for that type of advertising. The attention of Hoosier theater operators was called to the fact that direct plugs for Schlitz beer and Bromo-Seltzer were worked into the continuity of *Whistle Stop*. Besides a pictorial display, complained ATOI, actor Victor McLaglen gave the Schlitz product a verbal boost by stating in that movie, "That's a good beer." For these exhibitors it was obvious that the producers realized for themselves a "large chunk of change" from that type of advertising. With merchandise generally becoming much more available (after wartime shortages) this cinema organization worried that more manufacturers would seek to take the advantage of placing brand names on "the subconscious mind" of a prospective customer without resorting to direct advertising. A further worry, argued ATOI, was that some producers could go too far, further than good taste

*Vacation Days* (1947, actors unidentified). This movie was little more than an opportunity for Koret to display its fashions.

allowed, and "the public will resent being sold a commercial product in the middle of a feature picture, for it destroys the illusion and the picture is no longer entertainment." Other films, charged ATOI, had plugged soft drinks, automobiles, perfumes, and so on, in a similar fashion.[28]

Some 18 months later ATOI surfaced again with more complaints about alleged product placement. ATOI's bulletin reprinted a promotion circular of the National Brewing Company in which plugs in several pictures were mentioned as "a very important part of our national advertising program." Movies in which their product appeared and that were released in September 1947 were listed as *Too Late for Tears* and *Impact* (both from United Artists); *Maggie and Jiggs in Court* and *Shep Comes Home* (both Monogram); and *Thunder in the Pines* (Screen Guild). Such a frequency of plugs, believed the exhibitor organization, could only be accounted for on the basis that "some one has received compensation." In that case the exhibitors wanted to divide the advertising income or get an adjustment from the distributor on the rental terms.[29]

Less than a year after that Fox derided charges from independent exhibitors that it had received consideration for plugging *Look* magazine in its release *Mr. Belvedere Goes to College*. According to Fox officials, it received no money whatsoever from the magazine and had not even worked out a co-promotion deal, although *Look* "naturally gave the film considerable publicity." A sequence in the movie showed actor Clifton Webb holding up a copy of *Look*. Remarked one unnamed independent exhibitor bulletin, "What a short that was. The climax of the picture, with over 100 feet of spread on the screen, revealing the name of the magazine. What did Fox get back in money for that great ad? Why should exhibitors advertise other products on their screens unless they get paid for it? It looks like we all got stuck and should holler for a rebate." Explaining the sequence a Fox spokesman said the script called for a national magazine to be used and it was decided to feature *Look* rather than make up a phony name. The spokesman added that the exhibitors had not complained about the extra publicity the film got thanks to *Look* magazine.[30]

During this period the practice of stars endorsing products off screen was sometimes tied in by the studios to promotion of the film by the advertiser and to product placement. Writing in 1947, Mike Connolly noted that in the old days Hollywood stars always got cash for their offscreen endorsement deals. But by the time Connolly was writing, the studios handled all the deals and details and there was no deal concluded unless the star's recent film also got a mention. In return for that extra publicity for its film from the advertiser the movie producers, said Connolly, "are always looking for angles to return the compliment to the advertisers by giving the product a plug in the picture, feeling you'll 'Love That Picture!' more by virtue of that extra line in the soap ad— brought on, in turn, by a fleeting glance of a bar of that particular brand of soap in the film. And that's where the MPAA steps in to restrain the over-ambitious studios."[31]

Another journalist, Kay Campbell, recalled that in the past Douglas Fairbanks was paid $10,000 by a tobacco company for a cigarette endorsement. Today, wrote Campbell, Hollywood stars lined up to do Chesterfield ads for free—just for the publicity value and a mention of their latest movie. A decade before, she continued, endorsements enriched some of Hollywood's luminaries to the tune of an estimated $5 million annually. Shirley Temple reportedly collected $50,000 for endorsing puffed wheat and another $75,000 for a doll promotion while Jane Withers made $50,000 a year for similar endorsements. Deanna Durbin endorsed over 50 different products. Advertising agencies used to pursue the studios for tie-ups, said Campbell, but the situation had changed and the film business was on the offensive—it was initiating the promotions, and, "Frequently these demands involve the use of a product in a film in return for space granted." A company might say to a studio, for example, "If you'll use our watch in your production, we'll use [actor Danny] Kaye in our ads!"[32]

Campbell added that studios had their individual quirks when it came to endorsements. Paramount insisted that space devoted to a player in an advertiser's copy take up at least 30 percent of an ad; Columbia would not allow its players to wear or handle merchandise in the endorsement ads; MGM would not permit tie-ins with either liquor products or cigarettes for its players. Agreeing with many other observers, Campbell concluded, "When a product turns up as a prop in a picture, the manufacturer gets a big break." She cited the old examples of Clark Gable causing a fall-off in undershirt sales when he appeared without one in *It Happened One Night* and the spike in sales of pink champagne after Charles Boyer ordered that drink for Irene Dunne in *Love Affair*. And when Danny Kaye glanced—ever so briefly—at his wrist watch in *The Kid From Brooklyn* the manufacturer of Benrus watches observed his sales rising to a new peak. Venetian blinds, the one-hand telephone, and the elaborate bathroom were all given a lot of hype by Hollywood in its films and had become "prerequisites in the American home" because of that exposure, thought Campbell. Film audiences "are readily conditioned to the acceptance of ideas. Some wide-awake commercial firms, including Western Union, Remington Rand, Ford and the makers of Coca-Cola make their products and services easily accessible to film prop men." The Walter Klein organization in Hollywood then maintained a centralized borrowing warehouse stocked with $150,000 worth of "name" items which the studios could borrow at any time.[33]

One contemporary journalist who thought that little product placement took place in this time period was Ruth Inglis. Writing in 1947, she observed, that "Although occasionally high-pressure publicists for national products try to inject their sponsors' wares into films and at times bribe studio employees to achieve their ends, every effort is made to avoid unnecessary close-ups of radios and other items showing the name of the product, outdoor scenes showing advertising signs on billboards, and dialogue mentioning trade names." There was some truth in what Inglis said. Product placement was still fairly low-key in the immediate post-war period but the practice was quite a bit more prevalent than the words of Inglis implied.[34]

As World War II ended there was great optimism that cinema advertising was ready to experience strong growth. But it didn't happen. One reason was that Hollywood experienced hard times of its own. Film attendance experienced a drop of 20 percent or so before the effects of television were felt. Television's arrival sped up that decline and ensured there would be no recovery. One result of a decline in attendance was a drastic restructure of the typical film program. During the coming couple of decades or so the standard film program of two features (normally an A and a B film), a newsreel, a cartoon, perhaps an entertainment short, and trailers for coming attractions, would be reduced to nothing except a single feature film and, of course, those coming-attraction trailers. These developments combined to make motion pictures somewhat less attractive to advertisers. The predominant screen advertising method, the ad short, would be almost completely gone by the 1950s. Also, there remained much hostility within the film industry against any kind of screen advertising, including from the Hollywood cartel (at least opposed in theory and officially, if not in practice to the same extent). That hostility was from time to time very vocal and vigorous. Its effect certainly was to limit the amount of screen advertising. As the 1950s began those who dreamt of a big increase in screen advertising saw their enthusiasms dampened and this hopes shriveled.

# 5

# Television Ads
# Condition Filmgoers to
# Accept Commercials
## *The 1950s*

> To many people abroad, the motion picture is still the most excit-
> ing form of entertainment they know. Commercials, then, could
> almost be classed as 'entertainment' in some countries.
> —*Sales Management*, 1953

> The public has been strongly conditioned to accept advertising
> with its entertainment.
> —Theatre-Screen Advertising Bureau, 1958

> Why not improve the [film] script by inserting an entertaining TV
> commercial leading up to this hilarious high spot in the film?
> —Klingman and Spencer, public relations
> firm for Exquisite Form Brassiere, 1959

The idea that watching television, with all of its commercials, might
soften up the filmgoers and make them more accepting of screen advertisements was an often expressed sentiment in the 1950s. However, it
was based more on hope than on experience.

Merchandise tie-ins and licensing remained strong—continued testament to the supposed selling power of the cinema screen, and of the
small screen also, as licensing tie-ins spread to television. Name licensing for Cinderella dolls (film) or Hopalong Cassidy lunch boxes (television) or a multitude of others reached an estimated sales volume of $250
million in 1950. More than 150 manufacturers were then licensed to turn
out hundreds of items carrying the names and sketches of Walt Disney
characters with a sales volume of about $100 million annually. Hopalong
Cassidy was the latest rage in that field and in the space of eight months
in 1950 had licensed 73 manufacturers who collectively expected some

$80 million in sales that year. At least one observer believed the father of the licensing industry was Kay Kamen, who secured exclusive licensing rights to all Walt Disney characters in 1932, and increased sales of that material from $10 million in 1933 to over $100 million in 1949. When Kamen died suddenly in a plane crash in October, 1949, the licensing rights reverted to Walt Disney Productions, which began doing its own licensing.[1]

Ad shorts were rarely mentioned in the 1950s, although reportedly there were more than 200 production firms in the U.S. then competing for the $80 million annual gross of the industrial movie business. During 1956 Hollywood produced more than 250 entertainment shorts, about 30 percent of its 1935 peak. Typical of the independent industrial shorts producers was John E. Sutherland, a one-time scriptwriter who worked for Walt Disney and who made wartime training films for the government before going out on his own. He produced about 20 ad shorts a year (running from 10 to 45 minutes), at a cost to the sponsor of $50,000 to $300,000 each, for such varied industrial giants as General Electric (*A is for Atom*), United Fruit (*Bananas? Si, Señor*), American Telephone and Telegraph (*The Voice Beneath the Sea*), Du Pont (*The Spray's the Thing*), and the New York Stock Exchange (*What Makes Us Tick*). Sutherland was said to have gotten his client's point of view across with "suave indirection," although he did not find it an easy job to persuade tycoons that filmgoers resented "being pounded over the head with a sales spiel." Many sponsoring corporations, however, had so enthusiastically adopted the concept of "non-irritating hucksters," noted an account, that their names, as in Richfield Oil's 26-minute *The Conservation Story*, were never mentioned in the body of the film. The corporation merely got an opening credit that read "So-and-So Presents"—"an almost infallible sign of the industrial movie." Richfield's short was reported to have played in "dozens" of cinemas in western states. However, the vast majority of them never got beyond in-house usage. With the cinema film program cutting back on all shorts, the ad short had less change of being screened than the chances it had enjoyed in previous decades—not too likely even back then.[2]

As this decade began a reporter for *Variety* declared that more minute movies were being produced and more houses were showing them, although he gave no details. For one thing, he thought those ad trailers were better made than in the past and, for another, that "Sponsored programs on TV have softened up audiences to the point where they accept such product more readily." United Fruit's Chiquita Banana was cited as a prototype of the modern minute movie. At the time United Fruit had six different ads in release from its library of some 23 trailers. One thing the reporter did admit was that "the deluxe [cinema] chains look down on adpix."[3]

A surreptitious introduction of ad trailers, through newsreels, continued to be attempted from time to time. In 1950 the Century exhibition circuit reached an agreement with NBC-TV and the William Esty ad agency to carry the television program the "Camel Newsreel Theatre," on a two-week experimental basis, in just two of its New York houses for a start. That program was taken on a feed from NBC at the television show's regularly scheduled time, 7:45–8:00 P.M., Monday through Friday. During the experimental period Century eliminated its regular newsreel. The narrator of that newsreel was John Cameron Swayze. Century paid an unspecified "token" fee for the newsreel and carried it intact, including the commercials for Camel cigarettes. Since the two Century houses (one in Brooklyn and one in Long Island) were taking the program live off the air they had to schedule their regular film program around it. One reason for undertaking the experiment was that the television newsreel had consistently been able to beat the theatrical ones to the punch.[4]

Of course, that last fact doomed the cinema newsreel. Fox was concerned, in 1953, over the steady decline in the circulation of its *Movietone News*. To battle that decline the producer had devised a scheme under which exhibitors would seek local sponsorship for the reels. The way Lem Jones, Movietone sales manager, figured it, an exhibitor would approach one of the stores or banks in his community with a proposal of newsreel sponsorship. Newspapers, too, he thought, would go for the scheme. If handled properly, newsreel sponsorship could not only return to cinema operators their newsreel film rental cost but even produce a profit for them, Jones argued. Fox concentrated its drive on smaller communities since most of the newsreel cancellation in recent months had come from the small houses where, Fox believed, they tended to cut the newsreel as the first step in any economy move. One argument Fox raised was that exhibitors who canceled newsreels did themselves no favors since polls had definitely established that the public wanted them and enjoyed them. However, in raising that argument Fox was living in the past. There was no way the cinema newsreel could match the currency of its small screen counterpart. By the end of the 1950s cinema newsreels were a nostalgia item.[5]

Cinema ad trailers were much more common abroad than they were in the United States (but television ads were far less pervasive abroad). According to one reporter, a filmgoer in 1953 in Rio de Janeiro or São Paulo, Brazil, likely saw a 60-second ad trailer sponsored by a U.S. firm such as Pond's, RCA-Victor, Atlantic Refining, or Kibon Ice Cream. Later that evening an identical 60-second ad might appear on a local television channel. A similar experience could be had in the cinemas of Canada, Mexico, most of Latin America, England, Continental Western

Europe, South Africa, and Australia. That was because more than 40 major American advertisers were using ad trailers in overseas markets. In Latin America filmgoers were regularly subjected to minute movies from Procter & Gamble, Coca-Cola, Squibb, Johnson & Johnson, Socony-Vacuum, and General Electric; in Canada it was Ford, Philco, United Fruit, and many others. Kibon Ice Cream and Atlantic Refining used only cinema screens to introduce new products in Rio de Janeiro. Results were reportedly so gratifying that showings of those ads were expanded to include television.[6]

After pointing out the spread of U.S.–produced ad trailers to foreign locales the reporter argued that television viewers were passive while filmgoers were a captive audience and since they had paid money to get in they were inclined to sit the program out to get their money's worth: "Moreover, to many people abroad, the motion picture is still the most exciting form of entertainment they know. Commercials, then, could almost be classed as 'entertainment' in some countries." Another reason for using cinema ads abroad was the then spotty distribution of television in many foreign countries. According to Walter Ellaby, export manager for the Alexander Film Company (a producer of ad films) commercial trailers produced in the U.S. could be used anywhere in the world because "Theater audiences throughout the world have become accustomed to accept American scenes, actors, props." According to Alexander Film, if an advertiser booked 150 theater weeks in Mexico, including first-run houses, the cost to him for screening a minute movie would be $5,000 with an estimated audience of two million people. In Cuba, if 170 cinemas were booked for a week the advertiser's cost would be $5,000 with an attendance of about 1.5 million. Three hundred houses rented in Canada for a week cost $8,000 and delivered an audience of 1.7 million viewers. Cost to an advertiser to have a 60-second ad produced was around $600 to $700 for a black and white ad, $1,200 for color.[7]

A more realistic assessment of the ad trailer situation came in 1953 when an account noted that it did not appear to make much sense to invest in ad trailers for a dwindling audience. Cited also was the fact that many national advertisers were spending a lot of their advertising money on television. The sharp decline in motion picture attendance then underway did not help to enhance the medium in the eyes of those advertisers.[8]

Just a couple of weeks later a much more optimistic assessment was given—by someone in the business. Claude Lee, an executive with the Motion Picture Advertising Service Company estimated that cinemas then were collecting a "record" $5 million in revenue from ad films and those items were screened in about 15,000 houses. He added, "You can

costs of the ad trailer costing another $2,500 in total. Lewyt had hopes that as many as 5,000 cinemas would eventually join the plan.[15]

Then in the fall of 1957 there was a great, but short-lived, furor over a different type of screen ad—the invisible invader. A new technique for transmitting "invisible advertising messages" on television and movie screens had reportedly been developed by Subliminal Projection Company of New York, with the objective being "fewer interruptions for sponsor messages, more entertainment time." The infamous subliminal ad had supposedly been born. Subliminal was defined by the company as "below the threshold of awareness." In a test by the company two advertising messages were projected every five seconds during a movie program. One message urged the audience to "Eat Popcorn" while the other suggested the audience "Drink Coca-Cola" Reportedly, that invisible sell increased popcorn sales by 57.5 percent and Coca-Cola sales by 18.1 percent. The developer of the new process was James Vicary, owner of a marketing and opinion research firm. Vicary said subliminal advertising would not prompt a viewer to buy something he did not consciously want. Subliminal beer ads, for example, he suggested, would have no effect on non-drinkers. Boasted Vicary, "If we had used any stronger psychology in our theater experiments, the whole audience would have gotten up to buy popcorn or Coca-Cola." He explained that his subliminal ads flashed on the screen for one three-thousandth of a second and that people did not see them because they were below their threshold. "Why send through a whole barrage of advertising when a light touch is better?" he exclaimed. "Our advertising messages are shown when the whole audience is there. It's not like the regular commercial break. The message is given during the actual TV or movie program."[16]

Days after that dramatic announcement Vicary hosted about 50 members of the press who turned out for a media demonstration of the subliminal ads. During his opening remarks to the press he declared "The purpose of subliminal projection is to eliminate irritation, create consumer desire without fuss and feathers—no visual image, no audible word." Media members attending the demonstration saw a nature film *Secrets of the Reef* during which the words "Coca-Cola" were flashed on the screen subliminally. Twice, however, during the showing of the film the word "Coca" was momentarily visible. That, explained Vicary, was intentional, to give the reporters a hint of what was happening. Nevertheless, several members of the press expressed disappointment they had not seen a 100 percent invisible demonstration. Other questions were put to Vicary, many of which challenged the ethics of invisible ads and pointed out the unpleasant implications. Vicary felt his technique would not be limited to visual perception but would be expanded to other senses because "Low-intensity sound can get past your ear the same way that high-speed light can get past your eye."[17]

Vicary acknowledged a limitation for subliminal ads since they were best suited only to "reminder" advertising—that the process could not be used, say, to introduce a new product. He also said he anticipated that "the intellectuals will land hard on the idea," but he denied harboring any sinister intentions. As if to silence any critics in advance Vicary argued the use of his process should be subject to some sort of control, and should be linked to some method of telling the audience in advance that they were going to be subjected to invisible ads. Control could be exercised, he suggested, by some federal department or by the advertising agency itself.[18]

When *Newsweek* ran a summary article on the subliminal ads it headlined its piece, "The Invisible Invader." New York University psychologist George S. Klein offered the opinion that "There's no way of telling how a person will react to such an ad. He might actually form a dislike for the product."[19]

Within a few weeks of the issuing of its first press releases the Subliminal Projection Company announced the signing of a contract with a "leading chain of movie houses" for use of its system. However, it refused to name the chain involved, preferring to leave it to the chain to identify itself. According to Subliminal executive Richard Forrest, the movie chain would use subliminal messages "to stimulate sales of refreshments; to implant messages about coming attractions, and also to aid in promoting merchandise that the theater might offer in connection with movies."[20]

By that time critics of subliminal advertising were out in force. One was Norman Cousins, editor of *The Saturday Review*. In an editorial he spoke of the dangers associated with the process when he wrote, "If the device is successful for putting over popcorn, why not politicians or anything else?" He wanted no "bypassing the conscious and dealing directly with the subconscious" and suggested that the wisest thing would be to take this invention and "attach it to the center of the next nuclear explosive scheduled for testing." In California Dr. Maurice Rappoport of the Stanford Research Institute called the use of invisible advertising on television a "virtual social H-bomb." Speaking for the Institute for Motivational Research, its executive vice president Albert Shepard expressed concern and said that any application of subliminal ads without the express knowledge or consent of the audience would be contrary to the public interest. Lawyers for Hollywood's majors threatened to legally challenge anything that would detract, if only subconsciously, from the audience's absorption of a film. Said one of those lawyers, "Contracts with exhibitors generally require the showing of the picture in the form received. If there is interference, the producer has a right to object."

Another remarked, "Absolutely illegal! Anything that's done to the film is an interference with our product. Our pictures must be shown as delivered." In response to the objections from the Hollywood cartel members, Subliminal Projection declared, "That question has come up, but we see no problem. One projector shows the movie; another our commercial. We don't alter the film, and the message is invisible."[21]

Then suddenly the issue disappeared—because none of what Vicary had claimed was true. There had been no increase in the sales of popcorn and Coca-Cola. His findings, wrote Mark Crispin Miller, were "fabricated … a mere sales gimmick to promote the Subliminal Projection Company itself."[22]

Writing in the *New York Times* early in 1958 Alexander Hammer said an increasing number of national advertisers were using cinema screens to get their messages across through the use of ad trailers: "This is a comparatively new trend. For many years this medium was used almost exclusively by small merchants and retailers in their own communities." According to Hammer the number of national advertisers using the medium had risen from fewer than 100 firms in 1955 to about 200 in 1957, with those ad trailers being screened in the "vast majority" of houses. Studebaker-Packard was then using ad trailers to show its 1958 models; the Philco company was promoting its latest appliances in a series of 13 ads; the Rheem Manufacturing Company had just completed a series of ads for its room heaters; and General Motors had a series of 11 trailers promoting its GMC trucks.[23]

Also, the Bankers Life and Casualty Company of Chicago showed two trailers in a test attempt to sell its White Cross medical insurance. Those trailers ran for one week each in 81 drive-in theaters, spotted around the U.S. Linked to the ad trailer was an inquiry postcard that was handed to the driver of each car as he entered the drive-in. An announcer on the ad trailer referred to the card and told the audience they would receive a free booklet or a free sample policy by sending the card to Bankers Life. Results were said to have been so good that Bankers Life decided to undertake a national campaign in both drive-ins and indoor cinemas.[24]

Among the reasons for this supposed growth in the popularity of the medium, said Hammer, was that the ad trailers reached that all-important "captive" audience. There were no distractions and the impact was experienced by every viewer. Also, the circulation count—number of tickets sold—was readily available and accurate. Costs for reaching 1,000 filmgoers then ranged from $5 to $7, depending on length of the ad. Hammer added that some 25,000 local advertisers also used the medium. According to his figures in 1946 the total capacity of drive-ins was about 300,000 persons and only about 40 percent of them showed commercials. In 1956 drive-in capacity was 14,484,736 and about 95 percent of them ran advertising. Back in 1946 there were 11,661,937 seats in indoor theaters and about 70 percent showed ads; in 1957 the seating capacity was 12,191,472 and about 80 percent of those hardtop venues ran ad trailers.[25]

During the mid 1950s a consortium of five companies (led by the Alexander Film Company) formed the Association of Theatre Screen Advertising Companies, the first trade group for the screen advertising business. Reportedly, it was responsible for more than doubling the number of national advertisers running cinema ads from fewer than 100 in 1950 to some 225 in 1958. Sometime in 1957 that organization renamed itself the Theatre-Screen Advertising Bureau (TSAB).[26]

A year later, in 1958, TSAB argued that television, despite all the hardship it had inflicted on the motion picture business, was responsible for at least one benefit. Because of television, said the group, "The public has been strongly conditioned to accept advertising with its entertainment, leading to a phenomenal growth in the number of theaters available for theater-screen advertising." About 98 percent of America's drive-ins accepted advertising that year, as did about 80 percent of the 15,000 indoor cinemas, claimed TSAB, according to its own survey. The total sales volume for the five member firms of TSAB (all of whom produced and distributed ad films) was around $20 million. TSAB members said the prevalence of cinema screen advertising often came as a surprise to many advertising personnel, "who are located in downtown New York and Chicago, where it is not generally available." Chevrolet, one of the pioneer companies in that medium, had booked about 3,500 houses (the majority were drive-ins) for its 1958 campaign. Other national advertisers then said to be using ad trailers included: General Electric, U.S. Rubber, Carnation Milk, Coca-Cola, Rexall, Philco, B. F. Goodrich, Maytag, Skelgas, Rheem, Pepsi-Cola, Pet Milk, and Seven-Up.[27]

Another upbeat article in 1958 about the future of screen ads also spoke of the conditioning influence of television and that cinema ad proponents relished a comparison with television because "They point out that their pictures are hundreds of times larger, stereophonic sound commands more attention, distractions are fewer in the darkened theater than at home, and color is available for a small extra production cost." Also, those proponents felt the medium deserved more attention but admitted that decisions on media selection were often made by advertising people in New York or Chicago, "where downtown theaters don't show ads. The men who make the decisions are not regularly exposed to theater advertising and thus tend to overlook it in their plans." When the TSAB formed, one of its reasons for being was to carry its story to advertisers, to compile and disseminate information on its medium—information such as the fact that a theater ad could supposedly reach 35 million filmgoers over the age of 12 each week. Ad trailers were still said to be limited to a maximum of three per program. Proponents of cinema ads also stressed the selectivity of the medium—that an advertiser could target his audience by geographic location, by race, by income level, and so on. However, in reality that was a bit of a stretch since more selectivity could be achieved through television as the tracking system of the latter became more sophisticated. One survey from TSAB claimed that an ad trailer, run on a 13-week national schedule, was seen by 72 percent of the population. More sobering, and working against screen ads, was that American weekly cinema attendance in 1958 was about 46 million, down dramatically from the 85–90 million weekly attendance registered in 1946.[28]

French national Andre Pierre Albert Sarrut (a producer in France of ad trailers) arrived in the United States in 1958 to publicize an American agency that was handling U.S. sales of his filmed ads. He said that since "the public doesn't consider advertising an art, it is willing to accept revolutionary expression in an advertising short which it wouldn't accept in a feature film." Sarrut added, "The public likes original creation in advertising; it hates it in entertainment. It is getting so the advertising intermission in a theater has the appeal for the highbrows." He was one of the very few in this industry who argued that the audience in a cinema was not a captive one. Ads, he explained, were sandwiched between feature films with the house lights on; a portion of the audience was then on its feet and moving around to better seats, and hawkers were selling candy, soft drinks, and so forth. Ad trailers had a number of tasks that Sarrut broke down as follows: achievement of brand recognition, 65 percent; product message, 20 percent; and motivating function, 15 percent. With respect to the last task Sarrut said he and his personnel tested the selling capacity of a commercial by asking people, "Did you find the ad ridiculous?" They found that "if men—including advertisers and agency men—say yes, it will be successful among women consumers."[29]

Despite the number of upbeat articles about the growth of ad trailers on theater screens the reality was less optimistic. They continued to be mainly absent from all the cinemas that really counted—from the first-run houses in the downtowns of major cities, and generally from the large, prestigious, national cinema chains. Whatever growth that took place in the 1950s was mostly in drive-in theaters, the influence of which would start to wane in the 1960s and beyond. In fact, that lack of, or minimal existence of, screen ads was regularly used by cinemas in publicity as a point of advantage. During the 1950s when film attendance was in a steady decline cinemas regularly played up their lack of ads as a reason for going to the theater, compared to staying home to watch televi-

*Will Success Spoil Rock Hunter?* (1957, Jayne Mansfield, left, and Joan Blondell). Cited for conspicuously plugging the airline TWA, in this scene the film hyped a popular novel of the time, *Peyton Place.*

sion. A constant worry expressed by many in the industry was that cinema ads drove away patrons. A mail survey reported in 1951 by I. I. Raines revealed that ad trailers had little impact on movie attendance patterns. When asked "If advertising films were not shown how would it affect your attendance?" only 10 percent of the respondents indicated they would attend movies more often; five percent said less often; 85 percent said it would not alter their attendance patterns. Nearly all (91 percent) of Raines's sample reported they would not "be willing to pay a somewhat higher admission price" if advertising films were not shown. Thirty-eight percent of respondents were "strongly in favor" or "in favor" of cinema screen advertising; 27 percent had no opinion: and 35 percent were "opposed" or "strongly opposed." Of those opposed to screen advertising their reasons for opposition were broken down as follows: takes too long, 22 percent; the showing of ads is an imposition, 21 percent; uninteresting presentation, 20 percent; not interested in products, 19 percent; poor photography and sound, five percent; and other reasons, three percent.[30]

Within the product placement area, the practice had turned up in television shows by no later than early in 1951. An account that year declared the practice of radio and television payola had lately hit an "unprecedented high." It was said that virtually every public relations company in the business had a special emissary assigned to radio and television programming "specifically for the purpose of getting a plug on behalf of a client's product." Sometimes, in the case of sponsored shows, it led to embarrassment in the inadvertent plugging of rival company products. For example, on a major show sponsored by a brewery firm the star of the show was not aware that the supplementary plug worked into the continuity represented a conflict with one of the brewery's auxiliary products.[31]

Companies seeking product placement on television were reportedly paying those public relations middlemen from $150 to $250 per network plug, with the PR person passing on $75 to $125 of that total to the producer of the television show, or its talent, or writer who arranged the plug. In one reported instance a comedian doing a guest shot on a television program worked in half a dozen paid plugs, "which earned him more than his performing fee." A Philadelphia department store bought a mention on a network mystery program. For his fee the scriptwriter had the villain traced to that city, with a clue found in the store. One unnamed manufacturer, billed for five television placements (at $175 each) in one week, told his public relations contact to limit his activities to a maximum of two "insertions" per week. Supposedly it was that easy to get plugs.[32]

Product placement in the movies was profiled in *Time* magazine in 1951 under the heading, "The plug lobby." Noting first the power of films to sell, even inadvertently, the account cited the by this time classic examples of Clark Gable and undershirts, and Charles Boyer, Irene Dunne, and pink champagne. Also mentioned was that simply by wearing a cap in his pictures, silent film star Wallace Reid started men rushing out to buy caps of their own. According to this account, "Last week, as they have for years, high-powered Hollywood lobbyists were subtly slipping their wares into the screen's magic showcase." Lobbyist Bill Treadwell, who worked for Britain's Tea Bureau, claimed he had increased U.S. tea consumption 17 million pounds a year, largely by getting tea scenes in 83 movies in two years. His greatest coup was reportedly having persuaded Warner Bros. to change the name of its musical *No! No! Nanette!* to *Tea for Two*. In return Treadwell used some of the Tea Bureau's $2 million a year promotion fund to squire a couple of starlets on a 14-city tour as "Miss Iced Tea for Two" and "Miss Hot Tea for Two." The newest member of the plug lobby was reported to be the United Nations publicist Mogens Skot-Hansen, who persuaded a producer to make Dorothy McGuire a UN translator in *Mister 880*. "She is a nice, good girl and gives us a good name," explained the bureaucrat. Thanks to his efforts, Bing Crosby, cast as a journalist in *Here Comes the Groom,* was shown at work on a story about UN relief work; Joseph Cotton, playing a doctor in *Peking Express,* worked for the UN's World Health Organization. Skot-Hansen had no budget that would allow him to reciprocate by publicizing movies that plugged the UN but he could lend studios items such as Korean war film footage, and give producers publicity in UN publications.[33]

One sign that the practice of product placement was perhaps growing came in 1951 when the U.S. federal government's Internal Revenue Service (IRS) announced that the giveaways going to people for effecting a plug in the movies and on radio and television were henceforth to be taxable items. "It's an old Hollywood custom, in radio and television, too, to sneak in plugs for a price. The payoff, as often as not, has been in merchandise (never cash), either the sponsor's product or hard liquor by the case," observed reporter Jack Hellman. No fraud was charged by the government; it just wanted its "fair share of the loot." According to Hellman the customary payoff was "a case or two of choice spirits" with the giver writing if off as a legitimate business expense while the recipient writer, actor, or producer failed to declare the item as taxable income.[34]

Examples of product placements in specific films included Rosalind Russell dabbing on Charles of the Ritz perfume in the 1958 release *Auntie Mame.* Sales of Ace combs reportedly soared after James Dean swept one through his hair in *Rebel Without a Cause.* In the 1951 release *The African Queen* (Humphrey Bogart and Katharine Hepburn), cases of Gilbey's Gin were very evident. Hepburn dumped the gin overboard as she battled to keep Bogart sober. However, no deliberate placement may have been involved in that instance. Looking back at that film from 1995, Dean Ayers, a product placement executive, said he was pretty sure that no placement was involved. His guess was that it was purely a creative decision or some idiosyncrasy such as, perhaps, director John Huston being a drinker of that brand of gin.[35]

A 1957 account in *Variety* highlighted the placement situation and its supposed increasing prevalence. It was said, "After a period of supervised discretion film studios are again beginning to 'plug' specific goods and services on the screen." Sales pitches, while still "integrated" as much as possible into the story and action, had lately become "more obvious." Cited as a "glaring example" was the movie *Will Success Spoil Rock Hunter?* which went "all-out" in plugging the airline TWA. In one lengthy scene, a bright red TWA travel bag was kept in conspicuous view throughout, "with the TWA letters virtually dominating the screen." In *Love in the Afternoon* both Pepsi-Cola and Coca-Cola received plugs, complete with company slogans. A cigarette company reportedly received a "hefty free ad" in *Sweet Smell of Success*. Pepsi got another plug in *Pajama Game* while other unnamed films reportedly included plugs for cigarette manufacturers, beer companies, auto makers, and so on.[36]

From time to time exhibitors had complained about product placements such as those cited above, observed *Variety* "and in years past, there have been instances of theatres actually snipping such footage out of films." Executives at the majors argued that realistic props were needed to make realistic stories. "I'm not sure we'd get away today with using fake labels," remarked one. He agreed, however, that the wisdom of using brand names in a prominent way on the screen was questionable. This account concluded that there was a period when the studios carefully sidestepped the use of known brands. This changed with the rise of realism in filmmaking and the advent of television: "Not only household and other goods, but also magazines now appear regularly in pix."[37]

*Love in the Afternoon* (1957, Gary Cooper). After touting both Coca-Cola and Pepsi-Cola this film featured some alcohol products, although the brand-names were hard to read. Manufacturers were often disappointed with the quality of product placement they ended up receiving.

One example of product placement in a 1959 film began when Klingman and Spencer, public relations counsel to Exquisite Form Brassiere, Inc., happened on the script for *Happy Anniversary*, a United Artists movie starring Mitzi Gaynor and David Niven. As Klingman and Spencer read into the script they came to a scene where Mitzi and David tuned in their television at home to unexpectedly find their eight-year-old "daughter" on a children's program, detailing her "parents'" marital problems. Klingman and Spencer then arranged a meeting with Ralph Fields, producer of the movie, and said, "Why not improve the script by inserting an entertaining TV commercial leading up to this hilarious high spot of the film?" And, of course, the firm said they had the ideal ad for leading into that bit—one for Exquisite Form Brassiere. After negotiations, an agreement was reached with Exquisite Form earmarking a multi-million-dollar ad campaign to publicize the film within its own advertising. United Artists arranged special screenings of the film for department store personnel around the country. Both agreed to sponsor a *Happy Anniversary*-Exquisite Form contest with a prize of a trip for two to Hollywood. A 63-second Exquisite Form ad appeared as part of the movie.[38]

As the 1950s ended cinema advertising had still not lived up to the potential that many had envisioned for it. It was in a period of stagnation—a period destined to last for some time.

# 6

# Ad Trailers Make a Big Push
## *1960–1981*

It would indeed be a major pollution of the theatre screen if we were to pay for the dubious privilege of being molested by commercial pitches.
—A. D. Murphy, 1977

One of the most important competitive advantages the American theatre has is its ability to present entertainment without the encumbrance of commercial advertising.
—Richard Kahn, MGM vice president, 1977

It would be insulting to customers to make them sit through a commercial. We are not running them.
—Ed Knudsen, Redstone cinema chain, 1977

With regard to cinema advertising this period was one mostly of a continued state of stagnation, at least until the latter part of the 1970s when ad trailers made a move to obtain a greater presence on theater screens. They received more notice and attention than they had at any time in the past.

Merchandise licensing remained an important part of the Hollywood scene, at least with respect to some of the more publicized of the Hollywood releases. Fox formed its own licensing subsidiary in 1966. Prior to that it, and much of the Hollywood film industry, had been using Licensing Corporation of America (LCA), but Fox saw all the money LCA was making and decided to do away with the middleman. Said Fox executive vice president Seymour Poe, "Licensing is becoming an increasingly important factor in motion picture distribution...it is only logical that we extend our overall program of diversification to licensing with the creation of this new subsidiary." Sean Connery was then portraying James Bond in the first films of that series and had negotiated a piece of the licensing fee derived from the sale of Bond-linked products. LCA had more than 150 products licensed to use the 007 mark. In a similar line, within a couple of months of its television launch on the ABC network the series *Batman* had spawned nearly 150 linked products, LCA also handled the licensing in that case.[1]

Ad shorts were still around in the 1970s, but just barely. Leonard Sloane did a piece in the *New York Times* in 1971 in which he argued that the short subjects of old, remembered by filmgoers of the pre-television era, were returning to cinemas under business sponsorship. These ad shorts included companies such as Western Electric celebrating the centennial of the telephone, Kemper Insurance warning of the dangers of drug abuse, or Pan American Airways promoting vacation interest in the island of Bali. Because of the "virtual disappearance" of shorts that earlier generations grew up on—serials, newsreels, comedy shorts, cartoons, and so on, said Sloane—theater owners were then "happy" to show the "free sponsored films that meet their standards of quality and interest to fill the time between features." Peter J. Mooney, president of industrial film producer Audio Productions, remarked, "Films in theaters represent a soft sell for companies and often you don't see the name of the company in the picture at all. They've got to stand on their own," Sloane said some $135 million a year was spent to produce and distribute 7,000 sponsored movies, but that only a very small portion of those were aimed at regular cinemas. Most of those were one-reel items that ran for a maximum of 10 minutes. The cost of producing a sponsored picture ranged upward from $1,000 a minute, but most corporation figured on an expenditure of $40,000 to $70,000 for a 10-minute movie designed for cinemas, plus another $100 or so for each of the 50–100 prints that were required for a national program.[2]

Asked why a company would spend so much money on an ad short George P. Ducharme, director of advertising and public relations for Kemper Insurance, said, "I think it gives the public an increased awareness of our company. We can capture a thinking audience that way." William J. Fitzgerald, department chief for motion picture and television production at Western Electric, explained, "It can create an acceptance of industry, an empathy, a feeling of mutual understanding. But if it goes heavy on the commercial, you're defeating yourself." And that was because the "sophisticated and critical" movie audience "won't sit still for commercials disguised as industrial pix and presented in cinemas where they've paid as much as $5 a tix." One executive who made his living from sponsored films noted the movie industry started with shorts, "but they have always been a stepchild. We're looking forward to the day that sponsored films will be so good that they will be worthy of being rented."[3]

Several years later, in 1978, Judy Goldsmith, an executive with Modern Talking Picture Service (a producer and distributor of ad shorts) argued, not surprisingly, that the market for them was "great." Her company had arranged the "terrific" match of *Ridin' the Edge,* Allstate insurance's driver safety short, playing with the Hollywood feature *Hooper* (with lots of stunt driving). Manufacturer Hanover Trust's *New York City Marathon* played with *House Calls,* whose ads showed Walter Matthau and Glenda Jackson jogging. While both those articles were optimistic about the future of ad shorts the reality was much different. Those few cited examples were probably close to the total number of ad shorts screened. Their future was indeed in the past. After the 1970s the ad short was no longer mentioned in the media.[4]

When U.S. cinema advertising men went to Europe in 1960 to check out the situation they must have been more than a little envious, for they reported that ad trailers had developed into the number one non-print medium in many nations abroad. One reason for that success was that several countries, such as France, Holland, and Belgium, had no commercial broadcasting of television or radio while England was just then starting to sell via television. That vacuum was filled by ads in the print media, to an extent, but the screen ad gave a visual presence. "The European screen has become a lavish showroom with a wide range of products on display," declared a reporter. "The mass-consumption items, which make up the backbone of American TV, dominate movie ads abroad; soft drinks, beer, and even wines and liquors; candy, cosmetics and cigarettes; soap, cleansers, and toilet articles; food, petroleum and pharmaceutical products." Among the names familiar to Americans on European theater screens were the likes of Life Savers, Coca-Cola, Kraft, Brylcreem, Colgate, Gillette, Palmolive, Bayer, Vicks, Elizabeth Arden, Max Factor, Shell, Chevrolet, and Ford. "Radios and TV sets, furniture and clothing are among other higher-priced items sold on this mass-marketing basis," it was reported. In most European nations, nationally distributed brands made up about 50 percent of the screen ads; local advertisers (mainly retail outlets) comprised 25 percent and internationally marketed products made up the remaining 25 percent of the ad trailers. Typical production and distribution costs of ad trailers for European screens were reported to be very cheap, working out to about one cent per viewer ($10 per 1,000, which was close to the distribution cost alone for ad trailers in the U.S.). Also, cinema screen advertising was said to consume almost 20 percent of total advertising of all kinds in some European nations.[5]

In 1960 the trade journal *Printers' Ink* ran an optimistic piece about the state of ad trailers on American screens that spoke of a supposed "boom" in the field. Admitting the trailers' home was primarily to be found in rural and small-town houses and that the old-fashioned slide ads, crude by metropolitan standards, could still be called the "back-

*Boys Night Out* (1962, Kim Novak, James Garner). Among other items, Sunbeam appliances were placed in this movie. Note the toaster on the counter.

bone" of the business, the article nonetheless argued that more and more sophisticated ad trailers were being employed by top national advertisers. According to this report, in 1959 some 175 national advertisers and 25,000 local ones made their sales pitches through nearly 6,000 cinemas. Altogether they were said to have spent about $20 million in the medium.[6]

Going against that grain of undocumented optimism was an article in the *New York Times* in 1961 by Philip Shabecoff wherein he pointed out how minimal screen advertising was, and how it did not have a great future. Such advertising was very much the exception rather than the rule in New York, he observed, although he did agree that screen advertising was widely used in Europe and that in several Asian and African countries where illiteracy was widespread, the theater screen was one of the principal advertising media. Still, Shabecoff allowed that 90 percent of venues in the United States accepted ads to one degree or another and that it was only in some of the largest cities in America that such advertising was not prevalent. Cinema screen advertising was a medium of comparatively minor importance in the U.S.'s advertising industry since theater advertising made up only a fraction of one percent of total U.S. advertising expenditure, "ranking the medium on about the same level as match book covers." By comparison, in France, for example, 14 percent of the total advertising expenditure was placed in movie theater advertising.[7]

As to why screen advertising was such a tiny fraction of the advertising total, one executive told Shabecoff that a main reason was that the New York metropolitan area (America's number one consumer market) was almost devoid of such ads. He explained, "We're all eggheads in New York and sophisticated audiences tend to resent interruptions by commercials at the movies. In some areas, people prefer theatre commercials to those on television, but not here." New York, of course, was also the center of the advertising industry. Shabecoff agreed that in the years prior to World War II cinema screen ads were limited principally to the smaller towns and rural areas. After the war business dried up in a lot of those towns due to the spread of suburbs, shopping centers, and automobile ownership, with the result that a lot of small cinemas in rural areas shut down. The one bright spot in the post-war period for cinema ads was the growth of drive-in theaters, since most of them accepted cinema advertising. "Despite this cozy picture, however, theatre screen advertising is probably doomed to remain forever a comparatively minor medium," Shabecoff concluded. He felt that way because of a number of self-imposed limitations. For example, a maximum of four one-minute ads were screened at venues. It had been estimated, he said, that if all cinemas accepting ads sold every minute of available time, total billings would not be more than $50 million a year. Yet sales at that time "are well below that figure." Due to mergers and absorptions there were then only two major theatre screen advertising companies left in the U.S.— the Motion Picture Advertising Service Company of New Orleans, and the Alexander Film Company of Colorado Springs, Colorado. "There is little likelihood, however, that any new motion picture advertising company will arise in the near future," Shabecoff declared.[8]

For the 1966 model season Chevrolet offered its dealers film versions of 14 national television commercials. They were made available free of charge to the dealers with personalized dealer identification at the opening and close of the ad trailers. All the dealer had to do was to buy the time at local cinemas. Chevrolet had begun adapting its television ads during the 1965 model season; 730 dealers ordered those ad trailers. For 1966 Chevrolet hoped to have 25 percent of its 6,700 dealers participate.[9]

Another journalist who looked at the absence of cinema advertising in New York was Philip Dougherty, in 1972. Exhibitor Donald Rugoff told him it was that way "because the audience would tear down the theater" if ads were displayed. Carl Levine of the Brandt chain said that local theater owners "are reluctant to commercialize their screens, although we have been approached many times." But Sheldon Gunsberg of the Walter Reade chain was not willing to rule out the possibility it could happen in New York: "Someday, some advertiser if he's willing to pay the price and his message is not offensive. Well, I'm not saying it couldn't happen." One who did want to change the situation was Gene Weiss, vice president of the Motion Picture Advertising Corporation. He was said to work with 8,000 exhibitors, including some in every other major American city. Advertisers paid him from $3.50 to $8.70 per 1,000 filmgoers, with about one-third of that amount going to the theater operator for screen rental. Weiss claimed he never heard any criticism from audiences over being subjected to ad trailers and he would not be surprised if that was because television had gotten them used to the ad experience. He admitted that television had badly hurt the cinema advertising business. Generally, he explained, the arrangement with theater operators was "for the first 4 minutes after the lights go down and before the featured entertainment starts."[10]

Early in 1977 journalist A. D. Murphy argued for advertising-free screens when he observed, "In a world where, on any given day, a person's waking hours include being bombarded with literally hundreds—perhaps thousands—of commercial appeals, there has always been at least one place essentially free of the hardsell: A motion picture theatre." Putting aside the coming attraction trailers, he added, "there is a relative haven from the billboards, teleblurbs, bulk mail, panhandlers, radio pitches, Goodyear blimp, sound trucks, sandwich boards and such, hawking everything from jockstraps to Presidential candidates." A generation or two earlier, Murphy recalled, "In theatres playing 19th run or worse, one can remember a few minutes of screen advertising—little local shops...That was strictly smalltime stuff." Writing from Hollywood, he noted the *Los Angeles Times* had long pitched subscriptions on neighborhood cinema screens and sometimes a brief plug appeared for Universal Studios tours, and drive-in patrons were subjected to a lot of concession promotions. But apart from those "aberrations," a person paying an admission ranging from $4 down to 99 cents could buy some relief from the ad pitches. Murphy worried that if screen advertising were allowed to increase "It would indeed be a major pollution of the theatre screen if we were to pay for the dubious privilege of being molested by commercial pitches." Murphy concluded, "Exhibs would be well advised to keep the commercial junk off the motion picture theatre screen and allow folks to continue to be able to pay for a couple of hours of freedom from grubby mercantile rape."[11]

Several months after that, still in 1977, reporter John Cocchi wrote of the possible rebirth of the ad trailer business. William Woosley, president of the newly formed Cinemavision, Inc. (CI), the Nashville-based firm that was to distribute the ads, stated he had the blessings in that endeavor of both the National Association of Theatre Owners (NATO) and the National Independent Theatre Exhibitors (NITE) group. NITE president Tom Patterson cited a recent Gallagher Poll that found the majority of viewers preferred to watch films at home (on television) rather than in cinemas. It was a result that caused the NITE head to worry that exhibitors might not figure at all in the future plans of the Hollywood majors—that the cartel members would eventually release movies directly to cable television rather than to cinemas. To that end a plan had been developed by NITE and CI. Reportedly, by August, 1977, some 2,000 exhibitors had already signed up for an advertising program to run up to three minutes of "spot entertainment" (ad trailers) before the main feature, declared Patterson, as part of the plan. CI would pay revenues generated from the ads into a film financing fund. Direction of that fund was to be in the hands of the exhibitors, who would hire professional people to make films for their cinemas. A minimum of $9 per 1,000 patrons for each 30-second ad trailer was slated to go into the fund. Exhibitors signed up for the program would have first-run rights to the films to be produced, paying a maximum rental for those movies of 35 percent of the box-office gross (rental of movies from the Hollywood majors was usually 45 percent of the gross).[12]

Cocchi reported that an audience response survey supposedly indicated that 75 percent of the patrons had no adverse reaction to seeing commercials on a cinema screen. When told the CI ad program would help maintain admission and concession prices, the patron response was said to have jumped to 96.8-percent approval. Those ad trailers were projected to cost around $100,000 each to produce and would feature only major advertisers, "not cheap local outlets." Patterson explained that exhibitors had an option to put half the revenues into the film-producing fund and to keep the other half for themselves, although he felt it should all go into film production. While CI hoped to sign exhibitors to contracts that ran for several years an escape clause permitted the cinema operator to get out of his contract in the first six months if patron reactions to the ad spots was adverse. Woosley hoped to begin the program in September 1977 by showing 1.5 minutes of commercials in the 1,200 houses that had actually signed contracts for the service. A full-scale operation was expected by November of that year and Woosley confidently predicted that in 10 years, the revenue generated by CI's program could exceed $250 million.[13]

Delays pushed back the test start date of CI's ad program to Novem-

*Who's Minding the Store?* (1963, Jerry Lewis, Nancy Culp). In its time this film was cited as an example of excessive placement.

ber 1, with the plan being to launch the ad trailers in 1,000 houses in eight major markets—Los Angeles, San Francisco, Sacramento, Boston, Philadelphia, Portland, Colorado Springs, and Pueblo, Colorado. However, as of early October only one national advertiser, RCA Records, had committed itself to a one-minute ad. CI maintained, though, that others were "keenly interested" and that they were in negotiations with several. Patterson emphasized the 1,000 venues were just a start, with a hope to quickly move it to 4,200 houses and eventually to 10,000, with the latter number providing CI an annual revenue of up to $50 million. Advertisers were to be charged $18 per 1,000 admissions by CI. The initial response to the planned CI-NITE ad network from the Hollywood majors was, said a reporter, "generally negative." Many expressed fears the ads would alienate audiences and some had suggested the possibility of action—withholding film product from participating exhibitors—as one way to counter the ad network.[14]

Even before that network launched its test, it was announced that CI had a rival. A Frenchman named Roger Hatchuel had worked quietly for the previous 18 months toward an October 26, 1977, premiere of "a new U.S. national advertising medium." On that date moviegoers in some 1,800 cinemas across the country were slated to see—just before the feature started—three minutes of ad trailers for Chrysler cars, Seiko watches, and other nationally advertised products. And despite what he called "scare stories" in film trade papers that questioned whether audiences would "tolerate" commercials in theaters, Hatchuel was certain that both patrons and advertisers would. As general manager of Mediavision, a French company that sold $20 million worth of cinema advertising annually to European clients, Hatchuel and his partners invested in setting up a New York subsidiary, Screenvision, Inc (SV). "For 40 years," Hatchuel said, "ads in theaters have been standard practice nearly everywhere except the U.S. and Canada" and he believed it was time for that situation to change. Hatchuel was said to have commissioned a research study of audience reaction. A test in a New Jersey cinema in January, 1977, was followed by one in March and April in eight major cities. The absence of any adverse audience reaction stemming

from those tests was reported to have persuaded several major theater chains—including United Artists Theaters (600 screens) and American Multi Cinema (400)—to join the SV project. Exhibitors signed up for the plan were to receive one-third of SV's net revenues while the advertisers were to be charged $17 per 1,000 admissions by SV—a price, admitted Hatchuel, that "makes for an expensive medium in a country where TV advertisers are accustomed to paying $4 for each 1,000 viewers." He justified the extra expense by arguing the film audience was a select one—youthful (18 to 29), relatively affluent, and one that viewed less television. Hollywood argued against this plan also, pointing out again that a major selling point in inducing

*You Only Live Twice* (1967, Sean Connery, other unidentified). One of the early James Bond films, displaying its whiskey. In time the Bond films would engage in massive product placement.

people to leave their homes to see a film was the absence of commercials.[15]

Weighing in on the issue was the advertising-publicity committee of the cartel's MPAA lobby group. Richard Kahn, MGM vice president and chairman of that MPAA committee, disclosed a unanimously approved committee stand deploring the "rebirth" of screen advertising and urging exhibitors "to keep their screens free of non entertainment clutter." Kahn did not mention NITE by name but denounced screen ad programs as a serious threat to the ability of exhibitors to compete with television. While he acknowledged that no television-like interruption of movies for commercials was contemplated by a screen ad plan, he insisted that any commercial pitches on movie screens would be a "disastrous turnoff" for people who patronized cinemas at least in part for relief from advertising. "One of the most important competitive advantages the American theatre has is its ability to present entertainment without the encumbrance of commercial advertising," said Kahn. "To lose that competitive advantage would be heartbreaking." Screen ads inserted as contemplated, he added, would "outrage" filmgoers. "These things, if ever allowed to gain a foothold," he warned, "would be insidious and almost octopus like in what could ultimately happen...Keeping the screens free of advertising would be to the advantage of all concerned."[16]

Early in November the CI program got off to a start with NITE of New England exhibitors (150 houses in the six states). Edith Scott, executive director of NITE of New England, said the ads were strictly from national advertisers, not the local ads people might have seen in some drive-ins and neighborhood indoor houses. "They aren't like commercials, more like entertainment," she added. "It's definitely not a hard sell, but a 30-sec. or minute of entertaining film, sort of a subliminal approach."[17]

Tests by CI in the Seattle and Portland area reportedly showed that about 75 percent of 1,700 filmgoers opposed ads on theater screens. They were shown Olympia Beer and RCA spots in the Pacific Northwest testing (understood to be a forerunner of a CI tryout of beer and auto ads nationally). CI had been holding back on its plans to join SV, which was then running Seiko watch ads in selected theaters. Survey findings indicated that 87 percent of the group sampled was opposed to television commercials.[18]

More problems for screen ads surfaced in November 1977 when a federal consumer agency asked Seattle cinemas to warn customers in advance that commercials would be shown. In letters to the managers of the UA Cinema 70 and the Sea Tac Six Theatres, Federal Trade Commissioner William Erxleben said he considered it "unfair and misleading...to take someone's money without first informing them of the commercials." In part, that letter said "Americans are bombarded daily by commercial messages. Even in the privacy of your home, it is difficult to avoid mail, telephone and door-to-door solicitations. Many people, I believe, look to movie theatres as a sanctuary for entertainment free from commercial solicitation." Erxleben suggested the houses "disclose prominently" in their advertising and at the entrance to the venues that commercials would be shown. The UA Cinema 70 had played one commercial at each program the previous week, said William Shonk, division manager of the United Artists theater chain. According to him, no customer had complained about the ads. Erxleben said that as far as he knew he was the first FTC director to question the showing of ads in cinemas. He believed it was possible that showing such ads might perhaps violate some consumer protection laws against false or misleading advertising if the theaters did not inform customers prior to their buying a ticket that commercials would be shown. Erxleben added his request was made on the basis of disclosure. That is, it was a merchant's responsibility to disclose material facts about a product or service and that "failure to disclose" had been the basis of FTC complaints in the past.[19]

With regard to the 75 percent negative survey, CI vice president of marketing Paul Kegley said that the finding—"which the company fully expected"—was taken unfairly out of context. Kegley explained that the 75-percent objection to screen ads figure came from a simple yes-or-no question, noting, "When we asked people if they would rather have theaters close down at less than peak periods, or have higher box office prices, there was a complete turnaround to 96.8 % in favor of screen ads." (Of course, it was ludicrous to present the possibility of higher admission prices in the absence of screen ads, given the figures. Exhibitors got one-third of CI or SV grosses of $18 per 1,000 admissions. With a maximum of three minutes of ads per program it meant an exhibitor would receive at most $18 per 1,000 admissions, or 1.8 cents per admission ticket—hardly a reason to raise the ticket price.) CI planned to continue running tests until the firm's planned national start-up, then slated for January, 1978. SV, which had launched its national program at the end of October as planned, claimed to have found "no significant negative reaction" from exhibitors or filmgoers, seven million of whom had been exposed to commercials in cinemas since it launched. Hatchuel felt those opposing theater ads may have prejudged them as being in television's "irritating detergent and toilet tissue genres."[20]

Screenvision preceded its ad program with a "Screenvision presents..." logo. Between each spot, a short, animated sight gag appeared, and the trailer package ended with a "Thanks, SV." With regard to the FTC plea from the Seattle office for full disclosure, Hatchuel said some exhibitors involved with his company's program might want to put up notices but he felt it was all a "small thing." However, CI had prepared a notice for box office use at exhibitor premises where its program was being tried out. Whether the notice would be posted was up to each theater, said Kegley. No notice was planned to be appended to newspaper ads. (FTC regional offices had authority to begin investigations on their own initiative up to the commitment of 100 hours of personnel time. Once a project exceeded that limit the regional office had to get approval from the Washington head office to continue.) Advertisers then lined up by SV included Seiko watches, Chanel perfume, and Chrysler cars. While Screenvision had rejected cigarettes, alcoholic beverages, and other "controversial" categories of advertising, CI said its 41 accounts included cigarette companies, besides RCA Records and Olympic Brewing (those two were the only subscribing advertisers CI would specifically name). When reporters canvassed all the tobacco companies, each one indicated it was not part of the CI ad program. Screenvision reportedly then had 3,000 houses in its program and charged advertisers $17 per 1,000 admissions for a 60-second ad. To reach 15 million people in the top 100 markets via 2,202 screens an SV advertiser client would pay $127,278 for a 30-second spot.[21]

*Rachel, Rachel* (1968, Joanne Woodward, Paul Newman).

Cinema commercials did not get much of a reception from Philadelphia houses. Locally-based Sameric Theatres said it had been approached in mid 1977 to run ads but that it turned the proposition down "flat." For Max Weiner, head of that city's Consumer Education and Protection Association, commercials were a rip-off. "It's bad enough we have to watch TV ads, but at least there we still have the privilege of turning the set off," he said. "But what does the consumer do when charged admission so they can make money on us with advertisements? That's really carrying things too far." The Budco Quality Theatres in Philadelphia said it would not run ads at its houses; General Cinema Corporation (20 screens in metro Philadelphia) said it then had no plans to use them. American Multi Cinema (with eight of its 425-house circuit in Philadelphia) was then testing SV commercials in about half of its houses to observe customer reaction. United Artists cinemas, with 48 screens in a four-state area centered in Philadelphia, was the only place that looked favorable on commercials—all its houses screened them. Both of those latter two chains argued it was better to screen ads than to raise admission prices. However, both failed to point out that an exhibitor got at most 1.7 cents per ticket.[22]

*Pocket Money* (1972, Paul Newman). The fast-food chain A&W received prominent play.

Cinema ads drew a mixed reception in Boston, with the large chains refusing to run them and the smaller, independent houses more likely to screen them. William Moscarelli, an executive with the Sack chain in Boston, commented that lots of people in the business there were talking about the issue and carefully watching the houses that were running the ads. "But we are in the business of selling relief from the commercial saturation you get on tv," said Moscarelli. "We believe we are providing a release from that, along with a different environment. We're the escape from tv and all its commercials. We're providing entertainment that's not to be found in people's living room." Ed Knudsen, vice president at the Redstone chain, said, "I think it's all wrong. If you pay $4 to see a film, the last thing you want to be subjected to is three minutes of sell before the feature. It would be insulting to customers to make them sit through a commercial. We are not running them."[23]

Also divided were exhibitors in Colorado. Carmen Bonacci, district manager for Transcontinental Theatres, which operated the Colorado 4 and the Brentwood 4 outlets in Denver, said the houses were showing ads for Seiko watches on six of their eight screens prior to each feature. SV had plans to air three minutes of ads before each movie but Bonacci said his company had decided to go with only one 40-second spot to "see how the project works." He said that after running the ad for a week only one complaint from a customer had been lodged at his houses. "We'll watch it for three or four weeks and if people complain too much I'll recommend that we discontinue the program," he added. CI had a contract with Westland Theatres (located in Colorado Springs and Pueblo, Colorado, and also in Nebraska). Westland operational manager Clayton Cheever explained his company was showing ads on 17 of its 25 screens (technical problems on the other eight screens—all automated— was the only reason they were then not running the ads). Like many others, he argued the ad revenue would help to keep costs down. "Advertising revenues may be the ideal way of keeping prices affordable," he said. "We'll have to wait and see." Steve Hinkle, ad manager of Mann Theatres (12 Denver-area screens) said his company had run ads before, but just "Christmas greetings" from local merchants. "Patrons come to see a movie," Hinkle said, "not to be coerced to buy anything." Therefore Mann Theatres was not running ads. Sy Evans of Boston-based General Cinema (750 screens nationwide, about 14 in Denver) echoed the sentiments of most area theatre operators when he said, "We don't feel that the American audience is ready for movie advertising yet. We'll have to watch this thing and reevaluate our position sometime in the future."[24]

*Time* magazine reported in December 1977 that for the previous month SV had flashed 30-second ads for Seiko watches and Chanel perfume on 1,800 screens across America, with 1,200 other houses said to be under contract but not yet running the trailers, and that SV planned to expand its ad package to three minutes. Erroneously, it said that exhibitors received up to 75 percent of the SV charge to advertisers— also reported incorrectly—as $17 to $24 per one-minute ad per 1,000 viewers.[25]

At the very end of 1977 CI's partner in its program, NITE, lodged an official complaint with the U.S. Department of Justice accusing the Hollywood major distributors of an anti-competition conspiracy to discourage and prohibit onscreen commercial ads in cinemas showing major studio features. Hollywood's avowed and open hostility to the cinema ad program of CI and SV had hardened into action as the majors tried to impose anti-screen ad rental contracts on exhibitors.[26]

United Artists Theatres, although it stated it deplored the growing distributor efforts to restrict or penalize screen ads, had decided—for the time being, at least—to sign the anti-screen ad rental contracts under protest, reserving the right to challenge the agreements in court. That decision was revealed by Richard Goldman, the San Francisco-based counsel of the 700-house circuit (including 250 screens on the West Coast, 150 of them in California). Goldman attacked the Warner Bros. prohibition on screen ads during the engagement of *Superman* and Fox's move to share in cinema ad revenue by declaring it part of the house's overall gross [when a distributor rented out a film it received from the exhibitor a specified percentage of the gross ticket receipts] as "a great amount of overreaching being done by the film companies." He was especially worked up over the screen ad revenue clause that had been appearing in all Fox rental contracts since December 1, 1977.[27]

Warner Bros. was then thinking about a more precisely defined anti-screen ad policy and in the meantime, observed a reporter "the company has adopted an interim position of leaning heavily on the prohibition in the rental of selected films while all but looking the other way on others." That interim ambiguity came to light in rental contracts for two features opened to bidding after *Superman*. One of them, *Swarm*, carried with it a conspicuously spelled out restriction against screen ads while the other, *Capricorn One*, did not carry the same strong language banning screen ads from appearing on the same program. According to Warner sales vice president Larry Lashansky, the general rental contract already contained a clause forbidding "paid commercials" with the showing of Warner Bros. films and had done so for a long time. However, Lashansky acknowledged that it would be necessary to read the fine print to find the exclusion and, said a reporter, there existed "a notion supported by prima facie evidence that Warner has not been enforcing it." Lashansky argued the ban on screen ads during the engagement of *Superman* was spelled out more prominently because of the nature of the movie; the studio wanted no misunderstanding that its refusal to permit screen ads on the same program with its blockbuster release *Superman* was unequivocal. And, "despite the standing prohibition" in the general contract, the studio was still pondering an overall policy on which it would be prepared to demand exhibitor conformity. Confusingly, Lashansky added "We made it (the ban on screen ads) very specific in *Superman*. In the other situations, we're going according to our contract, which restricts it anyway."[28]

In March 1978, said journalist Aljean Harmetz, those screen ads ran into fierce resistance. According to SV executive Richard McIntosh, his company had signed the United Artists, RKO, Stanley Warner, American Multi, Video Independent, and Mann theater chains to three-year exclusive contracts. Three months earlier houses in some of those chains were "flooded" with SV ads for Seiko, Chanel, Revlon, and Chrysler, but now, said Harmetz, "There is, currently, no Screenvision commercial playing anywhere." Said McIntosh, "It's very difficult to launch a new medium in this country." SV's first ads were met with a "barrage of criticism" and the action, mentioned above, taken by Warner Bros. and Fox. The Fox letter to exhibitors declared that "the corporation regards all income from such advertising as part of the gross house receipts," as such to be shared with Fox. Of course, it was widely understood within the industry that Fox was not really interested in the money. Peter Myers, domestic sales vice president for Fox stated a few months earlier, "We don't really want screen advertising. I don't think it's inevitable. I don't think it's good showmanship for these few pennies that it brings to theaters." Noting that whether the studios had any legal right to do what they did remained to be seen, Harmetz said, "But, for the moment, the controversy has harmed Screenvision. That company is now having to demonstrate its effectiveness to advertisers by setting up a series of test markets." McIntosh said that SV hoped to have 15 or 20 test clients within a month. Jim Gallagher, vice president for United Artists Western cinemas, said that overall they had not had many complaints from customers about screen ads, "But there have been a great many complaints at a few theaters. At the Elmwood, an art house in Berkeley. And at the Metro, in a sophisticated shopping area in San Francisco." That chain started in November 1977 with an ad for Seiko. In the next four-week cycle they had a different Seiko ad and one for Chanel perfume. Robert Laemmle, co-owner of a chain of 10 Southern California houses, remarked that "we would never accept product ads. We have a class audience. They would react quickly and be very hostile."[29]

By the middle of 1978 exhibitors in Massachusetts were still reported to be divided on the issue; big chains said no. Sack Theatres (Boston) president Alan Friedberg declared, "We have not, we do not have and we will not have onscreen advertising in our theatres.... If people wanted to see ads, they'd stay home and watch TV." Boston's other large chain, General Cinema, also ran no ads. Even some of the small independent houses opposed the practice. At the tiny Galleria Cinema in Cambridge the manager said, "The public is very hostile to the ads. Some customers said in no uncertain terms that they wouldn't come back until they knew we wouldn't have ads." They did stop running them. SV continued to test market their commercials in various cities. "The reason why we haven't set up our regular program nationwide," said McIntosh, "is that

*Hardly Working* (1981, Jerry Lewis, left, Susan Oliver, Roger C. Carmel).

big business balks at new ideas, especially in advertising. They never move quickly on innovations." Because of some opposition, said NITE's Patterson, CI's commercials had been temporarily slowed from entering the theaters. A different but unidentified CI source went further and asserted "the majors' position has bullied some advertisers and theatres. Until we can clean up this mess, we're out of business."[30]

Paramount joined the other majors by publicly expressing its displeasure with screen ads. Frank G. Mancuso, general sales manager for Paramount, said, "We have only expressed our displeasure to theatres over commercials. They [commercials] will alter the magical experience films provide." With regard to informing the public that ads would be shown onscreen CI's Paul Kegley said his company was not involved in a hard sell and the consumer needed to know what was going on. Therefore "When we institute advertising, we will have lobby displays explaining that there will be no more than three minutes of ads before the main feature. If patrons want to wait in the lobby, that's their choice." Taking a different position on that issue was SV's McIntosh, who declared, "Why should we tell the public that our theaters have advertising? When you introduce new ideas to the public, they get shaken. No one else informs consumers that they are about to be bombarded with advertising." As 1979 began it was estimated that 7,000 of America's 16,000 cinemas were "willing and eager to unreel ads."[31]

Screen advertising, overwhelmed by opposition, was clearly in trouble by the end of the 1970s. CI had gone out of business and disappeared altogether. Looking around for a partner with "expertise," Screenvision agreed in August 1978 to sell 50 percent of itself to Capital Cities Communications. One of the first results from that arrangement was that SV did away with its price "inflexibility," offering discounts during slow months of the year, long-term discounts, and so forth. Nearly half of the 15 million admissions for the top 100 markets per month were in the 18–34 age group. To reach those 15 million people in the top 100 cities with a 30-second SV ad the cost to the advertiser was $103,899 per month. While

*Hardly Working* (1981, Jerry Lewis, other unidentified). This Lewis film was also cited in its time as a prime example of excessive product placement.

the cost per 1,000 viewers was higher for the cinema than it was for television, SV executive vice president Zachary Smith said that handicap was overcome because research also showed that audiences were not turned off by theater commercials if those ads avoided "the mundane, hard-sell and questionable content." With negative public reaction in mind SV still rejected cigarette and liquor advertisers and also refused such categories as detergents and headache remedies. Current SV advertisers as of the spring of 1979 included Foster Grant (in the top 30 markets), Saks Fifth Avenue (In New York, Chicago, and Los Angeles) and Dr. Pepper (in six markets for three months). Smith said auto makers, breweries, soft drinks, and fragrances were the advertiser categories most enthused about cinema ads. SV claimed it had 3,000 houses signed up for its program. Still, the industry could only look with envy at Europe where, in 1978, advertisers spent $100 million to advertise on cinema screens.[32]

After a lobbyist for the National Association of Theatre Owners (NATO) said the organization would not oppose the ban, a committee of the state legislature in Trenton, New Jersey, approved a bill in June 1979, that would prohibit cinemas in New Jersey from showing commercials on the screen. The bill, approved unanimously by the County and Municipal Government Committee, would levy a $100 fine against cinema managers who showed film commercials "unrelated to motion pictures or products sold at the theatre." According to NATO lobbyist Tom Leach, only a few cinemas were then running ads. Ed Wrightson, manager of an outlet of the American Multi chain located in suburban Lawrence Township, said his house had been running ads for around two months. An earlier experiment with more "hard-sell" ads had been abandoned a year earlier, he noted. New Jersey Senate president Joseph Merlin (D.–Trenton), who introduced the bill, said he acted after getting calls from constituents angry about the screen ads. Merlin felt people should be spared the irritation of ads when they had paid to see a movie. NATO's Leach did suggest an amendment to the bill that Merlin agreed to accept. As amended, the bill exempted drive-ins from the ban on screen advertising because, according to Leach, drive-ins were often marginal operations that had been showing commercials for years. That measure did not become law.[33]

Between July 1 and September 8, 1979, SV cinemas ran no ads whatsoever while the company forged and implemented a new strategy. SV's new contracts stipulated that no client's cinema ads could appear on television for at least 60 days and, once an advertiser used an ad on television, it could not be run as part of the SV program. Noting that big-screen commercials should be entertaining rather than displaying hard-sell tendencies, Smith cited the work of two of SV's new clients, Sony and Yamaha, as being of the caliber desired. Both took advantage of SV's production cost subsidy to clients, which enabled Screenvision to be "more forceful" in suggesting to advertisers ways to adapt to the medium. Under that subsidy plan SV paid the full $150,000 in ad trailer production costs for Sony and Yamaha. Smith acknowledged that his company needed to have repeat users in its program "to build a track record" for SV's concept. However, he admitted that as of late 1979, SV had not had a single advertiser who had been a repeat buyer of time.[34]

Ford Motor Company's Lincoln-Mercury division purchased a second ad on the SV network for the fall of 1980. It marked the first time SV could boast of a return client. SV was still trying to entice advertising clients by offering a subsidy on the cost of producing an ad trailer that could come to $60,000 toward making a 90-second national spot. An audience response survey commissioned by SV and carried out by Trendex revealed that 87 percent of SV filmgoers recalled a specific spot when contacted the next day and 78 percent remembered it two weeks later—well above the average television score, said Smith. Trendex was also said to have found that eight percent of its respondents thought cinema ads were "great" (two percent felt the same about television ads) and 65 percent "don't mind them" (40 percent for television). Just 27 percent disliked cinema spots enough to consider not returning to the cinema, while 58 percent disliked television ads. Of those respondents opposed to cinema ads 12 percent said that more entertaining or informative commercials might change their minds. Screenvision continued into the 1980s, but was in a markedly low point in its history in the 1980-1981 period.[35]

Operating independently, the *Los Angeles Times* as of 1982 had been running its trailer ads to sell newspaper subscription on Southern California theater screens for nearly 30 years. According to cinema chain owners, the *Times* was about the only advertiser that could get away with using ad trailers in their Los Angeles area houses. The only reason they could do it, they said, was that they had done it for so long that audiences did not seem to notice anymore. One theater owner, who requested anonymity, went so far as to say the *Times* had cinema owners over a barrel, forcing them to compromise their anti-advertising policies by screening *Times* ads. The *Times* gave cinema owners a trade-off, listing features in return for the ad screenings. A United Artists theater chain vice president expanded on that idea when he said, "I doubt if they would take a display ad without our showing the trailer." Those *Times* ads, produced in house by Gordon Phillips, were seen 52 weeks a year in 600 Southern California houses. Phillips said the ads began as a result of intense competition among the four Los Angeles newspapers in the early 1950s. In June 1981 the *Times* did away with "advertising" material in the trailers, said Phillips, in favor of a "public relations direction." Then in production were trailers on historical events. Only at the end of the trailer did the name of the newspaper appear. According to Phillips, there had been "virtually no response" to the *Times* trailers except for scattered "caterwauling and booing" in some Westside houses. He said he had received "about a letter a year and a dozen phone calls" in the 10 years he had been with the company. Robert Selig, Pacific Theatres vice president, said his group monitored the *Times* trailers carefully to ensure that they did not get "too commercial." Others reportedly watched those spots to make sure they did not get "political."[36]

Product placement in this period got off to a worrisome start for the Hollywood majors after the federal government passed a 1960 law against payola that stipulated that producers of programs who received any "consideration" for using commercially identifiable products or services in a program had to reveal that fact at the time a program was aired. Mainly, it was directed at an unidentified, and believed rampant, payola in the television industry. Hollywood was worried because its movies eventu-

*Honeysuckle Rose* (1980, Dyan Cannon, left, Amy Irvine). Note the unidentified actor on the right is displaying his beer in typical product placement fashion—visible, right side up, square with the camera, and so on.

ally made their way to the small screen. However, the majors took the official position that the federal government's anti-payola legislation did not apply to theatrical features even if they did show up on television. That stand was taken after the issue was studied by the MPAA's legal counsels. Failure to comply with the law was a criminal offense involving a fine up to $10,000 and/or imprisonment up to one year. Herb Golden, vice president of Hollywood major United Artists, explained that UA's production-distribution contracts with independents "always have carried a clause prohibiting undue identification of commercial products and services used as props or sets."[37]

Looking at the product placement practice late in 1961 reporter Kay Campbell gave her version of its history by first mentioning personal endorsements prior to World War II—such as Shirley Temple and Quaker Oats—which tended to benefit the endorser more than anyone else. During World War II, she explained, when film producers had lost much of their overseas box office receipts, the star tie-up became an industry rather than an individual affair and put on a barter system more to the benefit of the producer than a monetary basis more to the benefit of the star. Manufacturers swapped props and promotions for endorsements

*Superman II* (1980, Christopher Reeve). Superman poses before some brand names.

and the use of products in films. Property men readily recognized the budgetary advantage of free props. Campbell argued that a slowdown in product placement took place between 1955 and 1960 partly because of the rise of television and a shift in focus to that medium by advertisers and partly because of an increasing worry over payola, much in the news in the late 1950s. At one time, she reported, the Walter E. Klein and Associates operation maintained a central warehouse in Hollywood stocked with $200,000 worth of products that studios could freely borrow from at any time. However, in 1961 a large percentage of their business came from supplying complete sets—such as a police station, a gas station, a toy store, and so forth—to the film studios on a rental basis ranging from $1,300 to $8,000 per set. She argued the biggest plug a product had received in films since *Love Affair*, way back in 1939, was in *One, Two, Three* (1961) when Billy Wilder decided the soft drink company in West Berlin should definitely be a Coke distributor. Coca-Cola, of course, agreed to do a big advertising campaign tie-in. For Campbell, though, that period was a low point for product placement in the movies.[38]

There were placements around that time, though. The first movie in the James Bond series *Dr. No* (Sean Connery, 1962), featured plugs for the Aston Martin automobile and for Smirnoff vodka. Larry Dorn, president of a product placement firm in Los Angeles in the mid 1980s, recalled he had started in the placement business in 1957, with the Walter Klein organization. In the 1962 MGM release *Boys Night Out* (James Garner and Kim Novak) Dorn said his company placed a Nutone intercom system and some Sunbeam appliances. Writing in 1997, reporter Stuart Elliott went so far as to argue, "Products began to be placed in the late 1960s through a casually run cottage industry based on barter that exchanged merchandise for mentions," with the implication the practice was barely known before that time.[39]

The best example from the early 1960s of a film going overboard in product placement was the 1963 Paramount release *Who's Minding the Store?* (Jerry Lewis). Lewis played a troubleshooting salesman in a department store who worked in just about every area of the store, with obvious opportunities to involve consumer goods of all kinds. Jack Keller, exploitation and public relations chief for the Lewis organization, arranged all the many tie-ins. The biggest tie-ins (in terms of promotional budgets spent by advertisers) were with Sealy mattresses and Wembley ties. Sealy sponsored a big contest, with the first prize being a part in Lewis's next movie. Other plugs were arranged for the American Gas Association, Browning Arms, Brunswick sporting goods and boats, Channel Master televisions, Garcia fishing tackle, Honda motorcycles, Hoover vacuum cleaners, RCA Whirpool, Tappan ranges, and Universal appliances, among others. So many advertisers were involved, said Keller, that he had to get some of them not to buy too many magazine ads "because Jerry didn't want his picture on every page in every publication." He added, "The manufacturers supplied us with all the products used in the film—about $1,500,000 worth. We got $50,000 from Brunswick-MacGregor alone."[40]

When *Store* opened in New York in November 1963, there were few critical raves. The picture was accepted as harmless entertainment and that was the end of it. Except, observed *New York Times* reporter John Lee, "this is probably one of the most skillful movies ever made in at least one respect. That is in the use of commercial tie-ins." One viewer counted 20 separate brand names that were shown on the screen along with identifiable displays of the products; "There may have been more," Lee added. Brands mentioned here, but not in the above account, included Park & Tilford liquor and Planters peanuts. Paramount merchandise coordinator Lige Brien explained, "The quid pro quo here is that the manufacturers of the products that are to be plugged in the picture agree that in their advertising they will plug the movie." Thus, said Lee, an elaborate pattern of cross plugs was set up. "This has been going on for years, but the practice seems to have been refined in *Who's Minding the Store.*"[41]

Advertisers were happy over the opportunities available to them in *Store*. Daniel S. Roher, advertising manager of the Channel Master Corporation (whose radio and television sets got big plugs in the film) said, "Within the Paramount or Jerry Lewis organization, someone seems to have come up with the idea of doing a film which offered unexcelled opportunities for tie-ins of this sort." Full of praise for the technique, Roher continued, "The use of tie-ins openly, which naturally fit into the format of the picture, can generate enormous amounts of additional advertising for the movie." He was especially pleased that in the movie "We came up with two verbals"—that is, mentions of the product. In one scene a customer in the movie asked for a Channel Master by name; to which Lewis replied, "A 30-inch Channel Master?" Only one other product—a Browning gun—was mentioned by name; a line of dialogue had Lewis say, "That's the newest, finest Browning big game gun." Other movies for which Paramount's O'Brien had arranged product placements and cross plugs were *Come Blow Your Horn, A New Kind of Love, The Nutty Professor,* and *Hud*. For *Hud* the placement entailed making sure the Texas ranchers in that film drove Cadillacs. Reporter Lee concluded that "Persons familiar with these arrangements say that no money changes hands. One public relations man reports, however, a rock-'n-

*The Cannonball Run* (1981, left to right, unidentified, Dean Martin, Jamie Farr, Roger Moore, Burt Reynolds, Tara Buckman, Rick Aviles, Farrah Fawcett, Bert Convy). **Another movie mentioned as containing excessive placement.**

roll production offered to plug his client's drug product for $100,000. The offer was refused."[42]

Philip Dougherty reported in 1970 that advertising agencies in New York City had been receiving a letter from Warner Bros. that offered to put their clients' products in the movies. A maximum of 40 pictures a year were possible for such placements with the minimum contract being for plugs in 10 films. The letter, which estimated that 15 million people went to see the average movie, explained the products placed would be "shown in a good light," and in use or on display, or signage or a delivery truck could turn up in a particular scene. "I am sure you realize that your products would receive enormous public attention by a prestigious film company," said the letter. "They are made with established names and valuable scripts, all of which becomes an important vehicle public relations wise and sales wise, for your company."[43]

Associated Film Promotions (AFP), a product placement firm, was responsible for placing a Dynavite exercise machine in the 1979 release *Being There*. In that case AFP recommended enlivening what they thought was a dull scene with the president of the United States, played by Jack Warden, by having him ride the exercise machine in the Oval Office.[44]

A sudden change took place in product placement in the last couple of years of the 1970s and the first couple of years of the 1980s as the practice really did grow and increase dramatically. It was a lead-up to the modern era of placement that dated from *E.T.* in 1982 and its now legendary product placement. Product placement became pervasive at the end of the 1970s and has remained that way ever since. Business journalist Steven Mintz commented on many examples in his September 1981 piece. In the mystery thriller *Looker* (Albert Finney), actor Susan Dey announced she had to get up early the next day because "I am doing a Hawaiian Tropic commercial." Actually, of course, she had just done one. Tanning Research Labs, Inc., marketer of the suntan oil, had paid a sales promotion firm to get its product's name inserted into scripts. Other exposure for the suntan oil was received in *The Cannonball Run* and some half-a-dozen other films about to be released. When Clark Kent's earth family sat down to breakfast in their house in Smallville in the blockbuster *Superman*, a box of Cheerios was in plain sight, as arranged by General Mills. During the Chinese dinner scene in Alan Alda's *The Four Seasons*, a bottle of Kikkoman Soy Sauce was very prominent. According to Mintz, "Getting what you sell into a film or on a TV show was always a matter of discreetness...Today, it's brazen and an epidemic. It is so common, in fact, that it is now a part of many companies' formal marketing plans." Box-office bomb *Can't Stop the Music* was one of the more brazen examples mentioned, with plugs for Dr. Pepper; Famous Amos cookies (packages of which later showed up in retail outlets bearing a plug for the film); milk, in a dairy industry tie-in; and Baskin & Robbins, which created a new ice cream flavor for the picture, "Can't Stop the Nuts." Actor Gene Wilder ate Yoplait yogurt in *Stir Crazy* while a bag of Dunkin' Donuts sat beside him on the bench. *Kill and Kill Again* featured the Anheuser-Busch Clydesdale horses, a Quaker State T-shirt, and a Minolta camera. Across two years, it was reported, Anheuser-Busch products had appeared in 70 films.[45]

Another big user of film placement, said Mintz, was Royal Crown (RC) Cola. The role RC played in the films it had appeared in—among them *Rocky III* and *North Dallas Forty*—was intended to demonstrate, said RC marketing manager Larry Atseff, "that RC Cola products are part of the mainstream of the country." His company had included films in its overall marketing strategies since 1979. Robert Kovoloff, founder and president of Associated Film Promotions (AFP) declared that his company succeeded in placing its clients' products in eight out of every 10 films. It was "a new advertising medium that makes products look much more believable," he said, compared to television, which prohibited cigarette advertising, the onscreen consumption of alcoholic beverages, and the presence of brand names. Kovoloff, described then as "a major factor in film promotions," charged his advertiser clients a minimum fee of $25,000 for the first year, but the cost could escalate depend-

*Blow Out* (1981, John Travolta).

*Blow Out* (1981, John Travolta, other unidentified). **Note the cigarette brand is visible. Travolta, a non-smoker in real life, was one of Hollywood's most frequent on-screen smokers, with his characters lighting up in film after film.**

ing on how much time was spent on the account. Some accounts, such as Anheuser-Busch, paid an annual fee reaching six figures, for which AFP provided such tie-in services as film star endorsements and poster campaigns. A competitor, Larry Dorn & Associates, represented such clients as American Express, Pepsi-Cola, Pan Am, and Botany 500 for placements in films and on television. Dorn based his fee on several factors: 1) the nature of the product and how easy it was to place; 2) the particular studio and distributor; 3) the popularity of the film's stars; and 4) the writer and producer of the film. Once he had a product, getting it placed in a movie depended "100% on contacts," said Dorn, who insisted, as did others, that no "payoffs" were involved. Stephen Michaelis, advertising director of Tanning Research Labs, observed that "Exposure in a good movie can go on for years." In the movie *Blow Out* (John Travolta), J&B Scotch appeared frequently, always with the label on the bottle aimed straight at the camera. During one scene the bottle was used as a weapon; in another, an actor held it in plain view as he urinated into a toilet. J&B claimed no knowledge of how it got used and both the company and its distributor denied placing it or knowing how it got placed.[46]

About six months later entertainment reporter David Linck wrote another long piece on the sudden surge in product placement. (This account may have been the first to use the phrase "product placement" to describe the practice.) Linck pointed out that featuring brand-name merchandise conspicuously onscreen "has been around Hollywood for several decades," but had moved to a new and higher level, mainly because of the efforts of Kovoloff. "Remember in *The Formula* when [Marlon] Brando offers George C. Scott some Milk Duds? Well, that was my idea ... and it worked," bragged Kovoloff. "Not only did I get one of my clients' products mentioned by a star onscreen, but it actually helped the scene." Linck declared that Kovoloff and AFP had "virtually cornered the product placement market of late, successfully persuading producers and propmen alike to use an average of 12 of their clients' products in any film their firm handles." Kovoloff explained that filmmakers were

*Blow Out* (1981). Besides the Jeep Renegade pictured here, J&B Scotch also was featured prominently in this movie.

as happy as his clients that he was in the business. "Our company merely supplies products that would ordinarily be needed by the property masters," he explained. "However, those products are usually those of our clients! We merely bring the parties together." What his company did, he elaborated, "has always been done in films, but it was usually done under the table. Products were used as payoffs and property masters received kickbacks from companies. We don't operate that way. And our honesty is appreciated all the way around."[47]

Recalling his entry into product placement, Kovoloff said he recognized the need for his present service while working for American International Pictures in the mid 1970s. Working on a 1976 Peter Fonda film titled *Hiballin'* that dealt with the then national love affair with CB radios, Kovoloff found that several electronics manufacturers were desirous of getting their brand names onscreen whenever possible. Then, reported Linck, Kovoloff "not only brought the two factors together legally but created a method of introducing brand-names into films without taking artistic license." In explaining how his firm operated Kovoloff commented, "We take a script and study it long before it goes into production. This way we can see where our clients' needs can be served. We may just supply a prop or we may suggest a better way to use a product. The production people don't have to listen. Often now, they come to me with suggestions." Some of those suggestions had turned into script changes—changes that Kovoloff felt were "ultimately for the better." For example, Kovoloff suggested to Sylvester Stallone on the set of the upcoming *Rocky III* that Wheaties be mentioned by name in a speech Stallone gave to his son in the film concerning the merits of eating a good breakfast. So Rocky told his son to eat his Wheaties. Said Kovoloff, "Now, 'eat your Wheaties' has been around for years and years. And in this scene, it really works. It is this type of thing I'm proudest of." Even Kovoloff, though, admitted that some pictures had gone overboard by utilizing too much placement and becoming too commercial. Linck thought one of the most blatant examples was *Hardly Working* (Jerry Lewis), where Kovoloff's clients "seemed to crowd the screen at every turn, from Quaker State Motor Oil being prominently displayed in a lengthy service station sequence to an appearance of the Budweiser Clydesdales themselves." Kovoloff admitted, "That was overdoing it. But remember, it was the producers who suggested it...I probably wouldn't have done it if it were my film. But needless to say, the clients received some real exposure."[48]

Linck stated that even in the case of excessive placements filmgoers had not complained about the practice. Nor had the Hollywood majors because, as several studio spokesmen had said, "It works for everyone." Willie Nelson drank Budweiser in *Honeysuckle Rose* while

Cheerios filled up the foreground in *Honky Tonk Freeway*. Any time John Travolta grabbed for a beer in *Urban Cowboy* Kovoloff made sure it was a Budweiser. When a television commercial played in the background of *Looker* it just happened to be for Fruit-of-the-Loom, another AFP client. AFP clients signed up on yearly contracts. That way, Kovoloff explained, "We can in no way be accused of promising a client the use of his products in one certain picture by a certain star. We try to get as much play for our clients' wares as possible all year, fitting products in where they can be used. There is no guarantee that the product will be prominently used. But it will eventually be used several times a year." Current placements at the time Linck was writing included *Grease II* (Hawaiian Punch, Playboy magazine), *Blade Runner* (Quaker State, Kikkoman Soy Sauce), and *Cannery Row* (wherein actor Nick Nolte stated, "I wanna Budweiser"). In *Six Weeks* (Dudley Moore) the producers were going to use foreign cars and went to AFP for models. "We held out for a domestic brand, so now they're using Cadillacs instead of the imports," explained Kovoloff. "Now, that was satisfying."[49]

*The Formula* (1980, George C. Scott, left, Marlon Brando). In another scene in this film Brando offered Scott the candy Milk Duds. Even though a high-profile star such as Brando did not do commercials he could fall victim to its equivalent—a product placement pitch. A placement agency took credit for the bit.

*Rocky III* (1982, left to right, unidentified, Ian Fried, Talia Shire, Sylvester Stallone, Burt Young, Carl Weathers). This film featured a scene where Rocky Balboa (Stallone) admonished his son (Fried) to eat his Wheaties. A placement agency also took credit for creating the bit, and for inserting it into the feature.

As this period ended screen advertising probably was in a stronger position than it ever had enjoyed in the past, albeit a weak one in any absolute sense. Ad trailers had struggled to a greater position in the late 1970s before slipping back slightly at the start of the 1980s. Product placement had suddenly taken off at the very end of the 1970s although it was only drawing slight media attention at the start of the 1980s, because that surge was nothing new. The modern era in screen advertising can be said to have started in 1982, when the film *E.T.* was released, and continued to the present. There was nothing unusual in the product placement involved in *E.T.* It was actually just one of many, many movies that succumbed to placement in the 1978–1982 period when the surge in the practice took place. What set *E.T.* apart was the phenomenal results attributed to the placement of the candy Reese's Pieces in that movie. Soon the story took on legendary proportions. It would come to be cited as often—perhaps even more often—than the example of Clark Gable and the undershirt.

# 7

# Ad Trailers in the Modern Era
## *1982–2003*

> People say they don't want to see commercials…. But they see these [ad] trailers as romantic, entertaining, seductive, and so subtle that the products come away with a halo.
> —Terry Laughren, Screenvision president, 1989

> Advertising in theaters is destroying the moviegoing experience. It is insulting to a paying audience.
> —Richard Cook, president of
> Disney's Buena Vista, 1990

American exhibitors and advertising people continued to look with envy at the screen advertising situation in Europe in the modern era where commercials in cinemas were much more common and much more pervasive. Advertisers were estimated to have spent $20 million on cinema advertising in 1982 in Britain, where there were just 1,530 theaters.[1]

By early in 1988 it was reported that the two major UK exhibition circuits (Rank and Cannon) had virtually sold out all of their available advertising screen time for the rest of the year. Most cinemas then ran 13–14 minutes of ads on each of their programs. Ad agencies wanted the theater operators to extend that period but the exhibitors refused, for fear of alienating patrons or disrupting playing times. Screen ad revenue for 1987 was reported to have been $39 million.[2]

Cinema audiences in Britain were then described as young and upwardly mobile and a group who had plenty of money to spend. Some 78 million people were expected in British cinemas in 1988, up two million from the previous year; many of them did not watch a lot of television. And that led to a rise in demand for cinema ads; before 1988 was over all available time was sold out through the end of 1989, despite a rate increase of 15 percent. "Gone forever are the downmarket slide-and-voiceover advertisements for the local Indian restaurant," declared reporter Martin Hedges as he described the more sophisticated trailers then appearing on the screens. "Only a few years ago, Rank Screen Advertising Services and Pearl and Dean [the two main distributors of cinema ads] could not give the time away." Hedges felt the cinema ad had two major advantages: the cinema environment, and the scale of the medium. "People have made a decision to watch a film; they have paid money to see it; and they are in a more receptive mood than they usually are when watching the television," he explained. By scale he meant the big screen. Also, unlike in the U.S., cinema advertising was cheaper than network television. Exhibitors received 60 to 80 percent of the screen ad revenue (compared to the one-third U.S. operators received). With regard to the American idea that film audiences did not like cinema ads, Hedges said of the UK audience, "Any visit to the cinema will give the lie to this. The creative quality of most of the advertising is such that you can almost feel the audiences lapping up the commercial hors d'oeuvre."[3]

Several years after that, in 1997, British reporter Alexandra Frean remarked that "providing that the adverts do not last more than 13 minutes, audiences do not just tolerate them, they now frequently welcome them. Because of the dedicated, distraction-free environment in which they are watched, cinema advertisements are reckoned in the industry to be five times more memorable to viewers than television ads." Although about 70 million pounds sterling was then spent annually on screen advertising it represented just 0.8 percent of the total spent on all display advertising.[4]

As of 2002 the UK had an annual expenditure of 16 billion pounds sterling on all advertising, with less than 2 percent of that amount going to onscreen cinema advertising.[5]

During 1983 some $40 million was spent on cinema advertising in West Germany, with about 10 minutes of ads screened. For 1986 the amount spent on all advertising in West Germany was about $8 billion, broken down as follows: daily newspapers, $3.15 billion; illustrated weeklies, $1.4 billion; Sunday newspapers, $140 million; television, $750 million; radio, $300 million; and $72 million (0.9 percent) spent for commercials screened before the features in Germany's 3,000 cinemas.[6]

Onscreen ads, while they had long been a regular part of the European cinema scene, continued to remain relatively insignificant as they represented only a small percentage of total advertising expenditures, ranging in 1993 from 0.1 percent in Finland to 5 percent in France.[7]

Back in America Screenvision (SV) continued to limp along in the early years of the 1980s. Capital Cities sold their 50 percent interest in SV in 1981 to the FTTL Media Corporation. It remained the only company in the U.S. that distributed ad trailers on something that amounted to a national basis. Movie Media Network was formed in 1982 but it limited itself to distributing advertising posters for display in theater lobbies. Those posters used the same copy and illustrations as the advertisers' print, television and billboard campaigns. "The average person spends over two minutes in the theater lobby," said Movie Media president David Weiss. "People are trained to look at posters for coming attractions." Weiss's posters were said to be on view in some 1,500 theater lobbies across America. Both Weiss and SV insisted they had heard no complaints from filmgoers about advertising in cinemas. Movie Media Network quickly expired.[8]

Around 1986 things seemed to pick up for SV, as it announced it was doing better because of, for one thing, the advent of the 15-second commercial. The resultant clutter (a greater number of ads in the same amount of time) was driving advertisers to seek alternate media. One account that SV handled was Pepsi-Cola. A spokesman for Pepsi's ad agency said, "We made the judgment that the creative impact is greater [than television] due to the impact of the large screen in a dark theater." According to reporter David Kalish SV split its screen ad revenue 50/50 with the theater operators. It charged advertisers $18 per 1,000 admissions to screen a 60-second ad and $25 per 1,000 for a 90-second spot. Kalish observed that "most cinema advertisers seem to run with longer variants of existing tv commercials."[9]

A month later *New York Times* reporter Richard Stevenson argued that Madison Avenue was slowly chipping away at the resistance to cinema ads. Pepsi-Cola was described as one of the biggest users of that medium. Pepsi's advertising manager Jeff Myers said, "Just put Acme soap on the screen and you're going to draw hoots and boos and ill will." But if the advertiser presented something entertaining, he added, "The audience will react well and will remember the commercial more than it would a similar spot on television." However, many exhibitors remained holdouts. "A decision was made several years ago that we did not want to alienate our patrons," said Janine Dusossoit, a spokesperson for the General Cinema Corporation, the nation's largest cinema chain. "People come to us for entertainment. If they want to see commercials, they'll watch television." Ronald Kaatz, senior vice president at the J. Walter Thompson ad agency, observed, "It is an opportunity to get a very important demographic group with a very dramatic message in a captive setting with no competition."[10]

According to Stevenson, SV then had 4,800 screens under contract and put strict limits on the quantity and quality of commercials. A spot had to be at least 60 seconds long and no more than three minutes of ads were to be shown before any feature. Also, SV was said to review every commercial to make sure it was not going to "alienate" viewers.

Screenvision Cinema Network (as it was now called) vice president Marie Marcus explained, "We do not accept commercials that are not entertaining. I'd rather refuse an advertiser, if the commercial is going to offend a movie audience because it's too TV-like, than have another advertiser." Besides Pepsi-Cola, clients of the company had recently included General Electric, Dr. Pepper, Eastman Kodak, Lee Jeans, and Toyota. Stevenson did note, of the SV ads, that "sometimes they are the same as commercials aired on television." That meant that SV's long-standing ban on using a television commercial, as it was, on the big screen had been abandoned by 1986. With respect to the need to screen only "quality" commercials, SV president Terry Laughren stated, "We want to maintain the sanctity of the movie-going experience. If we didn't, we wouldn't have a business sometime down the road."[11]

When reporter Cyndi Dale spoke to SV late in 1986, it was still the only national distributor of "sponsored trailers" (a term it preferred to "commercials"). She received the usual story about the ads being tastefully entertaining, about the low audience resistance, and having a recall rate higher than for ads on television. She wondered, if that were all true, why had the medium not taken off in America; why was there so much resistance from cinema owners? "We're competing with television as it is and we're lessening that edge of competition if we start running commercials," said Ed Gross, a spokesman for the United Artists cinema chain. "We're trying to give people something they're not going to get at home, whether TV or video. We want to give them a motion picture experience rather than a large-screen television experience." Even some advertising agencies were skeptical about the medium. Robert Irvine, a media director at the J. Walter Thompson agency, explained, "When an environment that's always been commercial free becomes commercialized, people react to it. I think it has an opportunity to be a pretty effective medium, it just never seems to have taken off. There seems to be a lot of consumer resistance to it." Patrick McKeon, a media director at Bozell and Jacobs, agreed with that sentiment, adding, "How many commercials will they take is what it comes down to. Although I don't have any qualms about recommending it to certain clients. I think there will be negative reaction as more and more people get exposed and commercial lengths get longer." Of the 21,000 theater screens in the U.S. in 1986, SV had contracts with 4,500 of them. New York City was never portrayed as a good market for cinema ads but in this account Chicago was presented as the worst. SV vice president Anne-Marie Marcus said, "Chicago is our worst market. The majority of theaters are owned by only three companies—none of which are using our services right now."[12]

When SV marked its 10th anniversary in mid 1987 the company's western sales manager, Larissa Alexander, explained that her company

produced "sponsored trailers" or "minimovies that get right to the soul."
She distinguished them from regular television ads, which she called "just
radio ads with pictures." Research cited by SV had it that 87 percent of
viewers who saw ads at the movies would remember them the next day,
as opposed to 20 percent recall for television ad viewers.[13]

A milestone was reached by Screenvision over the summer months
of 1987 (June, July, August) when all of its nine commercial availabili-
ties (three ads per venue per month) sold out for the first time. According to Ronald Lesser (an exhibitor running the ads in his nine houses in
New York State), at first there were a "few complaints, but as the advertising production values improved, so did audience acceptance." SV president Terry Laughren went so far as to say that cinema commercials
"enhance the movie-going experience." It still charged advertisers $18
per 1,000 viewers for a 60-second spot, which was a premium price compared to network television. Laughren maintained that was an intentional
differential: "It is the price of a captive audience (one that doesn't have
its collective head in the refrigerator during the commercial break) that
is affluent, well educated and active." According to Laughren his company periodically checked audience response to screen ads by using "an
independent audit and survey firm" that reported a "96 percent positive
reaction to sponsored trailers."[14]

Malcolm MacDougall, vice chairman at the Jordan, McGrath, Case
& Taylor agency, thought SV was a good investment for a client who
wanted to reach a cross section of the population. "It's good for a sea-
sonal product, or one for young people. But I wouldn't recommend it as
the cornerstone of a marketing strategy," he added. "You can't drive your
selling points home, and after a while, you many start annoying people."
Although SV remained optimistic about its future others were not. Advertising agency executive Jan Rehder (who was involved in making ads for
cinemas) thought that if the situation in America got to be like it was in
Europe—where up to 15 minutes of ads preceded the feature—the
patrons might start arriving late at cinemas to avoid the commercials.
Candidly, Rehder admitted, "I really resent paying $6 to watch com-
mercials."[15]

As 1989 began SV still charged more for ad exposure than comparable prime-time television exposure. A 28-day run on the 5,583 screens
affiliated with SV cost an advertiser around $600,000 and reached an
average of 30 million viewers. One reason those cinema ads were finding
increasing favor, said reporter Bernice Kanner was "that the commercials are designed to be as dramatic—and memorable—as the feature."
According to Russ Klein, senior vice president of marketing at Seven-
Up, the large theater screens showcased those "mini-movies" without
clutter and away from competitive advertising. While moviegoers could

break away to get popcorn, or just look away, "zapping is not an option." John G. Clarke, senior vice president of marketing at Dr. Pepper, said, "the theater audience is by and large not distracted. They're in their seats with the lights off, watching a presentation whose quality is bigger than life. You've got a captive and captivated audience."[16]

SV still required that its ads be at least 60 seconds in length (said to be the minimum amount of time necessary to tell a story) and a maximum of three minutes of ads per program. "Research indicates that five trailers, no matter how wonderful, is the breaking point for audiences," said SV president Terry Laughren. "Four seems fine, so we hold it at three." Kanner stated the firm was still selective and that it routinely rejected hard-sell "TV-type" ads with "intrusive" voiceovers. And it would not accept even soft-sell spots for feminine hygiene products or condoms. From 1984, it had also stopped running tobacco ads. According to this report it had accounts with some 5,250 (30 percent of the 17,500 screens nationwide) outlets. However, many large exhibition chains still did not do business with SV, nor did it do business with any Manhattan cinemas because, said Laughren, "The fees are excessive." That is, the cinemas wanted more money to screen the ads than SV was willing to pay them. "People say they don't want to see commercials. We know that moviegoers have paid for a ticket and that we can't assault them," argued Laughren. "But they see these trailers as romantic, entertaining, seductive, and so subtle that the products come away with a halo."[17]

One chain that did not use SV's service was General Cinema. Russ Duncan, a regional manager with the chain, explained, "We've tried it from time to time in different parts of the country. The company felt the good will between the patrons and the company was somewhat compromised, and we valued the good will of the patrons more than running the ads." Richard Dodderidge, senior vice president for corporate marketing at the exhibition chain AMC Entertainment in Kansas City, Missouri, said that when AMC experimented with ads it was easy to gauge public reaction. "There was public displeasure indicated by thrown popcorn boxes at the screen and people wanting their money back," said Dodderidge and AMC ran no more SV ads. Yet both AMC and General Cinema featured the very old-fashioned ads on slides. Said Neil Katcher, Detroit district manager for AMC, "The slides are very low key. You don't have to watch them if you don't want to. Nobody complains about them." Those slide ads were all for local advertisers as national advertisers did not use slide ads for national campaigns, viewing them as out of date. Nevertheless, AMC (America's third largest exhibition chain with about 1,600 screens in 300 locations) sold display time in all its outlets while General Cinema used slides in only some theaters.[18]

A sold-out segment of three ads for SV in July 1989 consisted of ads for the following: ABC TV (ironically, advertising two of the shows on its upcoming fall schedule), the U.S. Marines, and the California Raisin Board. Journalist Ellen Conn said the exhibitors received 30 percent of SV's gross ad receipts. In New York SV had only five screens in three outlets. What hampered SV's New York City expansion, said the company, was resistance from large chains requesting "excessive fees." Cineplex Odeon (the U.S.'s second largest chain nationally and number one in Manhattan) had featured onscreen advertising since it expanded from being a Canadian-only circuit in 1985. While SV still remained the only U.S. company that distributed ad trailers nationally, Cineplex did not use SV's service but operated independently. It limited each spot (no more than two per program) to 60 seconds each. By booking its screens directly, Cineplex eliminated the middleman and kept 100 percent of its fee. National Cinema Network, a subsidiary of AMC Entertainment whose American Multi Cinema was America's third largest chain, supplied a slide ad package. Running 15 to 30 minutes in length, and playing on some 2,200 screens across the country it consisted of entertainment segments (trivia quizzes, puzzles, and so forth), local and national product ads, and public service announcements. Elements within the slide ad package could be changed weekly or run 30 to 60 days. UA theaters in Manhattan still used no ads, and neither did the Loew's circuit anywhere in the U.S. Asked for his company's view regarding onscreen advertising, Loew's executive vice president Tom Elefante replied tersely, "We don't do it. I'd rather not discuss it." Elefante denied the chain ever considered screen ads but another executive (who requested anonymity) said that one outlet did try cinema ads three or four years earlier and that "the phone calls and letters didn't stop. There was hell to pay." Ralph Donnelly, executive vice president of City Cinemas (Manhattan's second largest circuit), was also unequivocal in his response to the question as to whether or not his chain might screen ads. "Over my dead body! You can't burden the $7 ticket buyer with that."[19]

That same year, 1989, an editorial in the *New York Times* noted that someone had recently gone to see a film in a Manhattan cinema and been shocked to find the movie preceded by an ad for American Express. "And this in a theater for which she had just paid $7.50 for her ticket." Also noted was that Cineplex Odeon had booked ads for the likes of Coca-Cola, Nike, Dentyne, American Express, and others for all its 1,875 screens through 1990. Cineplex explained, like SV always did, that its screen ads, unlike television ads, had to be subtle and entertaining. However, the editor scoffed, "As though that mitigates the offense." In conclusion the editor declared, "Such screen advertising has been inflicted on European viewers for years but began in the U.S. just last year. Cineplex Odeon is the largest user." Being that out of touch with the screen advertising situation was perhaps evidence that New York City had been as completely isolated from the subject, relative to other U.S. cities, as most accounts had asserted.[20]

Even filmmakers complained about screen ads. "Commercials cheapen the medium and put the audience in a bad mood before they see the film" said director Phil Alden Robinson (*Field of Dreams*). He was, said reporter Gerald Clarke, "expressing the overwhelming reaction among producers and directors."[21]

SV claimed it would sell about $25 million in movie ad time in 1989, on the 5,711 screens (35 percent of the 17,500 total U.S. screens) with which it had contracts. Of course, Cineplex would also draw an unspecified sum from the 1,840 screens it booked independently. For a 60-second spot SV charged advertisers $600,000 to $700,000 for a 28-day screening. That meant a sold out period would generate $2.1 million at most; multiplied by the 13 28-day periods there were in a year, it indicated a maximum revenue for SV of $27.3 million. Given that a sold-out period was still definitely the exception rather than the rule, and that many of its ads were booked for less than a full, national exposure, SV's estimate seemed exaggerated. Laughren estimated that of the total of American theaters, one-third had no interest in screen ads "because they're philosophically opposed to it" and another third "is interested, but they want more money."[22]

At the beginning of 1990 it was reported that ad trailers then appeared on some 8,000 U.S. cinema screens; SV had 6,000 of the total 23,000 U.S. screens while Cineplex Odeon ran ad trailers on its 1,940 screens. Bill Smith, president of Certified Marketing Services (a film industry research firm that monitored in-theater advertising), said that only four percent of filmgoers polled had reacted negatively to the ads. Betsy Frank, director of new media at the Saatchi and Saatchi agency, observed of that filmgoing audience, "They are the kind of people who don't watch much television. It's a good way to make a big impact with an audience that's very hard to reach." She added that cinema ads were "an excellent strategy for advertisers who want to insure that their messages stand out from the pack," a reference to all the clutter of television where a dozen or more short ads of 15-seconds duration could appear rapidly one after the other.[23]

With the phenomenal growth of VCRs and movies on videocassettes, it was only a matter of time before producers and distributors starting placing ads on those videocassettes. Up until 1986 next to no activity took place in that area, wrote reporter David Kalish, because both the studios and the advertisers were afraid of antagonizing viewers. Then Pepsi-Cola showed it could be done "effectively" with its advertisement on the *Top Gun* (1986) videocassette, as the VCR penetration level of U.S. households passed the 50 percent mark. That ad had been created earlier for use on network television. In another deal, chocolate-maker Hershey placed a commercial in the video release of *The Princess Bride*.[24]

A major worry among advertisers was that in the case of videocassettes viewers would simply fast-forward through any ads placed on cassettes. Then Alexander & Associates, a New York consulting firm, did a telephone survey of audience responses to the videocassette release of *Dirty Dancing* (it contained a commercial for Nestle's Alpine White Chocolate) and *Platoon* (Chrysler's Jeep). Results were said to reveal that 51 percent of *Dirty Dancing* viewers reported they watched all commercial messages preceding the film (the Nestle's ad as well as some coming-attraction trailers). About 61 percent of *Platoon* viewers said they watched the ad; 15 percent said they saw parts of it; 21 percent said they watched none of it. Reporter Kalish added that one negative item was that roughly 67 percent of viewers stopped watching the tape altogether once the feature film was finished, "a potentially ominous sign for advertisers looking to stick messages after the film's conclusion." However, Jerilyn Kessel, managing director of the study, pointed out that "teasers" at the beginning of the home video could perhaps whittle down that number by inducing more to watch after the feature ended. Recall of the commercial messages on the videocassettes was reported to be roughly equal to the recall rates found for television advertisements. Nestlé spent about $300,000 to get its 30-second Alpine White Chocolate ad placed on *Dirty Dancing*.[25]

When *Rain Man* was released on videocassette in 1989, selling for $89.95, it included an ad for Buick. A new video release of the classic *The Wizard of Oz* around the same time started off with a one-minute ad for Downy fabric softener. Two companies then existed who added commercials to videocassettes for local businesses; those ads were in addition to those already inserted by the studios. Paramount, which started the whole phenomenon with its Pepsi ad on the *Top Gun* video, self-righteously brought suit in a federal court in Wichita to stop such interlopers. Proctor & Gamble, the makers of Downy, spent $8.5 million to advertise on *The Wizard of Oz* tape, despite the fact that two new surveys indicated that at least 67 percent of all cassette viewers (perhaps as high as 90 percent) did indeed use the fast-forward button when they spotted an ad.[26]

By around 1992 commercials had been added to the video releases of about 50 features. With *Moonstruck* (Snickers candy bar) it was estimated that 49 percent of those who rented the movie saw the ad; 24 percent fast-forwarded through some of it; and 23 percent fast-forwarded through all of it. A 1987 survey by Link Resources found that 51 percent of VCR owners expressed an unwillingness to buy videos that had commercials on them—a figure that was said to drop to 35 percent if the price of the tape was lowered by the placement of the ad. Yet another study was done of 200 patrons of a Midwestern video store between November 1988 and January 1990 with the aim of exploring consumer attitudes toward advertising on videocassettes. Questions concerning attitudes toward ads on videocassettes revealed generally negative feelings. Some 76.5 percent of the respondents disagreed with the statement that "commercials on tape are fun to watch," while 52 percent felt that "ads on tape are intrusive." More than half of the sample (52.5 percent), reported they recalled seeing an ad on a tape within the previous month. In 49 percent of those cases the ad appeared at the beginning of the tape. But when the commercial did appear just 19.5 percent stated they watched the entire spot, and 41.5 percent claimed they were somewhat or very inattentive during the commercial. Ads on videocassettes never did amount to very much for the simple reason that the viewer had far too much control over the situation. It was always very easy to skip the ad, and most videocassette viewers did just that.[27]

As onscreen cinema ads continued to exist through the 1980s, even if they did not make spectacular advances, the Hollywood majors decided to respond. In a surprise announcement at a movie industry convention at the start of 1990, the Walt Disney Company declared that starting in March of that year its licensing agreements with U.S. theaters would no longer allow commercials for products or services to be shown with its Touchstone, Hollywood Pictures, or Disney features. Obviously, SV and Cineplex were very upset. Tim Warner, president of the National Association of Theater Owners (NATO) said that if the practice of banning ads became widespread, it could result in higher ticket prices. Given the average exhibitor affiliated with SV received a maximum of less than two cents per admission that argument was false. Hollywood's major studios and their distributors did not share in any of that ad revenue but Richard Cook, president of Disney's Buena Vista Pictures Distribution, said the revenue was not a factor in Disney's objection to cinema ads. "Advertising in theaters is destroying the moviegoing experience," he said. "It is insulting to a paying audience." Disney's decision to ban advertising was not based on any formal research, said Cook. "When I would go to the movies I would hear people booing commercials," he explained. "It was clear the audience didn't like the intrusion."[28]

Soon after Disney's announcement Warner Bros. domestic distribution president D. Barry Reardon praised Disney's stance. Reardon said Warner had a no-advertising stipulation in its booking contracts since the release of *Superman* in 1978. Warner had not publicized its policy,

he said, but described Disney's high-profile position as "terrific." Commercials on the screen were "demeaning" to audiences who paid at the
box office "to be entertained," explained the executive. Fox domestic
marketing and distribution president Tom Sherak also supported Disney's action, but he stopped short of saying Fox would follow suit. Other
major studios offered no public opinion, but one studio executive said
anonymously, "The feeling here is that this is an issue that Disney is
going to have to fight on its own." Disney was one of four Hollywood
majors that did not own cinemas. Paramount and Warner Bros. jointly
owned the Mann and Trans-Lux chains; Columbia owned Loew's; Universal owned half of Cineplex Odeon.[29]

With regard to Disney's position Directors Guild of America president Arthur Hiller said moviegoers "sit through commercials, but that
doesn't mean they like them. We applaud Buena Vista's action." Direc-
tor-actor-writer Woody Allen remarked, "the odd thing is that it had to
come from a studio, when in fact paying audiences should have rioted
until exhibitors removed commercials. People should boycott the sale of
videocassettes that include commercials as well. It's exploitation of the
public in a shameful way." Exhibitors argued they needed the extra
income provided by the ads and that the public did not mind them
because they were entertaining, and so on. The largest chain to screen
commercials was reported to be United Artists Theaters, with ads run
on more than half of its 2,669 screens. Both UA Theaters and Cineplex
had been involved in recent disputes with Disney concerning bidding
policies on its films. Although both chains were said to have since then
forged an "uneasy peace" with Disney, some observers felt it was more
than coincidental that Disney's ad ban struck hardest at Cineplex and
the UA chain. Another suggestion was that Disney was also targeting
screen ads by archrival Universal for its competing theme park, on Cineplex screens. "That is not true. There are no ulterior motives," responded
Cook. "We want to preserve the quality of moviegoing."[30]

Stung by criticism that its ad ban was not based on any objective
research, the Disney company defended that policy by releasing, in April
1990, a study that concluded that 90 percent of moviegoers did not want
commercials in cinemas. Since it had first announced its ban Disney had
been criticized by advertising executives and exhibitors who insisted that
only a vocal minority rejected screen ads. With the announcement of its
ban Disney offered no evidence to the contrary. Said Jeffrey Katzenberg,
Disney chairman, "We naively thought we were dealing with an issue in
which the facts were self-evident." That survey, conducted for Disney
by the National Research Group of Los Angeles, a subsidiary of agency
Saatchi & Saatchi, found that 90 percent of 18,772 filmgoers pooled said
they did not want commercials shown in theaters. By way of contrast,

95 percent of the same group said they favored the showing of trailers for coming attractions. Conducted during the weekend of March 30 to April 1, that survey polled moviegoers at 40 cinemas across America. Katzenberg cited a second study, by the Roper organization, which found that only about half of those asked said they did not like television advertising. For Katzenberg that confirmed people were more willing to accept television ads because they understood commercials paid for programs. Movie advertising, on the other hand, which he maintained did little or nothing to hold down cinema admission prices, represented "freeloading" as well as being "intrusive," he argued.[31]

Warner Bros. announced in April 1990 that it was following the lead of Disney in banning commercials from movie screens where its films were shown. Barry Reardon, president of domestic distribution, explained, "If you pay $6.50 or $7.00 for a movie, you're entitled to see it unencumbered. They detract from the movie, and we don't want to run them." That decision was revealed one week after Disney released its study showing 90 percent of filmgoers opposed to screen ads. However, Reardon said Warner did not rely on the Disney study or anyone else's in making its decision: "Every theater I've been in you find the audience booing at the end of the commercials." He noted again that Warner had introduced a clause in its contracts that banned exhibitors from running ads back in 1978 with the release of *Superman*. Since that clause had remained in its booking contracts for all those years, Reardon tried to explain the seeming confusion by saying, "We felt over the years that the clause was implied, but we haven't enforced it. Now we feel it's our turn to step forward." John Neal, a spokesman for United Artists theaters, said his company would abide by the Disney and Warner bans.[32]

MCA owned Universal and 50 percent of the Cineplex chain. Universal and Disney had competing theme parks near Los Angeles and rival complexes in Orlando, Florida. Disney owned no cinemas. Another criticism leveled at Disney when it announced its ban was that at the same time it was vigorously soliciting companies for product placement in its films. MCA chided Disney on that account and sarcastically asked how much General Mills paid Disney to have its Cheerios breakfast cereal placed in *Honey, I Shrunk the Kids*. Katzenberg retorted, "We could have gotten substantially more money by featuring another brand of cereal. The offers were on the table. However, the director felt the Cheerios brand was necessary to give the scene its full comic impact, and it was his sensibility that determined our choice."[33]

Unhappy with the Disney survey was the trade journal *Advertising Age*, which was not satisfied with the fairly simple and straightforward question the Disney survey used—"Do you want commercials shown in movie theaters?" So *Advertising Age* did its own poll (in conjunction with the Gallup organization) that, they said, showed milder opposition. Gallup surveyed 1,000 people by phone in March and asked whether they had seen a movie in a cinema during the previous three months. The 435 persons who said they had were asked additional questions about ads shown before the feature. Of that group, 21 percent strongly favored a ban on screen ads; 23 percent favored a ban; 31 percent opposed a ban on ads; four percent strongly opposed a ban; and 21 percent were undecided. Sentiment against ads ran to 46 percent in men and 42 percent in women; 50 percent of those 55 or older favored a ban, versus 40 percent of those aged 18–34. Those who favored or strongly favored a ban on ads were asked if they would continue to favor a ban if it meant a 50-percent increase in the ticket price. In that case only half would continue to support a ban; if the ticket price went up $1 only 26 percent of those originally opposed still wanted a ban; only 15 percent continued to favor a ban if it meant a $2 increase in the ticket price. Of course, those questions were all nonsense since a full loss of ad revenue for a cinema was, at the most, two cents per ticket. Exempted from both the Disney and Warner bans were trailers for coming attractions, slide ads, and ads approved (by the studios) for charitable purposes. Cook announced that all the cinema chains in the U.S. had by this time agreed to honor Disney's policy.[34]

An editorial in the *New York Times* noted Disney's new policy on ad banning as something worthy of praise. Then, after talking about Disney's recently published price list for product placement in its films, the editor added, "If readily identifiable commercials are 'insulting to a paying audience'—a Disney executive's words—are covert commercials any less so?"[35]

Later in 1990 reporter Marcy Magiera observed that the Disney and Warner bans had been complied with by all major cinema chains except Cineplex Odeon, which emphasized it was not scheduling any new ads, just honoring previous ad contracts. National Cinema Network's Onscreen Entertainment slide program (which included ads) then ran on around 3,000 screens nationwide. Earlier in 1990 it said it was decreasing the emphasis on ads in its 13–15-minute movie program by adding more trivia questions, star biographies, and so on. The company said its goal was to make ads account for only about 20 percent of the slides in the program. National Cinema had never signed an advertiser to a national buy on its network, but marketers making regional or local buys included PepsiCo's Taco Bell and Campbell Soup Company. A four-week national run on the slide show would cost advertisers about $250,000. The bans did not apply to National Cinema's slide program.[36]

Paramount Pictures chairman Brandon Tartikoff, in a speech delivered in 1991 before the Broadcast Advertising Club of Chicago (who had named him "Person of the Year"), told an audience of 400 broadcasters and ad agency executives that cinema ads were an "intrusion" and gave them a strong thumbs down. Tartikoff said that after adding up all the costs of seeing a first-run movie—which could include hiring a babysitter and concession purchases—the last thing moviegoers wanted to see was a commercial asking them to spend more money. Remarked Pam Brown, a Broadcast Advertising Club of Chicago director, "I think most of the audience couldn't agree more. They'd rather see those ads running on TV anyway."[37]

A 1993 report said that SV then placed ads on 6,500 screens, with the average audience for a month-long run of a 60-second spot being 40 million. Cineplex Odeon remained the only other major player (it launched its own formal onscreen advertising arm, Cinespot, in February 1991). It ran ads on 1,057 screens nationwide. Reporter Mark Hubis noted that the Disney ban was still in effect and that "New York and Los Angeles moviegoers regularly hiss and boo in-theater advertisements." SV president Dennis Fogarty explained that "New York is a tough town. Manhattanites don't want to cooperate with movie advertising." Pat Cunningham, vice chairman at the Ayer ad agency, added that "New York isn't the same as the rest of the country. It's rougher and meaner." Fogarty argued that the acceptance level of the ads from audiences in 1993 was "extraordinary." As well, he said those cinema ads averaged 70 percent day-after recall, much higher than for prime-time television, which hovered between 15 percent and 20 percent. "The messages got through," boasted Fogarty. "Purchase intent scores were also four to five times higher than television."[38]

Around the same time reporter Marcy Magiera said that SV was then running ads on 6,600 screens (one-third of the U.S. total), up 16 percent from the 5,700 screens of 1990, despite the fact the Disney and Warner bans of that year seemed to herald the "beginning of the end" of screen ads. In a departure from the recent past SV was then, said Magiera, accepting commercials exactly as they had been used on television, breaking its old policy that SV used only spots especially created or edited for theaters. Besides that change, SV was considering increasing the length of its ad program from the long-standing three-minute maximum to four minutes. It was also testing 30-second spots (it had a long-standing policy of an ad being at least 60 seconds in length). Howard Lichtman, executive vice president of marketing at Cineplex Odeon, called those who booed and hissed at ads "an elite" group and insisted that well-crafted spots "please 98% of the moviegoing population." Cineplex still sold ad times on its own screens and ran a maximum of three spots, of up to 90 seconds each. Lichtman added that Cineplex continued to comply with the three-year-old ban imposed by Disney and Warner Bros. However, Magiera said, "But other theater executives privately say both studios have been lax in enforcing the bans, especially after the Federal Trade Commission looked into possible restraint of trade implications." SV president Dennis Fogarty said that "the theaters continue to stand out there as the last frontier of impact advertising."[39]

At the end of 1999 reporter Dade Hayes said the pre-show material at most theaters had nearly doubled in length in recent years, with the number of ad trailers having increased from two to three or four, or more, at some locations. Bans by Disney and Warner Bros. against the running of ads before any of their features remained in effect, at least theoretically. "I don't believe in advertising in a movie theater," said Dan Fellman, head of Warner domestic theatrical distribution. People get enough of that on television." SV's Fogarty blamed the coming attraction trailers, not the commercials, for the pre-show lengthening. He added that screen ads got high approval from audiences. "People below 35 don't complain because advertising is a part of their culture. They think it's cool. The only people who complain are the 49-and-older people. But they complain about everything," Fogarty declared. Loew's cinema chain had recently expanded its pre-show to 15 minutes from 10, but company policy required the five minutes of ad time within that 15 minutes should immediately precede the official feature time. So a showtime listed for 7:30 meant the ads should start at 7:25. (Coming attraction trailers actually started at 7:30, then the feature.) The exhibitor Cinemark USA had a three-minute ad segment it ran prior to the printed showtime. As in other chains Cinemark kept the house lights up during the ads, so as to differentiate them from the feature. Hayes remarked that most audiences looked more favorably on coming-attraction trailers (which the MPAA limited to two minutes each) than they did on ads: "But when some chains began showing up to seven trailers per show, some red flags went up."[40]

By late 2001 it was reported that of the nation's 37,000 movie screens, some form of advertising was shown on about 24,000 of them. Screenvision Cinema Network remained the only group that distributed ad trailers nationwide. It also handled a slide ad program, as did the National Cinema Network. Commercial Alert was a Portland, Oregon-based consumer advocacy group that was then urging lawmakers to adopt legislation so cinemas would be required to tell patrons exactly what time the feature started. "This industry is hammering movie patrons with ads," said the group's executive director Gary Ruskin. "It's a really bad deal because they don't tell us when the movie actually starts so we can make our own decisions and choose whether or not to sit through them."[41]

Throughout the modern period the screen ad trailer survived and perhaps grew somewhat, although it certainly experienced no spectacular increases. Hostility against the ads seemed to have lessened, in comparison with earlier periods, as they grudgingly remained a part of the scene. Still, their potential was always severely limited by the relatively small amount of ad time that could be loaded before a feature film. Moving from three minutes to four or five was felt to be a risky step. Nobody in America even remotely considered the European standard of up to 15 minutes of ads per program to be an American possibility. Screen ad expenditures remained overall a very tiny portion of the total amount of money spent in the United States on advertising. Spectacular growth in cinema advertising did take place in the modern era, but it was in the area of product placement.

# 8

# Hollywood the Ad—Product Placement in the Modern Era
## *1982–2003*

If the product doesn't end up on the cutting room floor and the manufacturer says he's satisfied, he pays the agreed fee.
—Chuck Asman, Fox Licensing president, 1983

The containers of Coke don't actually receive more close-ups than Miss [Margot] Kidder, but their close-ups seem more lingering and loving.
—Vincent Canby, 1985

We don't want to be associated with porn [films] or extreme violence or something that is making a social statement we don't want to be identified with.
—Ann Sauve, Compaq Computers, 1995

Product placement had been growing sharply in the period from roughly 1978 to 1981, but that growth had taken place fairly quietly. Then the legendary placement in the 1982 release *E.T.* was made. Its success for the candy product Reese's Pieces ushered in a period of spectacular growth in product placement—a growth that was very noisy and well reported on. New companies sprang up all over the Los Angeles area, firms that did nothing except to try and turn the products they represented into movie stars. Hollywood's major producers publicly declared themselves open for placement business. They even went so far in some cases as to publish price lists for potential advertisers. In the past the majors had sometimes engaged actively in placement, sometimes not. However, only rarely did they admit openly to engaging in the practice. Whatever may have been going on with regard to placement activities, Hollywood almost always maintained an official position that it was not involved. It was a position that ended in the modern era with product placement out in the open in all respects.

Producers of *E.T.* contacted the Mars candy company in 1982 to see if they would like their candy product M&Ms to be included in their film as the candy that cemented a friendship between the young boy, Elliott, and the extra-terrestrial creature. Uninterested, Mars turned the proposal down. Then the producers substituted Reese's Pieces, unbeknownst to the product's manufacturer, Hershey. When the movie was in production Hershey was contacted and asked if it wanted to put money in a tie-in promotion of the film and the candy. According to Dennis Eshleman, Hershey product manager, when Universal approached Hershey the film had no title at that point and all Universal could tell the candy firm was that it was a family movie directed by Steven Spielberg. Nevertheless, Hershey liked the idea and put up $1 million in promotion money. Sales of Reese's Pieces reportedly jumped 70 percent within one month of the film's release. Two months later more than 800 cinemas that had not previously stocked the product at their concession stands were then handling the item. As time passed the *E.T.* placement was cited again and again and became the reference point for product placement.[1]

Writing in the *New York Times* in 1982, noted journalist Janet Maslin commented on placements in a number of films and spoke of them as being "the handiwork of an up-and-coming entrepreneur called the product placer." In the days when Hollywood cared more for elegance, she thought, such a degree of placement might not have been possible because "Brand-name products onscreen would have seemed hopelessly déclassé. Even in recent years, the use of merchandise in movies was fairly random. But nowadays it's becoming an organized process, and the brand-name products that turn up as movie props are less and less likely to have landed there by accident." So common had the practice become by this time that there were even seminars about it. One at the Plaza Hotel, titled "How to Market Your Product in Motion Pictures and Turn the Silver Screen into Gold," attracted several dozen corporate representatives—who paid between $175 and $195 each to attend. As placement on this kind of an organized basis was a relatively new service, there were still only a few firms in the field. Biggest of those (and oldest at four years) was Associated Film Promotions (AFP). According to Maslin it then handled 160 products, for fees starting at $35,000 a year. In exchange for that fee a manufacturer was guaranteed at least five movie appearances for its products, although no guarantee was given that a product would be implanted in a specific film or handled by a certain star. In these exchanges between manufacturers and film studios, said Maslin, money did not "usually change hands." But, she added, "No one denies that a candy bar featured onscreen may mean free candy for cast and crew, or that a good shot of an airplane may mean free trans-portation for everyone concerned." A key part of the product placer's work was in cultivating filmmakers and developing friendships with them. That enabled him to see scripts before the filming began and to make suggestions about which of his clients' products might be planted in particular scenes. When the candy product Milk Duds was worked into *The Formula* (in that movie Marlon Brando offered the product to George C. Scott) and *Seems Like Old Times* (Chevy Chase held up a gas station and demanded the Milk Duds from a vending machine), sales of the product at lobby concession counters increased dramatically, according to AFP head Robert Kovoloff. Another advantage was that Brando, a star who did not do ordinary commercials, "had been induced to help out with a more indirect form of advertising."[2]

Maslin felt the advantages of placement to a manufacturer were obvious while Kovoloff added that seeing a product, even for a second, "in a realistic dramatic setting in which the viewer is already emotionally involved leaves an invaluable impression." As to why the studios went along with the practice, she felt that using brand-name products helped a movie look realistic. Another reason she gave was economics; it was less costly to use products supplied for free (of course, for small products such as Milk Duds or Coca-Cola, for example, that argument did not make a lot of sense). Firm in her belief that product placement could go too far Maslin cited *Hardly Working* (Jerry Lewis) as a picture in which the plugs were "virtually wall to wall" as "filmdom's most glaring example of merchandising overkill, even by product placers themselves."[3]

Also mentioned by Maslin were a couple of the more insidious aspects of the practice, wherein scripts were vetted by advertisers' agents before filming began—the thought being to avoid any film liable to be controversial and to ensure clients' products were used in only a "good" way. That is, left to seek its own level, product placement would result in having films made that were all mindless, content free, bland pap. An example of a film cited by Maslin as liable to be controversial, and therefore one to be avoided by manufacturers and product placers, was *Monsignor*. However, it could still use brand-name props without asking for permission and *Monsignor* did contain Campbell's soup and Hershey's chocolate (a central character was a black marketer). Watchdog aspects of product placement involved making sure the product was not used in a defamatory light. For example, when Walter Matthau used a Nikon camera in *Hopscotch*, the product placers made sure the actor was portraying a competent spy and not a inept one. Beer companies were especially sensitive about not wishing to see their products "misused" by violent or underage characters. According to Kovoloff, Anheuser-Busch turned down placements in *Making Love*—possibly because its bisexual love story had the makings of a controversy—and *E.T.*, because the beer was used for the questionable purpose of intoxicating a child and an extra-terrestrial. Kovoloff remarked that he wished he started this type of organization earlier: "It's too bad there was no professionally organized product representation in the old days of movies ... I'd like to see a T-shirt on every star and a logo on every T-shirt." At that seminar Maslin mentioned that an attendee from the Clairol corporation reported that someone had asked her firm for $10,000 in exchange for a plug in the movie *Smile*.[4]

In another interview Kovoloff described his service by saying, "We're like marriage brokers; we save film companies time and money." Budweiser beer was one of AFP's placements in *Poltergeist*, along with Royal Crown Cola, Wheaties, Stokeley Van Camp canned goods, and Cheerios. By Kovoloff's calculations, he estimated AFP's matchmaking saved the motion picture industry more than $3.5 million in 1981. Also, thanks to the work of AFP, Faye Dunaway as Joan Crawford served Cheerios for breakfast in *Mommie Dearest*. Glenfiddich Scotch, Dunkin' Donuts, and Cadillac all showed up in *Six Weeks* (Mary Tyler Moore and Dudley Moore). Mattel Intellivision, Maverick Jeans, Wild Turkey bourbon, and Frito-Lay snack foods all appeared with Jackie Gleason and Richard Pryor in *The Toy*.[5]

In *Cannonball Run* actor Dom DeLuise hurried out of a 7-Eleven store, its logo spread wide across the screen, and wolfed down a Big Gulp, the oversize soft drinks sold at 7-Eleven. "I'm having a Dr. Pepper Big Gulp!" he exclaimed to costar Burt Reynolds. To get its store and Big Gulp into *Cannonball Run* 7-Eleven agreed to mount a six-figure ad campaign to promote the film. As David Friendly put it in his piece on the topic in *Newsweek*, products then had their own agents. Dustin Hoffman drank Budweiser in *Tootsie*. Friendly reported that AFP charged its clients a minimum fee of $50,000 a year for a guarantee of placement of a product in five films. In 1983, he said, AFP expected it would place some of the 200 products it represented in more than 150 movies. Don Nunley, a former property master who founded a firm called Unique Product Placement, had more than 30 clients and said he would work on about 85 percent of all Hollywood movies released that year. Studios showed their scripts beforehand to people like Kovoloff and Nunley. Property masters were said to often drop by Kovoloff's warehouse in Los Angeles to borrow one or more of hundreds of items, from cowboy boots to surgical gowns. Friendly accepted the idea that the main advantage of placement to studios was that it held down the cost of props—and the advertising tie-ins that were often part of the deal.[6]

In one scene of *Buddy, Buddy*, Jack Lemmon was supposed to drink champagne. Prop master M. C. Ayers had verbally agreed to use Dom Perignon champagne, but later he was approached by an agent for Piper-

Heidsieck, who pleaded that he had been unable to place his product any-where. "The guy was in a real bind," said Ayers. When the scene came up Ayers told director Billy Wilder he thought Dom Perignon was too sophisticated for Lemmon's character. In the end, remarked Ayers, "Lem-mon drank Piper." Coca-Cola had worked hard for years for placement arrangements, often sending free cases to producers, said Friendly, in hopes of maintaining good relations. Coke's advantage over rival Pepsi-Cola (which had lagged behind and not been aggressive in seeking its own deals) was especially noticeable in the movie *Missing* in which Jack Lemmon was often seen sipping Coke, while the stadium in which prisoners were brutally tortured was serviced by a Pepsi machine. Forced into action by that example, Pepsi hired Brad Brown in 1983 as a product-placement consultant. One of his first placements was with actor

*Risky Business* (1983, Tom Cruise, Rebecca De Mornay). The wearing of Ray-Ban sun-glasses by Cruise was credited with reviving a dying model and driving its sales to new levels.

Jennifer Beals in *Flashdance*. Brown described that im-plant as just what Pepsi was looking for—"close associ-ation with the principal in the movie and a sympa-thetic portrayal."[7]

According to Brown a man claiming to represent the producers of *Superman II* offered "significant expo-sure" for Pepsi in that movie for $150,000, but Pepsi-Cola refused. Robert Sim-monds, associate producer of *Superman II*, said he did not know if Pepsi was approached, but stated that "other companies, such as Pentax cameras, did agree to pay for an appearance in the film." Some manufac-turers wanted to limit the type of picture their prod-ucts were used in—only in movies rated for general audiences, for example. When they said something like that to Nunley he told them jokingly, "Fine, we'll

*Cannonball Run II* (1984, Marilu Henner, left, Shirley Maclaine). One of many, many placements engineered for Miller beer.

put you in both of the ones that come out next year." No one could quantify the benefits of such plugs, observed Friendly, but the placers insisted the placements had powerful effects. "If Burt Reynolds drinks a certain beer in *Hooper*, so will a lot of people who want to be like him," said Nunley.[8]

As 1983 ended 20th Century–Fox became the first Hollywood major to officially and publicly offer manufacturers a specific display of their brand-name products in movies in return for cash. Fees ran from $10,000 to $40,000 for a play in one of their movies. "We've signed contracts with Miller beer and Snauwaert tennis equipment and we're in final nego-tiations with Chivas Regal and Puma sports shoes," said Chuck Asman, president of Fox Licensing and Merchandising Corporation. "I envision a dozen or more such arrangements in areas like soft drinks, trans-portation, hotels, foodstuffs, bicycles and housewares," explained Asman. "If the product doesn't end up on the cutting room floor and the man-ufacturer says he's satisfied, he pays the agreed fee."[9]

Reporter Aljean Harmetz commented that plugging products was then an established practice but that a new, more intense phase was underway in what once was regarded as "casual barter." Dozens of prod-ucts were sometimes being placed in a single movie by placers who got fees from manufacturers, said Harmetz, that ranged from $5,000 to

$10,000 for each product. Studios had been saving money on props when they used the product agents but now, like Fox, were trying to earn money by cutting out the middlemen and dealing directly with the manufacturers. MGM/UA was said to be only a few steps behind Fox in following the same path. "It used to be a tradeoff, but now the studios want money," said Irv Ivers, MGM/UA president of marketing. William Minot, MGM/UA's director of national merchandising, added, "I already have agreements in principle with an airline and with soft drink, beer and computer manufacturers." The other Hollywood majors remained on the sidelines for the moment, cautious observers. According to Herbert Wallerstein, Fox production management vice president, product placement began to increase some 15 years earlier (1968) for two reasons: suddenly there were a lot of independent (non-majors) films produced, with the principles keen on saving money, and "At the same time, Hollywood switched to making movies on location. If you were using a real bar in some town, it would cost money to rip out the neon signs and put in phony bottles." No evidence supported either reason, nor was there any evidence to support the idea placement started to increase significantly in 1968; 1978 was the more likely start date of an increase.[10]

Harmetz argued that until the mid 1970s product placement remained a haphazard practice where set dressers and property men scrounged to save a few dollars by getting props free. In addition, they could usually convince a soda or beer maker "to throw in 30 cases of drinks for the actors and crew." Then came the rise of placement firms. Reportedly, they were not worried about competition from the majors or about being squeezed out by them. "How many pictures do MGM and Fox make a year," asked Nunley (he then represented 40 products including Coors, Levi's, and McDonald's). "Perhaps a dozen. We worked on approximately 200 movies last year." Kovoloff estimated he had worked on 160 movies that year, placing an average of 20 products in each film. Fox's Asman agreed it was not worth the studio's time and energy to scramble for products that were not used frequently. "If we need a Jeep, we save time even more than money by letting a product broker supply it," he explained. "Most of these people have warehouses full."[11]

When Coca-Cola purchased Columbia Studios in 1982 a memo was quickly sent to studio executives forbidding the use of Pepsi-Cola and Seven-Up at any Columbia events. Forbidden products also included Miller and Lowenbrau beers—produced by Philip Morris, the owner of Seven-Up—and Stolichnaya vodka and Frito-Lay potato chips, all owned or distributed by PepsiCo, Inc. It was also understood that none of these products should appear in any Columbia movie. Executives of other major studios said their own firms would shy away from using Coke and its allied products at their functions and in their movies. As might have been expected, Coca-Cola and auxiliary products turned up regularly in Columbia movies at least until the late 1980s, when Coca-Cola sold the studio.[12]

With respect to whether or not product placement infringed on a film's integrity Fox's Ivers commented "We'll pursue products if it makes sense without compromising the integrity of the film. We're a creative medium, not an advertising medium." All agreed the practice could go too far; cited as one of the worst examples of excessive placement was, once again, *Hardly Working*. Harmetz concluded, "Yet no executive sees any likelihood that the practice will stop because it serves the needs of both the movie producers and what the [film] industry calls 'Corporate America.'"[13]

Early in 1984 Fox released *Unfaithfully Yours*, which featured Dudley Moore and TWA, from whose jet plane the actor emerged, accompanied by some clean shots of the airline's logo. TWA paid Fox at least $10,000 for the plug. Paramount's Dianne Mandell said she would now review final scripts to see what products were needed and then the studio would negotiate fees for manufacturers to obtain name-brand access to the screen. Still cautious was Warner Bros., with spokesman Dan Romanelli saying the studio worried that the public would grow suspicious of product plugs. Romanelli added that Warner planned to play each script by ear.[14]

Another placement firm was Advertising in Movies (AIM), based in Astoria, New York, and headed by Frank Zazza. Out of a reported total of 25 such firms in 1985 (up from none in 1977) Zazza said AIM was the only one based in the East. For a $50,000 fee AIM guaranteed at least 10 placements in feature films or television network productions. Zazza's approach to product placement began by sending an extensive questionnaire to clients, enabling him to get an idea on how they would like their product to be seen. Ad strategies, ad philosophies, demographics, and psychographics were also covered. Meanwhile, a steady stream of film and television scripts flowed into AIM's office. Each was studied and broken down, with possible props for each shot lined up. Then Zazza supplied the set decorator and prop master with a list of clients willing to participate, based on the guidelines received. He stressed to clients that products placed should be established brands—that it was not a medium in which to establish a new product. "You want to get the person who has been using it to continue using it," Zazza observed. In his view the practice had been around since the silent movie days but had only become a "businesslike procedure" about five years earlier. Before that, he said, a set decorator would call up a manufacturer's agent and say, "Listen, send me $2,000 and two cases of beer and I'll get your product shown." However, the movie might have been released without the product appearing (edited out or not placed at all) even though the money had been paid.[15]

Movies as commercial vehicles was a subject studied by advertising agency Saatchi & Saatchi in 1985. In a memo to his staff, senior vice president Stephen Fajen observed that more advertisers were integrating their products into movies and television shows. He described AFP as "a firm that screens scripts, selects appropriate vehicles, works with the production crew, helps develop the creative product, oversees the shoot on the set, and prescreens the result, at a cost of roughly $50,000." Fajen added that the object "is to have the product endorsed by a star, in a sympathetic environment, to cause the audience to emulate the action in the marketplace. In many cases it works." That memo made it appear the product placer had far more power to alter a film than anyone else in the business—either a studio or a placement firm—cared to admit.[16]

In *Power* Richard Gere played a political consultant watching election returns on television—but first he had to sit through a commercial for AIM toothpaste. Gere and AIM both got their parts through an agent. Six months earlier Lever Brothers hired AIM to place their toothpaste. *Brewster's Millions* showed Richard Pryor bestowing gift cases of Dom Perignon champagne on his friends while in *Desperately Seeking Susan* Madonna used a Polaroid camera. Business reporter Susan Spillman remarked, "But in the old days product placement was a lot more casual. Property masters at studios just called up Coke and asked for a couple of cases or sometimes they went to the grocery store and bought it themselves." However, in 1985, said Bill Minor, vice president of merchandising for MGM/UA, "Now it's chaos. You've got at least 25 companies acting as agents, bidding against each other for parts." Typically a manufacturer paid one of those specialized placement firms a yearly fee of from $25,000 to $50,000 to get parts for their products. A few of the large manufacturers—Coca-Cola and Pepsi-Cola, for example—had their own full-time employees devoted to product placement; they had eliminated the middlemen. The California Raisin Board paid over $25,000 for a bus-stop sign and a raisin-eating scene in Steven Spielberg's *Back to the Future*. Pepsi also got lots of visibility in the same picture because it supplied Spielberg with the hard-to-find Pepsi items he needed to decorate a 1950s soda fountain, where many scenes were shot. First, though, Pepsi had to buy back many of the needed items from a Southern California collector for $3,000.[17]

Spillman felt the rising interest in product placement was fueled by rising media cost in advertising, a new afterlife for movies on pay-television and videocassettes, and perhaps a growing belief that movie place-

*Murphy's Romance* (1985, James Garner, second from left, Sally Field). The bar-becue sauce faces the camera.

ments actually worked. Like many other observers, she cited the successful example of Reese's Pieces in *E.T.* And how the unknown Mumford High School in Detroit sold $1 million worth of school T-shirts after Eddie Murphy wore one in *Beverly Hills Cop.* AFP used a research company to conduct surveys of its placements. That research company went to a cinema line-up for a film and got the names and phone number of moviegoers waiting in those line-ups. Three to five days later the filmgoers were phoned and asked what products they remembered seeing in the film. Of the 1,600 people queried about *Rocky III* it was said that nearly 60 percent recalled actor Sylvester Stallone eating Wheaties but only one percent remembered a quick shot of a Glenfiddich scotch bottle. According to Columbia executive Joe Whitaker, his studio saved about $1 million by borrowing high-tech television monitors and computers from Sony to fill a newsroom set in the Sean Connery flop *Wrong Is Right.*[18]

Picking films that depicted a positive environment for a product was crucial, said Spillman. AIM vice president Rich Gore remarked that he discouraged MasterCard from participating in *Death Wish III.* He advised against a placement even though the film had a major star—Charles

*Living Daylights* (1987, **Timothy Dalton**). **Dalton, as James Bond, displays a blurry and hard-to-read cigarette package.**

Bronson—and was expected to be a sure hit because "it takes place in the ghetto and shows lots of people getting blown away. I don't think that would do Master-Card any good." Product placement was easier in motion pictures than it was in television because in the latter, network codes prohibited the placing of brand names for most products. (Just about the only placements that could easily be arranged for television were for cars and airlines, which were hard to depict generically.) Cited as an example of excess was the film *Little Treasure*. In a review in the *New York Times* Vincent Canby grumbled, "The containers of Coke don't actually receive more close-ups than Miss [Margot] Kidder, but their close-ups seem more lingering and loving."[19]

Besides wearing the aforementioned T-shirt in *Beverly Hills Cop* Eddie Murphy also drove a Mercedes sports car, the 380 SL. Placement of Mercedes was mostly handled through its West Coast public relations specialist Herman Hadler, who started out in the business doing placements for Chrysler, back in 1955. "I read the trades—*Hollywood Reporter, Daily Variety* and all the rest—and find out what the studios are planning. If a feature sounds promising, I make a few phone calls and visits," he explained. On behalf of Mercedes Hadler maintained a pool of more than 35 cars of various sizes, models, and colors, all available for free on loan agreements to producers. To counter a worry that his product could be used in a way that was "detrimental or even defamatory," Hadler carefully reviewed a script before offering one of his pool cars and that "assurances are given by the producers that the product will be shown in a manner that is tasteful." Ford Motor Company's manager of western public affairs, Robert Harner, said his company did not want "heavies" behind of the wheel of any of its cars. Another taboo was cars that crashed and burned. Hadler added, "Mercedes is adamant about having only the white-hat boys drive their cars." When asked about the heavy who drove a Mercedes 500 SEL in *Beverly Hills Cop*, Hadler pointed out that the car was rented by the studio and not placed by him.[20]

Coca-Cola was mentioned as a cautionary story of a manufacturer getting carried away with excess placements when it was in a position to create as many as it wanted—as it was for Coke during much of the 1980s, when it owned Columbia studios. Another reviewer of *Little Treasure* wrote, "It gets so that watching for the Coke ads, as they persistently amble by, becomes more interesting than the picture itself." Regarding the effectiveness of plugs, Ford stated that sales of its Mustang automobile "notched upward" as a result of Steve McQueen's chase sequence in *Bullitt*.[21]

In the original version of the James Bond film *A View to Kill* actor Tanya Roberts simply mentioned she was going to feed her cat some Whiskas. For the German release of the film Roger Moore (James Bond) asked Roberts a question that was not in the U.S. version, whether there really was Whiskas cat food. According to reporter Hazel Guild, "The extra plug was set up in Germany when the film was dubbed, but no one will say just how much it cost for the extra mention of the pet food." Also, in that film auto maker Renault paid "several hundred thousand dollars" to show Bond in a chase that used one of its autos and James Bond's use of Bollinger champagne "involved a considerable fee."[22]

Business reporter Kevin Higgins said, in the fall of 1985, there were more than 30 firms involved in product placement. Pan Am Airways, Jim Beam and Johnny Walker whiskies, Coleman lanterns, and Igloo containers all paid a consideration for appearances in *Volunteers*, starring Tom Hanks and John Candy. Besides Pepsi, Bank of America, Cadbury candy, and Toyota trucks appeared in *Back to the Future*. Three scenes displayed Swensen's ice cream containers in *Goonies*, and not only did the characters consume ice cream, they even talked about it. One character exclaimed, "I smell Swensen's," while passing a restaurant's freezer. Another scene in which Swensen's containers appeared was used in a

television ad for the movie. "While placement in this movie will generate millions of viewers' impressions nationwide, our goal is to generate
store foot traffic and sales," the Swensen's Advertising Association
pointed out in a letter to franchisees. Thus, the association provided in-
store promotional material and a flavor-of-the-month tied to the movie.
About 40 movie scripts were evaluated by Swensen's before it decided
to throw in with *Goonies*. That movie's family appeal made it a perfect
pairing, according to Carla Denham, senior account executive with
Stoorza/Smith, Swensen's Los Angeles advertising agency. She credited
the placement of Reese's Pieces in *E.T.* with opening the eyes of advertisers to the potential of this field.[23]

According to Warren Weideman, cofounder of Krown, Inc. (a product placement firm in Beverly Hills), because of international distribution, pay television, and videocassette rentals, the typical movie reached
more than 100 million consumers, which made placement more attractive. His partner Russ Krasnoff said, "The toughest thing is to not make
the situation look forced. If you see people in the audience elbowing each
other and saying, 'I wonder how much they paid for that?' you've done
a poor job of positioning the product within the film." In his view not
more than half the scripts making the rounds in Hollywood had any real
promise for placement. Such scripts had to be "youthful, upbeat, and
not overly violent or sexual," he explained. Krasnoff also believed that
for a film to be a prime candidate for placement it should be made or
handled by a major studio, otherwise national distribution was not likely.
And it should feature an important star or director and have an appropriate release date—a summer release for *Goonies* was critical to an advertiser like Swensen's ice cream.[24]

Tony Hoffman, director of product placement for Walt Disney Productions, echoed a common theme among the practice's proponents
when he said, "Placing consumer products in a film lends a more natural environment. Generic products can look very silly on the screen and
undermine the aura of authenticity." All that was in contrast, said reporter
Jim Gluckson, to yesterday's filmmakers, "who insisted on using generic
products instead of brand names, contemporary producers and directors tend to put an emphasis on reality." Don Nunley, president of
Unique Product Placement (UPP) was another in the field sensitive to
making sure his placements showed his clients' products in a favorable
light. In *Moscow on the Hudson* Nunley said he "worked out a part where
the Robin Williams character lands a job at McDonald's"—a UPP client.
On the other hand, Nunley chose not to use a men's magazine client in
a film scene where a young boy masturbated. He also passed on the movie
*Scarface*, exclaiming, "I'd rather have five seconds in another film than
10 minutes in that one."[25]

Yet another placement firm was a Pasadena, California, company called International Film Promotions (IFP). As of 1986 it was five years old. It was started in 1981 by Donna Estes and partner Carol Hilson with no staff and nothing more than a telephone. By 1986 IFP had 30 regular clients signed up at $50,000 each per year—and a staff of 18, including six based in London, England. Estes estimated IFP would place products in about 120 movies a year. She guaranteed her regulars a placement in six domestic releases each year; if she failed she promised to rip up the client's contract. "So far, that hasn't happened," she added. "We usually meet our quota three and fourfold." Additionally, Estes had "a slew" of irregular and one-shot customers. Peter Rainer, movie critic for the *Los Angeles Herald Examiner*, said, "I wouldn't say product placement has become the major source of money for movies, but it's certainly become a significant source of funding. The studios wouldn't do it unless it was worth it. And they're doing it now—big." One admirer of the practiced as a form of marketing was Ben Enis, professor at the University of Southern California School of Business. "This is a form of advertising that you simply can't buy elsewhere. When advertising is labeled as advertising, it is fulfilled by consumers," he explained. "You process the information differently, your guard is up. But in the movies you can have the hero or heroine implicitly or even explicitly endorse the product. It's quite effective."[26]

The process Estes used to place a product was the same as that used by other companies in the field. First she obtained a script for an upcoming production and then broke it down scene by scene, noting in the margin where one of her clients' products could fit in. Next she contacted the appropriate party at the studio to request a placement. "It varies who is in charge of it. Sometimes it's the director, sometimes the producer, sometimes the executive producer, sometimes the prop master," she said. For some clients IFP would pay over cash to a filmmaker, if there was a "guarantee" of a good placement. "On a really big film, for a solid placement, written into the script, and if the client wants it, it does happen," Estes admitted. Reporter Benjamin Cole added, "The delicacy with which Estes discusses cash reflects the low-esteem in which most product-placement companies are held." According to Estes there were then about 40 firms in the business, although she felt many were fly-by-night operators who appeared, got advances from some advertisers, and then disappeared when promised plugs did not appear in the named films. Kovoloff and his AFP remained the largest such firm, said to place products in two-thirds of all domestic releases and representing more than 80 of the Fortune 500 firms. Many worried that pictures could evolve to be little more than showcases for consumer goods. One who had those worries was film critic Rainier. "You get the feeling if the *Wiz-*

*Mac and Me* (1988, Jade Calegory, left, Jonathon Ward), Coca-Cola was everywhere in this critically savaged effort.

*ard of Oz* were made today, the yellow brick road would be brought to you courtesy of Carpeteria," he said. "A product placement can destroy a magical moment in a movie, by bringing you back down to earth with a thud." For Cole one of the worst examples of placement overkill was *Back to the Future,* "a film so loaded with products that one scene had a family sitting around the table with two brands of beer and a soft drink—and one member of the group wore a McDonald's restaurant uniform."[27]

One thing that was unique about product placement as it started its dramatic increase in the late 1970s was that there was no opposition to it from within the industry, which at least partly explained its continued surge. In the past cinema advertising of whatever type—ad shorts, ad trailers, or product placement—had always had some opposition from one or more elements from within the industry, such as the Hollywood majors themselves or exhibitor groups not to mention outside opposition from, for example, the newspaper lobby. Product placement in the modern era generated no opposition except, on occasion, from relatively powerless outside groups. In a letter late in 1985 to MPAA head Jack Valenti two organizations charged product placement as being blatantly unfair to audiences. They should be informed at the beginning of a picture that seemingly incidental depictions of consumer products actually were paid promotions, said the letter from the Center for Science in the

*Days of Thunder* (1990, Robert Duvall, left, Tom Cruise). Another movie cited for excessive placement.

Public Interest (CSPI) and a group called Doctors Ought To Care. Valenti was urged to advise MPAA members that the practice was beyond the bounds of fairness. "If the studios decline to end paid placements, one alternative would be to require an advertising disclosure at the beginning of the affected films," suggested the letter. Dr. John Richards, of Doctors Ought To Care, commented, "The 20 references to Marlboro cigarettes in *Superman II* and Burt Reynolds' quaffing Budweiser in *Cannonball Run*, a film in which several people drive fast and recklessly, are outrageous." Michael Jacobson, executive director of CSPI, argued the rampant advertising in films "mocks the artistic abilities of the writers and performers and is blatantly unfair to audiences."[28]

Predictably, Valenti dismissed any notion movies should carry a warning notice. In his response to the CSPI complaint that youth were enticed with unhealthy products such as liquor, beer, cigarettes, and junk food, Valenti went so far as to dispute whether such a problem existed. If it did, he argued, it was magnified "far more visibly" in sports by famous athletes who "use and wear equipment and clothing paid for by those who make and market those products." A finger could also be pointed at television celebrities who promoted products they might not even use, he noted. "Moreover," Valenti continued, "The producer, writer and director of films/tv programs are the captains of their creative ship. They would resent telling them how to shape their creative design."[29]

James Bond vehicles continued to be favorite locations for place-ments. In the 1987 release *The Living Daylights*, Bond was seen drinking Bollinger champagne, playing with high-tech Philips electronic equip-ment, driving an Audi Quattro 2000, and escorting women who wore Cartier jewelry. British reporter Roma Felstein called the technique "lifestyle product placement" wherein "The aim is not simply to get a product on the screen; it has to be the right movie with the right stars and the right image." Derek Coyte, who handled marketing and pro-motion for the Bond films, argued, "He has to drink someone's cham-pagne. So I use products that fit in with the 007 image." He added that in *Daylights* they needed a car that was known in both the East and the West and one with a trunk big enough to hold a body. "Not every car fits that bill," remarked Coyte. "So we went to Audi, and once we knew they were interested we discussed ways in which they would promote the film worldwide. Marketing the picture is every bit as important as mak-ing the picture."[30]

One thing that bothered many media buyers about film product placement in the late 1980s was that it was an alternative whose effective-ness was hard to document. Said Rick Markovitz, senior vice president of the J. Walter Thompson advertising agency's Entertainment Group in Los Angeles, "It's hard to talk about the effect of product placement in a movie compared to quantifiable media like tv and magazines. Prod-uct placement by its very nature is supposed to be in the background of the movie. The recall aspects can be dubious." But, said Russ Krasnoff, managing director of Krown Entertainment, a product placement firm he founded that by then was a subsidiary of ad agency Young & Rubi-cam, "We've gotten past the honeymoon stage. The vast majority of For-tune 500 companies are involved in getting their products placed." To address concerns about documented effectiveness the industry was then trying to generate numbers, often in a bizarre fashion. A movie that grossed up to $50 million at the box office was assumed likely to sell 200,000 videocassettes; a film grossing over $50 million meant a sale of 300,000 cassettes. Still more assumptions followed, including that a top feature film cassette was rented over five times a week, adding another 25–30 million "impressions" (viewers). Then there were cable television assumptions to be added on, and so forth. Krasnoff concluded from all that that the advertiser's placement cost per 1,000 viewers typically ranged from 50 cents to $1, "with the average placement in a major studio-dis-tributed star movie costing advertisers anywhere from $25,000 to $100,000. Much depends on whether the product is actually handled by the movie's star or simply appears in the background." Edward Mintz, president of the placement company CinemaScore, boasted of his firm's use of research data that measured audience recall percentage for products implanted. "This type of thing protects the clients. If [recall] falls under 15%, they don't have to pay," said Mintz. "We don't even like the words 'product placement.' We call it a media buy." To get its logo in *Coming to America* (Eddie Murphy) British Airways donated the use of its Kennedy Airport terminal in New York for an overnight shoot. In the movie *Cocktail* star Tom Cruise was shown drinking from bottles of Miller beer during several bar scenes. Reportedly, no direct fee was involved but in exchange Miller donated jackets, threw parties for the crew, and helped to promote the movie in its own marketing efforts.[31]

Trade writer Lenore Skenazy nominated producer R. J. Louis as "producer of probably the most product crammed film in history." *Mac & Me* was slammed by the critics as an open rip-off of *E.T.* The Louis film was about a little boy who befriended a space alien who existed on Coca-Cola. Besides being full of Coke cans, obviously, the movie was full of McDonald's and Sears, Roebuck scenes. Louis explained that he used things people could "relate to" in order to create a "realistic" movie. Denying any money changed hands, he said, "I've heard that people pay to have their products in pictures, but I don't do that." Louis added, "The intention was not to even focus on a product. They're props. I think that, after a while, you just forget about the Coke can." Yet when Louis commissioned the screenplay for *Mac & Me*, reported Skenazy, "he specifically asked writers Stewart Raffill and Steve Feke to make McDonald's integral to the plot."[32]

The placement frenzy continued when a scene in *Cocoon: The Return* was re-shot so that Quaker Instant Oatmeal could be displayed more prominently. Film director John Badham, who incorporated Alaska Airlines, Apple computers, Bounty paper towels, and Ore-Ida frozen French fries into his film *Short Circuit*, said, "If we can help each other, and it doesn't intrude on the movie, it's fine." Badham added that film budgets had become "increasingly high," with the result that people like himself were always looking for ways to save money. "From a producer's or a director's view, product placement is a great way to reduce the budget and keep the studio quiet." One example cited of the effectiveness of product placement concerned the company Ray-Ban (maker of sunglasses). The sales of its Wayfarer model sunglasses were said to have tripled in the year after Tom Cruise wore them in *Risky Business* while sales of its Aviator model increased 40 percent in the seven months after Cruise sported them in *Top Gun*. On the other hand McDonald's was said to pay its placement agency to keep its products out of films that might alienate customers by "offending the family unit." That is, as placers read through scripts before any shooting began (to find spots for clients' products) they might also find a reference already there (put in with no placement involved, presumably for "artistic" reasons) that showed a client's product in a bad light. In those cases the placer might badger and hound the producer to remove the reference, sometimes successfully. That part of the placement field came to be known as "product displacement."[33]

Another assault on product placement came in the spring of 1989, this time from the U.S. Congress. Representative Tom Luken (D.–Ohio) wanted an answer to the question of whether or not product placement in movies was paid advertising. And in the case of tobacco companies, if it was paid advertising, did that violate the congressional intent of keeping cigarette ads off the nation's airways. Luken asked U.S. Attorney General Richard Thornburgh to investigate whether Philip Morris Company and the Liggett Group broke federal laws by paying filmmakers to display their cigarettes in feature films. In his request letter

Luken cited three incidents in which the two companies paid to get their cigarettes into the movies—*Superman II*, *Supergirl*, and James Bond's *Licence to Kill*. Representative Luken felt there was no difference between a product placement and a 30-second commercial. Calling the arrangements a "prostitution of the movie industry" he said he felt the deals could be called a "conspiracy—a contract to do something illegal."[34]

According to documents provided by Luken, in September 1988 Philip Morris paid $350,000 for prominent placement of Lark cigarettes in the then upcoming Bond film (Lark was marketed by Liggett in the U.S. and by Philip Morris in international markets). It

*Die Hard 2* (1990, Bruce Willis). Note that Willis has nothing in his hands. Tool making company Black and Decker also noticed that fact and, since they had paid $20,000 to have Willis perform a hands-on usage in "heroic" fashion with its cordless power tool, it sued.

also paid $42,500 in 1979 for placement of its Marlboro brand in *Superman II*, while Liggett paid $30,000 in 1983 to have its Eve cigarettes appear in *Supergirl*. Because tobacco

*Pacific Heights* (1990, director John Schlesinger on the set with Melanie Griffith). Pest-control company Orkin did receive its $20,000 placement in this film but sued Fox, Schlesinger, and producing company Morgan Creek after it felt the placement was detrimental to its image.

ads had to carry federally mandated health warnings, observed Luken, any ads lacking the warnings violated the Federal Cigarette Labeling and Advertising Act. Also, no cigarette ads were allowed on television, and movies eventually showed up there. Luken acknowledged his placement protest would not apply if there were no contractual agreements and if there were no payments between the tobacco companies and the filmmakers for the placements. Steve Weiss, manager of media relations at Philip Morris USA, said placement was not advertising but product promotion, stating the money to pay for the two placements cited by Luken "probably came from the promotion budgets, not from the advertising budgets." John Kochevar, vice president of corporate affairs for the firm, earlier responded to Luken by saying it was not corporate practice "to make such payments in connection with the placement of its products or signage," with the implication those were isolated incidents. Also, he denied that Philip Morris had tried to "influence producers or script writers to include ... scenes in which smoking or related products were to be depicted."[35]

Around the same time CSPI appeared again to join the attack on product placement. CSPI petitioned the Federal Communications Com-

mission (FCC) to rescind an exception to its rules and require broadcasters to air sponsorship disclosures with any movie containing "paid
product placements." The Washington-based self-described consumer
advocacy group urged that the disclosure be superimposed on the screen,
as were subtitles for foreign-language films, with every paid appearance
or mention of a product or brand in a movie. For over 25 years, the FCC
had limited payola in programs produced directly for television by requiring that the practice be disclosed to the viewing public, explained Bruce
Silverglade, CSPI legal director. "Now that payola is rampant in Hollywood films, the FCC should apply the same standard to Hollywood films
when they are shown on TV," he added. Charles Mitchell, CSPI staff
attorney, said, "We think it is important that people know when advertising material is appearing in broadcast movies."[36]

At the same time CSPI also called on the FCC to assist the Justice
Department in investigating the issue initiated by Luken, whether paid
placements involving cigarettes violated the statutory ban against advertising cigarettes on television. In a related move, CSPI asked the state
attorneys general to determine whether product placements in movies
constituted deceptive advertising in violation of state laws and urged
them to work for sponsorship disclosure in cinemas. Under the FCC's
rules implemented in a 1960 sponsorship identification statute, the television stations had to make disclosures—"Promotional consideration paid
for by..." was the standard language for products and brand names in
programs if the stations (or program producers) received some consideration and if the products or brand names were not "reasonably related"
to the programs. The rules made an exception for movies produced principally for theaters, however. "The waiver is no longer in the public interest because circumstances have indeed changed," said CSPI in its
petition.[37]

CSPI lawyer Mitchell argued further, "It's an insidious form of
advertising. It hits the consumer when he doesn't expect it, when he
doesn't have his guard up. But advertisement should not masquerade as
entertainment. People have a right to know when a message has been
paid for, and who's trying to persuade them." Placement agencies argued
that manufacturers did not pay a film producer to use their product.
Rather, those makers paid them. The Entertainment Marketing Group,
a New York–based placement firm, took a relatively small annual fee and
then billed the client depending on the degree of exposure. For example, $2,500 for a product that was shown in the background of a scene
or $18,000 for "hands on use" of the product, together with a "verbal
mention." That company scored for its client in *Wall Street*, in a bar scene
where actor Martin Sheen yelled to the bartender, "Get this kid a Mol-
son Light!" Writing in *American Film*, Jon Silberg expressed his dis-

pleasure with the field when he wrote, "Some purists are already convinced that the situation is very serious. A movie, after all, should be a full dramatic experience.... There are few places left in life where we hope to find sanctuary" from ads.[38]

Requests and petitions from Luken and CSPI sparked a good deal of debate. Business journalist Ann Lallande worried that more was at stake than just semantics—that once placements were declared advertisements they became subject to a variety of regulatory requirements and rulings. Barry W. Lynn, legislative counsel for the American Civil Liberties Union, argued Luken and CSPI were stretching the definition of advertising and "it would intrude on the recognized artistic freedom of motion picture producers to force them to run a collection of warnings subscripted over the movie or even before the movie." On the other hand, Siva K. Balasubramanian, assistant professor of marketing at the University of Iowa's College of Business Administration and co-signor of the CSPI petition, commented, "We are watching the fringes of a phenomenon that will permeate across several art forms like a disease." If that happens, he warned, "We won't be able to recognize what is art and what is advertisement."[39]

All the furor raised by Luken and CSPI produced no results, except perhaps one. When released the James Bond film *Licence to Kill* contained in the closing credits a warning against smoking. Luken said the warning was placed in the picture because of his earlier complaints. But Saul Cooper, a spokesman for the film's producer Michael G. Wilson said the warning label was attached because the James Bond character had reverted to smoking heavily after several films in which he had not smoked. "There's a sense of social responsibility," explained Cooper. He denied the warning label had been prompted either by Luken's campaign or the Justice Department. "We were not compelled nor even requested to put it on by anybody," insisted Cooper. Noting that such a warning in a film was unprecedented, Benjamin Cohen, a spokesman for Luken, observed that "it seems strange that the only time this would happen is when $350,000 changed hands."[40]

It wasn't a scriptwriter who chose to showcase Mumm's Champagne in *Moonstruck*. "In the script, another champagne was used," explained Sam Baldoni of the Baldoni Entertainment placement firm, who represented Seagram's (Mumm's), "and we asked them to change it." They did. Typical of the industry mindset was the view expressed by Russ Krasnoff: "If an advertiser is willing to pay money and support the marketing effort on a film to have his product appear rather than a competitor, I'm all for it." Angelo Anastasio, national entertainment promotion director for Adidas, managed to place a whole Adidas commercial in Orion's *Johnny Be Good*. "It tied in visually so well," said Orion executive Jan Kean. "You didn't even know you were seeing a commercial." Why would film producers and studios sell out to the product placement firms who usually dictated their products be shown in a "positive manner," wondered reporter Lois Sheinfeld. Observed Rusty Citron, vice president of marketing at New World studios, "At a time when sky-rocketing costs are making it more difficult than ever to finance films and market them effectively, the clout of corporate America is a valuable resource."[41]

Entertainment reporter Edmond Rosenthal wondered what the cost-per-1,000 (or CPM, in advertising jargon) was if Batman took a swig of a specific maker's beer in the latest movie. Well, he figured, for the movie alone that cost could be $10 to $15 per 1,000, but if you factored in foreign release, videocassettes, pay television, and network television, it could be more like a cost of 10 cents to 15 cents per 1,000—provided the network did not cut the scene for the television broadcast. That was what, he said, product placement was coming to: "Although advertising agencies are yet to recognize its validity, product placement brokers are starting to come up with research that's on the same wavelength as TV advertising." Television networks had various rules to follow, Rosenthal explained, so placement there was less pervasive. Under those regulations the networks had to disclose on air in a program's credits if fees or other consideration had been accepted in exchange for placement: "The networks all claim they go well beyond this, even to the extent of cutting gratuitous product exhibition out of theatrical movies when they can do so without disturbing continuity." Alan Gerson, vice president of program standards and marketing policies at NBC, said that some of the theatrical movies being offered to his network had been vetoed altogether by the Standards and Practices department because they were over-commercialized."[42]

Mary Barnum, director of national promotion at Fox studios, was responsible for coordinating all product placement in the company's films. She told Rosenthal she knew of "few" straight fees that came near the rumored highest-ever payment of $250,000 and that for Fox "fees of $5,000, $10,000, $15,000 and $50,000 are more realistic." Rob Friedman, president of worldwide marketing at Warner Bros., noted that most suppliers paid cash for their involvement in Warner films and that there was a sliding fee scale based on quality of exposure. "Almost all of Warner movies have some product placement," he added. Although it was not a formal rule, Friedman explained, "We're not in the cigarette business" and "We're cautious in the way alcohol is used."[43]

As the MGM/UA film *Rocky V* began its shooting schedule early in 1990 Bill Minot, a special consultant to the studio, was handling national product placement in *Rocky V*. He said there would be the opportunity

*Bye Bye, Love* (1995, Randy Quaid, Paul Reiser, Matthew Modine, left to right). McDonald's played a major role in this movie.

to show 10–25 product logos during the film, but some might end up on the cutting room floor. Negotiations were then underway with many firms. Marketers were said to be especially eager to have their products seen in *Rocky V*, noted an account: "It's the final chapter in a great American story. It's safe, it has an upside to it…. You can see exactly what you're getting in your mind."[44]

As 1990 began Disney launched its new policy of banning onscreen ad trailers, with the resultant heavy publicity. At the very same time its Buena Vista distribution unit was soliciting paid product placement in its new film *Mr. Destiny*. Companies such as Campbell Soup, Nabisco Brands, and Kraft General Foods Group had reportedly all been contacted. Many executives were angered by the action and the perceived hypocrisy since they saw little distinction between product placement and an onscreen ad. Said one executive at a major consumer products company contacted by the studio, "Disney won't allow commercials in theatres, but the film can amount to one big ad." A marketing director at a Fortune 500 company who had worked with Disney in the past commented, "Disney is showing its ability to talk eloquently out of both sides of its mouth." Buena Vista was then offering marketers product placement in *Mr. Destiny* (James Belushi) at prices ranging from $20,000 to

$60,000. The cost structure, as outlined in a letter to marketers, was broken down as follows; $20,000 for a visual, $40,000 for a brand-name mention, and $60,000 for an actor to use the product. Screenvision president Alex Szabo asserted, "In the industry, Disney is widely known for broad product-placement opportunities, which is a very subversive form of advertising." Some advertisers applauded Disney's move to ban screen ads while still allowing placement. Explained an executive at one of the country's largest food companies, "It gives companies getting product placement exclusivity. They are assured that their placements will not be next to a cinema commercial for a competing product."[45]

With the help of its in-house placement arm, the Pepsi-Cola Entertainment Marketing Group, the Pepsi trademark appeared in close to 70 films in 1989, according to executive vice president Brad Brown. Among the more noteworthy, in his view, were *Back to the Future II* and *Big* (1988), in which actor Tom Hanks had a Pepsi vendor right in his living room. While a visual placement was good, a verbal mention was even better. "Verbal mention will usually be more effective and will stand out more in the minds of the people who have seen the film," said Brown. However, he was quick to point out that Pepsi was not in the business of rewriting scripts: "I would like to say that we got it into a script, but in most cases it's already there. If we did, it would be very expensive." Doug Christoph, manager of motion picture and video entertainment at Miller Brewing Company, said Miller's trademarked brands had appeared in over 50 movies in 1989. According to him Miller was very careful about the way its product was depicted: "If it's a scene involving drinking and driving we'll either try to change the scene or pull the product."[46]

Paramount's *Days of Thunder* (Tom Cruise) had heavy placement involvement, including firms such as Chevrolet, Hardee's, Coca-Cola, and Exxon. According to placement firms, companies tripped all over each other to get into the film because *Thunder* "is like a harmonic convergence—it's a perfect marriage of movies and advertising." While Paramount agreed that "big deals" had been made on the movie, it would not discuss specifics. In *Teenage Mutant Ninja Turtles*, the heroes not only ate Domino's Pizza but they also got a discount when the pizza came late—standard Domino policy. According to sources, said reporter Michael Fleming, "The script was doctored slightly to include the humorous plug, for which Domino paid a sum in the mid-five figures." That type of practice annoyed Peggy Charren, president of Action for Children's Television (a group that monitored children's programming), who said, "It's wrong that the picture people get paid for putting Domino's in the film. It has gotten to the point where it influences the story, where they'll say 'Let's do this instead of that, so we can make 20 deals.'" According to

Joe Allegro, co-owner of Entertainment Marketing Group which, he said, placed products in about 150 films in 1989, "The average film can realize $200,000 in product placements."[47]

When a reporter analyzed Universal's *Back to the Future II*, he concluded, "The heavy-handedness of the product-plugging dominates the first half of the movie." At least eight different brands turned up in the first 10 minutes. It led *Adweek* to warn that if the trend continued, "There won't be any movies as we know them, just prolonged ads." Journalist James Bone added that "no important picture is untouched," by product placement.[48]

Goldie Hawn whipped out her gold MasterCard 12 times in the movie *Bird on a Wire*, an advertising ploy paid for by MasterCard. However, the credit card company would not reveal how much it paid. According to Eva Steortz, director of marketing services at Cato Johnson Entertainment (the ad agency that offered the deal to MasterCard), American Express also was approached for the spot but lost the bid to MasterCard. Ted Jablonski, a spokesman for the credit card, said the spot fit the image his organization was trying to project. Hawn's character, said the account, "is a well-to-do lawyer who uses her card to buy everything from gas to chic clothes in pricey boutiques."[49]

Scholar and media critic Mark Crispin Miller, head of media studies at Johns Hopkins University, concluded in 1990 that mainstream cinema had become another mechanism for moving products. And in Hollywood of the day, even classic fairy-tale plots were subject to advertisers' dictates. *The Little Mermaid* originally had a very sad ending, said Miller, but "It was junked for the sake of the movie, and it's no coincidence that the movie was in a tie-in for a fast-food chain." Happy endings were always thought to be more conclusive to consumption and purchasing.[50]

When Ray-Ban placed its Wayfarer model sunglasses on Tom Cruise in *Risky Business*, those glasses, a 1952 design, were felt by their maker to be at the end of their life, with annual sales having dropped to 18,000. But after *Risky Business* was released it took sales to 360,000 in 1983. By 1989, after a number of films featuring Wayfarers, sales had reached the four million mark. Mark Smith, manager of David Clulow's eyewear shop in King's Road, Chelsea, London, said "As soon as people see a pair they like in a film, we start selling. When *Top Gun* came out, Ray-Ban sales went crazy." Using a placement firm, Ray-Ban was said to be able to implant its glasses in 160 films a year. Gary Mezzatesta, vice president of Unique Product Placement, was the agent who tried to get Ray-Ban into films. He denied that Bausch & Lomb, which made Ray-Bans, paid its way into movies, only to admit later that "in one or two cases" it was true. Other sunglass makers were said to be trying to do the same thing.

One of them, Persol, claimed that the producers of *Scenes from a Mall* (Woody Allen's latest, unreleased film) had asked "a very high fee" to have Allen wear Persol sunglasses in that film.[51]

Bill Derasmo, vice president of marketing for the Best Western hotel chain, said his company first considered film advertising two years earlier, in 1988. (Arnold Schwarzenegger plugged Best Western—and Hilton—in a trip to Mars in *Total Recall*.) At that time he sought out product placement firms for advice and guidance. Two years later, as a known film advertiser, he worked with placement firms like Motion Picture Marketing and received roughly 30 scripts a month. Negotiations for placements were typically completed with unfinished scripts, explained Derasmo, and he was presented with a number of page options. Often, though, where a product actually turned up in the film changed from start to finish, due to the unfinished nature of the project. "You don't want to hit the public over the head with your product. We are striving for subtle introductions of our logo into places where it belongs," added Derasmo. "*Total Recall* did not accomplish this for us. The film company decided to put us elsewhere in the script." (The Best Western sign showed up in Venusville, Mars's red light district.) "There is a tremendous risk in this business because you don't have total control of the final product," he warned. Derasmo felt that way because he discovered that, during the creative process, film content could change significantly. He had been under the impression that *Total Recall* was not supposed to be that violent. "In the future, we will stick to family entertainment." Prior to the making of that movie Derasmo bartered $10,000 worth of hotel rooms with Tri-Star Pictures in exchange for five seconds of screen time. Because Best Western lost 2.5 seconds of that exposure to the editing room floor, Tri-Star promised the hotel chain screen time in a future release.[52]

Clearly Derasmo was not happy with at least one of his company's placements. Others felt the same, and went so far as to launch legal action. Late in 1990 Black & Decker Corporation (B&D) started a lawsuit against Fox and a division of the Young & Rubicam ad agency (Krown/Young & Rubicam Marketing Group, known as the Cato Johnson Entertainment Group at the time of the suit) for failure to follow through on a product placement involving the summer 1990 hit film *Die Hard 2*. B&D alleged the non-placement cost it more than $150,000 that had been invested in a promotional campaign tied to the appearance of its Univolt cordless drill in the film starring Bruce Willis. Damages of $150,000 were sought.[53]

When Krown first approached B&D on Fox's behalf, the company initially declined to get involved, according to court documents. "We were reluctant to participate because of past experiences ... where we

*Men in Black* (1997). More famous for its Marlboro cigarette placement, other items also appeared, such as Hanover's Hard Pretzels.

jumped through hoops ... and our products didn't make it," into the movies, said Ellen Foreman, ad manager for B&D's power tools division. But discussions continued with B&D reportedly seeking a Fox guarantee of placement. Also, they discussed the promotion and ad campaign that B&D would undertake to tie together the product and the movie. In an October 18, 1989, letter to B&D Krown noted the cordless drill would be used by Bruce Willis to unhinge an access door to tunnels Willis had to crawl through to thwart the bad guys. "This hands on usage is a heroic effort that will make a memorable impact upon the film's audience," said the letter. "Research indicates that this type of film exposure results in brand recall 2 1/2 times greater than that of advertising." That letter also advised B&D that its $20,000 placement fee was "contingent upon B&D achieving prominent and identifiable brand identification with hands-on usage of the drill." Finally, around January 16, 1990, Black & Decker obtained a firm commitment from Fox that guaranteed the placement and appearance of the B&D product, "including a close-up photographic show of the product within the film." Thinking that the deal was finalized B&D began planning its promotional efforts in March 1990. A January 16 letter from Susan Todd, associate producer of *Die Hard 2*, said the studio would commit to a "close-up shot of the B&D drill ... with

*Twilight* (1998, Paul Newman, Susan Sarandon). Note the pack of Camel cigarettes.

the understanding that B&D will commit to a summer promotion supporting our film." After Fox had worked with B&D to create copy and mechanical art for the campaign, according to the suit, Fox cut from its movie the portion of the scene that contained the implanted B&D power tool. "This is a chronic problem in the industry. We have decided that we won't get into a paid product placement anymore," declared Foreman. "It's a crapshoot ... time, money and energy that doesn't pay out. But if a film calls and asks for a product for free, we'd send it."[54]

An editorial in the trade journal *Advertising Age* complained about there being too much product placement in motion pictures and that something like the B&D lawsuit was bound to happen sooner or later. With regard to the $20,000 fee paid by the power tool company, the editor declared "Money-grubbing for that pittance of extra revenue doesn't seem worth the possibility of distorting a fragile story line to accommodate a 'placement.' Let the movies be movies, not the Home Shopping Network."[55]

Product placement firms worried the B&D suit might hamper efforts to recruit new corporate clients to the world of placement, especially as the lawsuit came just after legal action by Orkin, the pest control firm. The Orkin suit was filed against Fox, Morgan Creek, and director John

Schlesinger in September 1990, following the release of *Pacific Heights*. Unlike B&D, Orkin received its placement. However, the company was shown failing to rid an apartment house of cockroaches. Samuel V. Baldoni, owner of the placement firm Baldoni Entertainment, grumbled, "The corporate world must realize that we're not making commercials, we're making movies."[56]

Reportedly Orkin paid $20,000 for its implant into *Pacific Heights* and then sued for an alleged breach of contract in which the movie did not honor its commitment to portray the company in a favorable light. Orkin felt there were "disparaging references" to itself in the picture and that the defendants failed to make promised script changes to protect the company's reputation. Not only did the Orkin man fail to get rid of the pests, but in one scene he exclaimed "Oh, shit!" as he opened a cabinet and a horde of cockroaches rushed out. Later, the audio expletive was eliminated when the movie was released on video. Said Orkin spokesperson Judy Donner; "That experience has certainly made us gun-shy with product placement. We've been approached (by other filmmakers seeking product placement), and we're reluctant to take that risk again." Both the B&D and Orkin suits were eventually settled out of court, with the terms not revealed.[57]

As cigarettes came under increasing fire the Tobacco Institute (lobby group for the makers) announced, late in 1990, a series of voluntary, youth-oriented restrictions on cigarette sales, movie placements, and other marketing practices. Those voluntary steps came in the face of pending and threatened federal legislation. The Institute declared its 13 member firms would end the practice of paid product placement of tobacco products in films. However, it added that the unpaid placement of tobacco products in movies would not be affected.[58]

A growing scrutiny of the practice reached the point in 1991 where Federal and state lawmakers were being compelled to take notice. Already feeling the pressure, cigarette makers had told the Federal Trade Commission (FTC) that they had eliminated paid implants. The latest salvo came in May that year when the Center for the Study of Commercialism (CSC—a Washington, D.C.-based group founded in 1990 to oppose "the overcommercialization of American life") announced it would petition the FTC to declare placement an unfair business practice and to require the onscreen disclosure of products advertised in the films. The Tobacco Institute had adopted its policy after the FTC began investigating such questions as whether films containing cigarette placements required health warnings and whether such films violated the ban on broadcast tobacco advertising when those pictures appeared on the small screen. Michael Jacobson, cofounder of CSC, argued, "We contend that there is an economic harm. Moviegoers are being persuaded to develop a highly favorable opinion of a product by having the product associated with the glamour of Hollywood and the fame of actors. That obviously accrues to the advantage of the marketer, because moviegoers are likelier to buy that product."[59]

CSC called product placement "stealth advertising" and "plugola." Jacobson declared, "We're asking the film studios to just be fair to the public. Don't pretend you're showing art when it's really advertising." In its petition filed with the FTC the CSC asked the agency to probe product placement in five of the six top-grossing movies in 1990. Those films (*Ghost, Pretty Woman, Home Alone, Teenage Mutant Ninja Turtles,* and *Total Recall*) were said to have a combined total of 148 references to brand name products. Also, CSC suggested the disclaimer it wanted to see before each film advising viewers of any paid (advertising) should be "clearly displayed" and "clearly audible" and could read: "The motion

picture you are about to see contains paid advertisements for the following products or companies." Joining the CSC in its plea for FTC regulations was the Consumer Federation of America.[60]

However, in December 1992 the FTC announced it had denied the CSC petition. Lee Peeler, associate director for advertising practices at the FTC in Washington, D.C., said the commission had found a lack of a pervasive pattern of deception and would consider those matters "on a case-by-case basis."[61]

Prior to the release of that decision the placement industry was under enough pressure that it felt a need to polish its own image. To that end, industry executives formed the Entertainment Resources and Marketing Association (ERMA) in September 1991, a trade group designed to improve the image

*Boeing-Boeing* **(1965, Jerry Lewis, Dany Saval). According to tobacco industry documents, Jerry Lewis was one of many Hollywood celebrities given free cigarettes in the 1980s for personal use in the hope that such people would smoke more often in their films, and include more smoking scenes.**

of, and set consistent standards for, product placement. Still in the formative stages, the group had an ad hoc committee of 10 people (from nine placement firms and one advertiser, Anheuser-Busch) who were attempting to create "a code of standards and ethics and a mission statement," said organizer Frank Devaney, a vice president at Rogers & Cowan. Devaney denied the association was in response to the FTC's investigation. Mostly, he said, the organization wanted to clear up the image because consumers "only know what people tell them, and that's mostly been that product placement is sleazy. I want to be able to say that it isn't."[62]

Two months later the fledgling ERMA was urging its members (now with 17 members, 15 placement firms and two advertisers—AT&T being the other) to place "positive social messages," along with the brand names in films and television shows. For example, Anheuser-Busch urged filmmakers to incorporate responsible drinking messages in scenes where its products were placed. All 17 members of the group planned to start to promote "social issues in general," such as safe sex and anti-gang messages in scenes where they were appropriate, said Devaney. A waiting-room set, he suggested, could be decorated with posters warning of the dangers of smoking or gang violence, instead of generic artwork.[63]

A report on how advertisers could make their ads work better, called "The 15 Best Ideas for Improving Media and Marketing Effectiveness in 1992," was released by Myers Marketing and Research at the start of that year. One of the report's recommendations was to "recognize product placement in movies as a new medium." Jack Myers, president of the firm and author of the report, felt that recommendation might be the most controversial aspect of the study. Despite the criticism of placement, Myers said it was "really interesting" to him how many clients mentioned placement to him as a worthwhile idea.[64]

One of those critics was Sid Bernstein, chairman of the Executive Committee of the trade journal *Advertising Age*. He worried about the increasing spread of product placement in films and warned, "As I said some months ago, the single most public objection to advertising is its pervasiveness; if we keep this up we may well endanger the acceptance of and belief in all advertising. That could be serious indeed."[65]

Coca-Cola's aggressive courtship of Hollywood enabled it to leave rival Pepsi-Cola with no tie-in to a big summer release (a key selling time for soft drinks) in 1992. Coke outbid Pepsi for promotional partnerships with what were expected to be the hottest movies of 1992—Warner's *Batman Returns* and Fox's *Home Alone 2: Lost in New York*. In Hollywood Coke was said to be known as an accommodating tie-in partner, allowing its brands to act in a supporting role to the movies. On the other hand, Pepsi had a reputation for insisting on starring roles. An unidentified

Hollywood promotion executive remarked, "Coke is more part of your life, while Pepsi want you to be a part of their life."[66]

A 1993 survey asked 171 people how they felt about placement in the movies. Researchers Eugene Secunda, of Baruch College in New York, and Israel Nebenzahi, of Bar-Ilan University of Israel, said the results suggested filmgoers did not object to paid product placements if they were "unobtrusive." Those respondents also preferred placements to onscreen ad trailers, which were described as "annoying."[67]

Another new high in product placement was reached with the summer 1993 blockbuster, PG-13 rated, *Jurassic Park*. It had over 100 corporate tie-ins. Usually, marketers preferred family pictures (rated G or PG) for product placements. "The family entertainment segment is definitely growing," said Sid Kaufman, president of MCA/Universal merchandising. "Studios can cross-collateralize the assets created from a movie into their various businesses. Creating properties is creating assets." A source from the Ogilvy & Mather ad agency in Los Angeles added, "With a film like *Beverly Hills Cops*, you get the tees and sweatshirts, but not the lunch boxes."[68]

Free ad plugs also appeared on television in great frequency, according to a study by Northwestern University for the trade journal *Advertising Age*. Monitored by the researchers were the four broadcast networks' owned-and-operated stations in Chicago (ABC's WLS, CBS's WBBM, NBC's WMAQ, and Fox's WFLD) for a 24-hour period in April 1993. Ad plugs were defined as any mention of a service, brandname, or company that was not a paid product placement—that included coverage in news or feature stories, editorial reviews, game show, dramas, talk shows, and every other type of non-commercial programming. Plugs for not-for-profit organizations and charity groups were not counted, nor were any paid placements (theoretically identified on the credits, as required by law), nor were infomercials. Excluding the Fox outlet, the three other stations had a total of 904 ad plugs in the 24 hours (up 10.5 percent from 818 in a 1990 study). With Fox added the total was 1,035. The ABC station had 31.6 percent of those plugs; NBC, 30.8 percent; CBS, 24.9 percent; and Fox, 12.7 percent. Types of plugs, as a percentage of the total, were as follows: brand-name shown, 49.8 percent; brand-name spoken, 34.8 percent; label/logo shown, 9.5 percent; and design identifiable, 6.0 percent. Types of programs on which the plugs appeared, as a percentage of the total, were as follows: evening news, 39.9 percent; morning news, 15.5 percent; talk shows, 15.2 percent; one-hour drama series, 7.1 percent; news magazines, 6.8 percent; half-hour sitcoms, 4.8 percent; game shows, 2.7 percent; daytime soap operas, 2.5 percent; non-fictional dramas, 2.4 percent; movies, 1.7 percent; feature news, 1.1 percent; and children's programs, 0.3 percent.[69]

Warner Bros. *Demolition Man* opened in late 1993 with Sylvester Stallone and Wesley Snipes playing cops and robbers in the year 2032. Thanks to product placement by the Oldsmobile division of General Motors (through the placement firm Vista Group), 18 futuristic "concept cars," valued at over $69 million, appeared in the film, bearing the contemporary brand markings of models such as Buick and Chevrolet. Vista president Eric Dahlquist remarked, "We felt like being involved in this movie, set in the future, would send a subtle message to the public that G.M. was alive and well in 2032."[70]

According to a 1993 account by reporter Bernice Kanner, Pampers paid $50,000 to be featured in *Three Men and a Baby*, Cuervo Gold paid $150,000 to be implanted in *Tequila Sunrise*, and Exxon paid $300,000 for placement in *Days of Thunder*. Danny Thompson, president of the product placement firm Creative Entertainment Services, remarked that no money was paid up front, so if a product wound up on the cutting-room floor, there was no cost to the marketer. In *Demolition Man* Stallone and Snipes ate a futuristic burrito from Taco Bell, supposedly the only restaurant chain left. (It was also reported to be the largest fast-food restaurant willing to appear in an R-rated movie.) "Product placement is less intrusive than paid ads because the products are so realistically used," argued Patti Ganguzza, vice president of entertainment marketing at AIM Promotions. "It's subtler than commercials, and while the scenes may seem fleeting, TV syndication, reruns, and home video give them a far longer viewing life. What's more, because they're part of the show, they won't get zapped." Dahlquist added that product placement used to be a "black science." But then it became more business-like, more systematic. "Product placement isn't conducted from the corner phone booth anymore."[71]

Frank Devaney, senior vice president of product placement at the Rogers & Cowan agency—who had worked in placement since 1956—said in 1994, "Today it's very sophisticated. We read all the scripts, we go to the sets if we are allowed, we watch it being shot and we track it all the way through edit. As early as we can, we try to see a print and we'll have a report for our client on whether they're in (the movie) or not."[72]

Cigarette placement in the movies came under scrutiny again when internal memorandums from the Brown & Williamson Tobacco Corporation revealed the company spent $1 million over four years to place its cigarettes in the movies. Those internal documents, which came to light in 1994, were audits the company conducted to see if it was getting its money's worth in placing images of cigarette packs and billboards in movies. It concluded it was not. Company spokesman Thomas Fitzgerald said the $1-million expenditure "was a total failure." According to the documents the way it worked was that Brown & Williamson asked an intermediary in Hollywood to seek out directors and producers to arrange for the placement of cigarette packs and billboards in films, and in some cases to show actors smoking. The producers then designated who was to receive money or gifts. In one deal, Associated Film Promotions (AFP was then out of business) arranged with Sylvester Stallone for Brown & Williamson cigarettes to appear in a "significant way" in five of his films and to "incorporate personal usage for all films other than the character of Rocky Balboa in *Rocky V*, where other leads, will have product usage," possibly at ringside. For the five films the price tag was $500,000. The films, and their proposed titles in 1983, were: *Rhinestone Cowboy*, *Godfather III*, *Rambo*, *50/50*, and *Rocky V*. Mainly, the money was delivered in the form of expensive gifts. For example, $24,200 in jewelry was listed in the audit as given to Stallone; he also was listed as receiving a $7,290 watch, a $97,000 car, and an $80,000 American saddlebred horse. Cash payments of $2,000 and $8,000 were made to the property master and the producer of one of the Stallone films, according to the audit.[73]

Also according to the audit was that deals had been made for 22 films between 1979–1983 with the Stallone deal by far the largest. Among the larger payments were $100,000 for *Harry and Son*, which included $50,000 in air travel tickets and a $42,307 car for Paul Newman. About $20,000 was paid for the James Bond picture *Never Say Never Again* (Sean Connery), with jewelry for Connery listed as having a value of $7,170. Other films and the amount spent for placement in them included: *The Tempest*, $70,000; *Shaker Run*, $5,000; *Blue Skies Again*, $7,500; *Smokey and the Bandit III*, $10,000; *Tank*, $25,000; *Where the Boys Are*, $100,000; and *Sudden Impact*, $50,000. According to the tobacco company's auditors, there were no written agreements about product placement with movie companies or producers and the placements received were often disappointingly fleet. For example, in *Never Say Never Again* the auditors stated that a pack of Super Kool Lights appeared onscreen for one or two seconds but that it was not possible to read the word Kool. Brennan Dawson, an official of the Tobacco Institute, said all the major tobacco firms had agreed since 1990 not to do any paid placements of tobacco products in films. Fitzgerald declared the practice had been stopped by Brown & Williamson about 10 years earlier (about 1983). "Obviously, it is something we tried but it just didn't work for us," he explained. "It didn't seem an effective way of spending our money." Ellen Merloe, a spokeswoman for Philip Morris USA said the domestic branch had never paid for placement in the movies. However, another subsidiary, Philip Morris International, had paid for placement in movies made outside the United States. Films that included those paid cigarette placements from the Philip Morris International subsidiary were

*Superman II* (character Lois Lane chain-smoked Marlboro Lights) and the James Bond movie *Licence to Kill.*[74]

Fox's *The Chase* (Charlie Sheen and Kristy Swanson) had a script that called for Sheen to kidnap Swanson and head for the Mexican border in her BMW. So the auto maker supplied three of its autos. Writing in *Business Week*, Ron Glover described that movie as "an unabashed 88-minute commercial for BMW's $32,000 325is." BMW spokesman Thomas McGurn observed that his company had turned down starring roles for its cars—for instance, when they would be used by drug dealers.[75]

ERMA, the product placement lobby group, remained alive and in 1995 had 25 product placement

*The Sting* (1973, Paul Newman). For allowing cigarette placement in his film *Harry and Son*, according to tobacco industry documents, Newman received a car valued at $42,307.

firms among its 48 members. Dean Ayers, president of ERMA, claimed, "Product placement has become institutionalized. Research has shown again and again that the American consumer does not mind product placement as long as it is not overdone." Seeing that a product was not "misused" in a film remained a major function of the placement firms. Cliff McMullen, chairman of the placement company UPP, remarked, "If we see something represented negatively, we'll drop a line to the studio production company, and most of the time they'll honor your request to remove that name." According to reporter Joan Oleck there were two reasons why that happened: "One reason is the fear of aggravating the agency, the other is litigation." When *Demolition Man* opened abroad Taco Bell was deleted, thanks to computer technology, and Pizza Hut showed up instead. That was because Taco Bell, unlike Pizza Hut, had no presence overseas so the reference would have been lost on foreign audiences.[76]

Dean Ayers, besides being president of ERMA, also worked full time as a product placer for one company, Anheuser-Busch. More typical was Norm Marshall of Norm Marshall & Associates, who had over 25 clients, from Ralston Purina to Chevrolet, from BMW to American Airlines. Even though Marshall and Ayers competed, they also cooperated if either saw a movie or television script with potential "image" problems. "The objective is to get good visibility. We're constantly monitoring the industry, reading scripts in advance and sometimes notifying the producer if we see something that's a problem," explained Marshall. "Like it's probably not a good idea to have a script where a 16-year-old is drinking beer and driving a car. We might suggest they use a soft drink. But we specifically keep them from using our beer. And I would call Dean and warn him." Placement took on added importance in light of the fact that some 80 percent of films shown in foreign countries were U.S. releases. So something like beer, which faced advertising restrictions in other countries, "can get their product visibility in these movies," remarked Ayers. Susan Monesco, research director for the Center for the Study of Commercialism said the CSC did a study in 1990 that revealed in *Total Recall* there were 55 references or exposures to 28 different brands, while *Home Alone* had 42 references to 31 products, either visually onscreen or in the dialogue.[77]

Business reporter Damon Darlin said in *Forbes* magazine in 1995 that product placement in films could run as high as $40,000 for an implant. The Subway sandwich chain and PepsiCo spent well over $5 million combined to promote their products along with Jim Carrey's *Ace Ventura: When Nature Calls*. In return, a Subway shop appeared incongruously in Africa, where the picture was set. Subway and Pepsi got to use clips from the picture in their ads. Ford Motor company clinched its appearance in the smash hit *Jurassic Park* by supplying 10 Explorers that retailed for about $35,000 each. An executive at one agency read the script for Columbia's 1993 *In the Line of Fire*. It contained a scene in which Clint Eastwood ate ice cream with costar Rene Russo on the steps of the Lincoln Memorial. Breyers Ice Cream won the bid (over the likes of Haagen-Dazs and Ben and Jerry's). According to Darlin, Breyers only cost was "enough ice cream for a cast and crew party." In *Tin Cup* (a movie about golf) golf equipment makers were "falling over each other" trying to get their products placed in the movie. Carlsbad, California's Taylor Made got its stuff placed in that picture; it paid a fee of $50,000, in addition to lending the equipment. Nearly one-quarter of the 1995 release *Bye Bye Love* was set inside a McDonald's restaurant. In return, the chain supplied an authentic set for the 15 days of shooting, said to be worth several hundred thousand dollars. Additionally, that movie (a bomb) had several dozen other products implanted in it, "from Cuisinart to Kettle Chips." Darlin also remarked, "Smart product placement people play another role: keeping products out of the movies." For example, liquor companies emphatically did not want their products to be shown in *Dolores Claiborne*, a movie that featured an alcoholic wife-abuser. AIM Promotions Patricia Ganguzza claimed she talked Woody Allen out of cracking a joke about having a heart attack on a StairMaster in *Scenes From a Mall*. Staying out of a film could be as important as getting into one, argued Darlin, and manufacturers had some clout in that respect. For one thing, it could be defamatory if a product were used in a way that would damage its reputation. "Studios routinely try to clear every product anyway," with the maker, said Darlin. "If they can't, they sometimes 'greek,' or obscure a product label."[78]

As of 1995 New York–based Apple Computer, Inc. had a full-time product placement person on its staff to get the Apple name and logo into films and television shows. As a result Macintosh computers had been featured in various movies including *Star Trek IV*, *The Firm*, *Jurassic Park*, *Sliver*, *Indecent Proposal*, *Get Shorty*, and *Assassins*. Suzanne Forlenza, the Apple placement executive, said Apple did not pay for implants but did provide "loaner" equipment. She thought the placement in *Assassins* was one of the better exposures for Apple because of the number of scenes featuring star Antonio Banderas working on his laptop. Forlenza described that deal as "a perfect example of what we strive for in product placement." Three computer companies (Apple, IBM, Compaq) had representatives that reviewed scripts to see how the computers would be used and how prominently they would be featured. Compaq spokeswoman Anne Sauve stated, "We want to be really careful. We don't want to be associated with porn or extreme violence or something that is making a social statement we don't want to be identified with."[79]

Graeme Atkinson, of the placement firm Prop Portfolio, declared, "Watch any film and 98% of the products are not there by accident." When the producers of *The Firm* decided to feature Red Stripe lager—instead of "the ubiquitous can of Budweiser"—its sales were reported to have jumped 50 percent.[80]

Another business writer, David Leonhardt, said in 1996 that script changes to accommodate product placement were becoming a far more accepted practice. MGM/UA wrote in an entire scene revolving around James Bond's BMW in *Goldeneye*. J. Sheinberg, the producer of *Flipper*, observed, "There are some [actors] who say, 'Wait a minute. We don't want to be connected with products.' We'll respect that decision, but often we want to find somebody who does." In *Flipper*, one scene contained a crumpled Coke can on the dock. After it was shot the producers signed a marketing deal with PepsiCo's Pizza Hut. So the crew of *Flipper* returned to its high-tech editing room and digitally changed the can label to the familiar Pepsi one—at a cost of roughly $40,000, shared by Pepsi and the film studio.[81]

Another deal that went wrong involved the hit movie *Jerry Maguire*. Cuba Gooding Jr. played Rod Tidwell, a football player who nursed a film-long grudge against Reebok for ignoring his talents and not giving him an endorsement deal. Tidwell's tirades against the firm continued until the closing credits when, with the help of his agent Jerry Maguire (Tom Cruise), he achieved his dream: a Reebok endorsement deal, promoted in an elaborate commercial in which Reebok declared, "Rod Tidwell. We ignored him for years. We were wrong. We're sorry." At least, said reporter Stuart Elliott, that's how Reebok executives said they thought the picture would end. But the film ended without any kiss-and-make-up Reebok spot. As a result, Reebok initiated a lawsuit against Tristar Pictures (Columbia/Sony) claiming the studio reneged on a promise to present Reebok in a positive light. Damages of some $10 million per complaint were asked for the 12 complaints in the "breach of contract" suit. Reebok said it provided Tristar with more than $1.5 million in merchandise, advertising, promotional support and other benefits.[82]

During the dispute Reebok insisted it was promised that highly complimentary ad, while Tristar stated it was understood that such an ending could finish up, as it did, on the cutting-room floor. According to the *Jerry Maguire* suit, the Reebok-Tristar agreement, reached in April 1996, called on Reebok to "flood America" with tie-ins that consumers would see before the film opened on December 13. There were tags on Reebok products promoting the film and a sweepstakes that customers could enter at sports stores; ads for the sweepstakes were placed in *Sports Illustrated* and *USA Today*. Former Reebok president Roberto Muller remarked that product placement could be "the greatest gimmick in the world. It's the aggregate of continuous exposure of your brand and your logo that separates you from the rest of the pack." Brenda Goodell, vice president for U.S. marketing communications at Reebok, added, "We live in a world where consumer products can define, or at least be outward badges, of a person's character." She had overseen what had been defined as successful Reebok placements in other movies, including: *A Time to Kill*, *Tin Cup*, and *Independence Day*. According to Goodell "A great deal about a brand's image gets defined by who's wearing it and using it. That's part of the fabric of who we are." *Jerry Maguire* had grossed around $116 million at the box office by January 1997.[83]

According to the lawsuit the only perceptions about Reebok that the film might instill in viewers were "highly derogatory and negative." The suit charged that Reebok's participation was contingent upon the movie having a happy ending. But on November 27, said the suit, just 16 days before the picture opened, Reebok executives were notified that the Tidwell happy-ending spot—shot by Reebok at the company's expense— had been edited out because it "no longer fit creatively in the film." That notice came after many of Reebok's tie-in promotions had hit the marketplace. The ending had Tidwell use a four-letter epithet to dismiss the company. Said Muller; "The swearing about Reebok sits in the minds of consumers. It's almost as if it were scripted by Nike." Reebok was only one of more than two dozen firms that implanted products in that film All the others, said Columbia Tristar, "couldn't be happier they were associated with it." Mark Workman, senior vice president for strategic marketing at the Columbia Tristar Motion Picture Group, observed that product placements must "balance the needs of advertisers with those of film makers. A sophisticated soft-drink or shoe maker realizes film makers at the end of the day have to be true to their visions."[84]

A ruling in February 1997 on whether to dismiss the *Jerry Maguire* product placement lawsuit had to be postponed because the U.S. district court judge making the decision fell asleep while watching the film. Then, later in 1997, on the day before the trial was to have started in Federal

*Rhinestone* (1984, Sylvester Stallone, Penny Santon, Dolly Parton, right). According to tobacco industry documents Stallone agreed, in 1983, to allow cigarettes to appear in a "significant way" in five of his coming films, for a total consideration of $500,000. One of them was *Rhinestone*.

court, Reebok and Tristar announced they had reached an out-of-court settlement, the terms of which were not disclosed.[85]

When the latest James Bond film, *Tomorrow Never Dies* (Pierce Brosnan) opened in December 1997, it did so after MGM/UA and a slew of high-profile promotional partners had put together a $100-million global marketing campaign. It was the most ever for a Bond film and twice as much as was spent on 1995's *Goldeneye*. After introducing its Z3 roadster in *Goldeneye* BMW expected to receive 5,000 preorders for the $29,000 vehicle. It received 10,000. One product placer in this movie was the clothing manufacturer Brioni. Marci Sutin Levin, Brioni marketing director, observed, "Here was a chance to clothe the world's best-dressed man. You see him running from an explosion in our cashmere coat, and he couldn't look better." Bond drove BMW's new 750il sedan, used an Ericsson cellular phone as a remote control device, detonated bombs with his Omega Seamaster watch, and used Smirnoff vodka in his cocktail of choice. With regard to a worry the film could be little more than a two-hour commercial, Karen Sortito, MGM/UA's executive vice president of worldwide promotions, commented, "That's a real fear. But each of our product placements is integral to the story. Nothing happens without the producers' okay." David Korb, vice president of marketing at Ericsson, added, "Bond movies don't bomb." BMW supplied the movie with about a dozen vehicles and used clips from the film in its multi-million-dollar ad campaign. Ericsson provided a centerpiece gadget: a phone that doubled as a stun gun, a remote control for the BMW, and a safe opener. The company undertook a multimillion ad push in 130 countries starring 83-year-old Desmond Llewelyn (a long-time regular in the Bond series, who played gadget creator Q). Smirnoff devoted its entire holiday ad campaign to *Tomorrow Never Dies*, including the distribution of recipes for Bond-themed cocktails. Visa credit card produced one of its most expensive television commercials ever for its tie-in—a 30-second high-tech "mini-movie" that starred Brosnan and Llewelyn. Omega timepieces worn by Bond and Bond girl Michelle Yeoh were publicized by the watchmaker in print and television ads. Trailers from the film played in 7,000 Omega stores. L'Oreal's new 007 cosmetics line—which featured eye shadow, nail polish, and lipstick with names such as Bond Bordeaux—were promoted in ads starring Yeoh. Heineken's multimillion-dollar campaign featured real people named James Bond. Both the beer and the credit card were seen in the movie.[86]

When the director of *Tomorrow Never Dies*, Roger Spottiswoode, was touring BMW's Munich, Germany, factory prior to shooting the film he took a liking to a prototype BMW motorcycle that he saw there. So, said reporter Joshua Hammer, "He promptly went back to his storyboards—and added a BMW motorbike chase through the crowded alleys of Ho Chi Minh City." As to the possibility of commercial overkill, Spottiswoode said, "It doesn't make me happy, but with large global production there's really no choice anymore."[87]

During 1997 the Clinton administration carried its crusade against tobacco to the film industry with the goal of curtailing gratuitous smoking onscreen. Vice President Al Gore addressed the issue of onscreen smoking at a private session with studio and network chiefs early that year in Los Angeles and requested a follow-up. Gore felt it was wrong to glamorize smoking, thereby making it appealing to youngsters. In the course of a single week viewers could see characters played by John Travolta, Julia Roberts, Meg Ryan, Brad Pitt, Bruce Willis, and Arnold Schwarzenegger smoke onscreen. Not only were the hip alien creatures in *Men in Black* seen to be smoking, but they also carted off identifiable cartons of Marlboro cigarettes to their home planets. A study published in the *American Journal of Public Health* in 1994 found that 38 percent of the lead characters in movies were portrayed smoking in the 1960s; 29 percent in the 1970s; and 26 percent in the 1980s. Study coauthor Stanton Glantz, professor at the University of California at San Francisco, said that while a follow-up study of the 1990s had not then been done, "We've seen a dropoff of brand placement in movies, but a big increase in smoking in films." Donna Shalala, U.S. Secretary of Health and Human Services, also met privately to express the administration's concern about onscreen smoking. One of the box-office draws then perhaps most associated with smoking was John Travolta, a non-smoker in real life. His characters could be seen smoking in *Get Shorty*, *Broken Arrow*, *Michael*, *Pulp Fiction*, and *She's So Lovely*.[88]

Tobacco companies, hoping that smoking scenes in Hollywood movies would increase sales, worked hard through the 1980s and early 1990s to get as much screen time for cigarettes as possible, according to a British medical report released in 2002, and at least one company went so far as to provide free cigarettes to actors and directors who might therefore be more inclined to light up when the camera rolled. Released by *Tobacco Control*, a British medical quarterly, the report was based on more than 1,500 formerly secret tobacco-industry documents that became available as a result of the master settlement agreement between tobacco companies and states' attorneys general in 1998. "In many ways it confirmed what we suspected all along," said Curtis Mekemson, a consultant for the American Lung association and the study's principal author. "The tobacco companies were well aware of the benefits of having audiences, especially young audiences, see their favorite stars smoking onscreen."[89]

Mekemson said at least one firm, R. J. Reynolds, worked through a Hollywood publicist to provide free tobacco in the 1980s to actors and directors including Jerry Lewis, John Cassavetes, Liv Ullmann, and Shelley Winters. "That was really one of the most insidious revelation," said Kori Titus, director of anti-smoking programs for the American Lung Association of Sacramento. "They wanted to make sure Hollywood stayed hooked on tobacco, because actors who smoke are more likely to smoke in public or want to smoke onscreen." The documents listed 188 actors, directors, and other celebrities, but it was reported to be unclear whether others might have received free cigarettes or when the program ended. Yet nothing in the report contradicted previous statements by tobacco companies that they ended paid product placement over a decade earlier. Researchers who studied the industry documents (which ended in the mid 1990s) were unable to find any evidence that tobacco companies continued providing free cigarettes or paying to place their products in films or television shows. But that had little impact on the frequency of smoking scenes, concluded the researchers. "Tobacco use in movies, which was falling through the 1970's and 1980's, increased significantly after 1990," said the report. "While there may be various reasons for this trend, the extensive groundwork laid by the tobacco industry in the 1980's and early 1990's certainly played a role." Titus said her group's effort then was to convince Hollywood to include warnings about tobacco use in its film ratings, a move vehemently opposed by Jack Valenti, as head of the Hollywood cartel group, the MPAA. [90]

As the 1990s progressed corporations were said to be turning more to independent (non-majors) films for product placement opportunities and those independents, said reporter Karen Hudes, "hope to form tighter bonds with sponsors than Hollywood ever has." Paul Speaker, director of marketing for The Shooting Gallery, the independent production company responsible for *Sling Blade*, remarked, "For independent film, we're really just scratching the surface of what we can do with corporate alliances." The key, he continued, "is not only to find opportunities to seamlessly place products, but more importantly to associate brand to the entire film relevance." An example of that direction was the independent film *The Faculty* (directed by Robert Rodriguez, released in 1998 by the Miramax/Dimension division of Disney), about high school students fighting off alien invaders. Clothing maker Tommy Hilfiger promoted the movie in a $10 million ad campaign. That deal came about when Hilfiger, a designer very popular among teenagers, heard the movie was in development and approached Miramax with a comprehensive proposal, seeking to provide most of the wardrobe. Hudes commented, "When Miramax joins Mr. Rodriguez for what could be seen as a feature-length commercial, it suggests that all barriers are down." [91]

Ted Hope, who helped found the independent production company Good Machine (which released *The Ice Storm* and *Happiness*), said, "We struggle with product placement all the time, and I know other producers and directors struggle with it. I actively discourage it now on our movies, but there are times when I contradict myself." Jim McKay, who directed the 1996 release *Girls Town*, believed "We're entering a period now in which sponsorship is just going unquestioned." In some cases, he said, free products had been helpful, but he noted that when filmmakers used them, "on some level or another, they're making an ad." McKay noted that the real problems came when directors made creative decisions based on sponsors' interests, and when those interests began to overwhelm the film. Another observation McKay made was that in the case of a truly independent film, a firm like Tommy Hilfiger would have nothing to do with it because a truly independent film was "about risk and difference, and something that doesn't conform."[92]

Apple remained king of computers in Hollywood in 1998. Macintoshes and PowerBooks turned up that year on 34 network television shows and 120 movies, compared with about 20 television shows and 22 films featuring computers from IBM. James Wooten, IBM product placement director, remarked, "We've had an aversion to things that are on the edge. We wanted to be careful not to endorse the wrong message." According to reporter Jennifer Tanaka, Apple paid no money for its placements but if a film or television producer would not make the brand identifiable on the screen, he would not get Apple products. Apple also liked its products to be associated with the good guys, like Tom Cruise in *Mission Impossible*. Suzanne Forlenza, product placement coordinator for Apple, commented, "Sometimes we are presented with ideas that are inappropriate. I was pitched a movie where the PowerBook was going to be used as an explosive device."[93]

One filmmaker not pestered by placement firms was Todd Solondz, the director of *Happiness*—a dark comedy about, among other things, a pedophile father—who chuckled, "There were not many product companies competing to have their merchandise in my movie." Kraft Foods, maker of Jell-O, initiated discussions with the makers of an upcoming film called *Jello Shots*, about a night of debauchery fueled by Jell-O. "Wary of such an unsavory linkage, Kraft wanted to ensure that its products would not be mentioned anywhere in the film—an act, if you will, of product displacement," said reporter Brian Palmer. Susan Safier, Fox vice president for product placement, declared, "At Fox we don't do handguns; we don't do cigarettes; we don't do hard alcohol. I don't go out and solicit companies to participate in these kinds of activities." Smith & Wesson (gun makers) used a placement firm, International Promotions, to puts its wares in the hands of stars. The company scored with the television show *Brooklyn South* and the film *For Richer or Poorer*, but fearing a bad press reaction the gun maker soon severed the arrangement.[94]

One of the latest films to be cited as exemplifying an excess of placement was the 2002 Steven Spielberg release *Minority Report* (Tom
Cruise). Elvis Mitchell, film critic with the *New York Times*, said, "The
movie turns product placement into omnipresent white noise," while
Christopher Goodwin, in the *Times* of London wondered if it was "A
movie or the world's most expensive advertisement?" According to a
report in *Variety*, 15 major companies paid as much as $25 million to
have their products featured prominently in the movie. That amounted
to 25 percent of the movie's budget. *Variety* called the placements "one
of the most extensive displays ever of this phenomenon." Among the
firms included were American Express, Gap, Guinness, Lexus, Nokia,
Pepsi, and Reebok. Professor Robert Thompson, director of the Center
for the Study of Popular Television at Syracuse University, New York,
described product placement as the only workable model for advertising on television with the existing technology that allowed viewers to
bypass commercials. "Product placement will become more prevalent
and more sophisticated," he said. All the major studios and television
networks had product placement divisions and, said Goodwin, the business may be worth as much as a billion dollars a year. "Having the leading character driving a car that you want to sell, or using a perfume, or
drinking a soft drink, is even better than a normal commercial," said
Thompson. "You are getting two things at once: a product message and
an endorsement from a movie star who won't normally endorse anything." In the James Bond films BMW was thought to have paid $20 mil-
lion so that Bond would switch from driving an Aston Martin to its new
sports car for the 1995 movie *Goldeneye*. Subsequently, Aston Martin
bought its way back in—Bond drove a Vanquish (worth 158,000 pounds
sterling) in the 20th Bond film *Die Another Day* (2003). From the tobacco
documents it was revealed the producers of the 1982 Bond film, *Never
Say Never Again*, were paid so that Sean Connery would smoke Camels
on the screen.[95]

# 9

# Conclusion

Advertisements in some form were present in cinemas from the very beginning of the motion picture industry. However, ad trailers and product placements hardly existed in the silent movie era. Ad shorts of one to two reels in length were the most dominant type of ad in this period. Still, even those were not very prevalent. One reason was that the mass advertising industry was just getting underway. Another reason was that the film industry was still in its infancy and as such was not very appealing to advertisers; there was not much money or potential in the medium at the time. Also, Hollywood's dominant cartel was not organized until 1922. The industry was still engaged in internal rationalization. During this early period the endorsement of items by movie stars, in off-screen media, became well established. Production and usage of industrial films (for in-house use only) by large manufacturers also grew and flourished. Both endorsements and industrial films helped to establish and reinforce the idea that motion pictures, and their stars, could be potent devices for causing the sale of consumer goods, fashion styles, and so forth, both directly (as a result of exposure to ad shorts and industrial films) and indirectly (from the exposure to the incidental appearance of such items in regular entertainment films).

Some observers felt there was little difference in the selling potential of those types of films; the obvious and direct pitch found in an ad short or the obscure, accidental pitch found in an entertainment film. Another piece of conventional wisdom to develop in the period, especially in the 1920s, was that ad shorts should be designed to look like entertainment films—that is, they should not be obviously advertisements. Thus, throughout the silent-film part of the 1920s advertising was relatively infrequently encountered in cinemas. Instead there was usually an ad short that went out of the way to convince the viewer that it was not an advertisement at all.

The coming of sound films in the 1927–1932 period ushered in a heightened enthusiasm for a union of advertising and motion pictures.

In some quarters the prospects seemed boundless. Ad trailers made their first appearance in an organized and systematic fashion, but only for a brief time, in a small number of locations. Their time had still not come. Product placement was somewhat more visible but still took a back seat to ad shorts. Agents for product placement briefly surfaced in the 1929–1931 period before disappearing for decades. Enthusiasm for talking ad shorts become great enough that the Hollywood cartel got officially involved with some of the majors producing ad shorts and exhibiting them in their owned theater chains. Independent producers of those ad shorts placed their output only in the non–Hollywood controlled cinemas. That split in the industry guaranteed no ad short could receive a true national distribution (as it could in magazines or on the radio) and that was one reason why the big national advertisers lost interest in the medium.

Paralleling the increased enthusiasm for ad shorts was a growing critical reaction. Newspapers threatened the cartel if it persisted in introducing ads into the cinema. Exhibitors and the public also complained. Fear set in and Hollywood backed away. Majors not involved with ad shorts criticized the majors who were involved. Hollywood worried there would be a public backlash if ads showed up in movie houses. Thus, a frightened cartel introduced rules for itself that imposed a ban on all advertising in the movies, whether an onscreen ad trailer or a product placement or anything else. However, the rules were vague enough to allow for exceptions. Another worry on the part of the Hollywood studios was that the independent firms involved in cinema ad production might take the next "logical" step and produce full-length feature films that would be supplied free to exhibitors, thus undermining the cartel's dominant monopoly position. It meant that if Hollywood could not control cinema advertising it would bar it altogether from every place it directly controlled, pressure everyone else to make sure that no non-cartel source would ever be more than a minor player in the field, and assure that cinema advertising itself would never grow. However, the cartel presented those actions in a different light, arguing, in altruistic fashion, that by barring all ads from the screen it was upholding the right of the public to receive 100-percent pure entertainment.

A period of stagnation marked the cinema advertising field until the end of World War II. Dissatisfaction with the fact that no national distribution system existed for the relatively few ads that existed could be seen in the occasional attempt by a national manufacturer, frustrated by a lack of national distribution, to try and develop a system away from cinemas completely—the free show at a rented hall, for example. Ad trailers experienced some growth and the advocacy or institutional ad short (selling Americans on the virtues of the U.S. capitalist system, for instance) made its appearance—a business response to the social unrest of the Depression era. The ads that did make their way into movie houses almost always did so in second-, third-, or later-run cinemas, and in small towns. That is, the prestigious first-run houses, and those in large cities, tended to not screen ads at all. It was yet another reason for major advertisers to not bother with cinemas.

A return to a post-war economy after 1945 led to more enthusiasm as the future for a union between ads and films once again seemed to be bright. But that all quickly collapsed as motion pictures suddenly experienced a sharp decline in their attendance, in a period before television was a factor. With the full arrival of the small screen, that attendance drop increased dramatically and became permanent. Advertisers quickly shifted their focus, attention, and ad budgets to television. Like radio, television came "free" to people and therefore, it was believed, the public accepted that a lot of ads would be involved. On the other hand, the filmgoer paid the full amount of the cost of a movie, through the ticket price, and thus it was felt he would not tolerate any advertising. As television caused a filmgoing decline, Hollywood responded by altering the film program it delivered. The short—including the ad short—was destined to be soon nothing more than a memory.

Stagnation in cinema advertising marked the field in the 1950s and 1960s as national advertisers continued to focus on television. A vain hope in the cinema world was that viewing all those ads on television would soften up people to the point where they would accept advertisements in theaters. Even product placement shifted focus to television. Things got so bad on the small screen that rules against payola had to be implemented—one reason for advertisers to reassess the big screen.

During the 1970s ad trailers underwent a small surge. Two new groups were formed to do more-or-less national distribution of onscreen ads. Both were vigorously opposed by the Hollywood cartel and one disappeared quite quickly. Also, there was still much exhibitor hostility towards onscreen ads, based on worries over an audience backlash. As a result onscreen ads were beaten back and were at a fairly low point around 1980-1981. Product placement underwent a surge of its own, starting around 1978. Leading that surge was the reappearance of product placement agencies (firms that acted as middlemen and tried to place products in the movies). This time there was no hostility to the practice from any industry elements. Because of that the surge was not beaten back. Growth in the practice of product placement continued. Placement agencies bragged they could go so far as to cause scripts to be altered to accommodate a placement, at least to a minor degree.

Within the modern period the onscreen ad made some headway but still faced hostility from some exhibitors and from at least some members of the Hollywood cartel. A studio could order a ban on onscreen ads run with any of its features while at the same time aggressively soliciting product placements for a fee for those features, without seeing any hypocrisy in those actions. What gains that did take place came from the fact the cartel opposition was not unanimous as it once had been—some of the majors then owned a lot of cinemas themselves. Yet onscreen ads made up a miniscule amount of the total money expended on advertisements in the U.S.—less than one percent, on the order of the amount spent on matchbook covers. Inherent limitations (such as no more than a maximum of about three minutes of ads before a feature films) indicated onscreen ads would likely never amount to much. Still, they stubbornly remained part of the scene.

What did flourish in the modern era was the practice of product placement. Hardly a film was released without the placement of items within it, often dozens of items. Hollywood studios were very open about the practice, even going so far as to sometimes issue price lists outlining how much it cost for a verbal mention, or hands-on use by a star, and so forth. Critics of the practice were all outside the industry and carried no weight at all. Lining up manufacturers to have their products placed in a film took on almost as much importance as did the lining up of a big-name star and director. Some critics worried that movies might become little more than long commercials. The later films in the James Bond series were prime examples. While onscreen ads never amounted to much in American cinema, that lack had been more than compensated for by the huge increase in product placement in the last couple of decades of the 1900s as the movie capital shifted from being Hollywood the Dream Factory to being Hollywood the Ad.

# Notes

## Chapter 1

1. "Breaking into the movies." *New York Times*, August 23, 1929, p. 20.
2. "Shoes advertised in movies." *New York Times*, October 13, 1913, p. 13.
3. "Food investigators to report Monday," *New York Times*, August 29, 1914, p. 14.
4. Darwin Teilhet. "Propaganda stealing the movies." *Outlook and Independent* 158 (May 27, 1931): 113.
5. "Camera! Action! Sales!" *Business Week*, May 27, 1939, p. 43.
6. *Ibid.*, p. 38.
7. Patricia Murray. "When advertisers tried films." *Printers' Ink* 205 (November 19, 1943): 25–26.
8. Bruce A. Austin. "Cinema screen advertising." *Boxoffice* 121 (April 1985) 29; Charles Musser. *History of the America Cinema: 1 The Emergence of Cinema: The American Screen to 1907*. New York: Charles Scribner's Sons, 1990, p. 360.
9. Dwight Wardell. "The business movie industry." *Dun's Review* 49 (October 1941): 24; William Bird. "Enterprise and meaning: sponsored film, 1939–1949." *History Today* 39 (December 1989): 26.
10. "Film pictures raise wages." *New York Times*, February 9, 1913, sec. 3, p. 13.
11. "Motion-pictures as business boosters." *Literary Digest* 65 (April 3, 1920): 92, 94.
12. "Film service for stores." *New York Times*, May 8, 1921, p. 11.
13. "Free industrial films." *New York Times*, June 25, 1923, p. 16.
14. "Films in business." *Times* (London), September 5, 1921, p. 6.
15. Lynn Meekins. "World markets for American manufactures." *Scientific American* 119 (December 7, 1918): 456.
16. *Ibid.*

17. David McFall. "The friendly way after the war." *Scientific American* 120 (June 21, 1919): 652.
18. Lewis R. Freeman. "Movie signboards." *Saturday Evening Post* 192 (June 17, 1920): 13.
19. *Ibid.*, pp. 13, 61–62, 67.
20. *Ibid.*, p. 67.
21. "Movies and foreign trade." *New York Times*, April 12, 1922, p. 4.
22. Julius Klein, "What are motion pictures doing for industry?" *Annals of the American Academy of Political and Social Science* 128 (November 1926): 79.
23. *Ibid.*, pp. 79–80.
24. Frank A. Tichenor. "Motion pictures as trade getters." *Annals of the American Academy of Political and Social Science* 128 (November 1926): 89.
25. "Collecting on picture names." *Variety*, February 14, 1919, p. 56.
26. "Seats' backs for ads in theatres." *Variety*, January 23, 1929, p. 1.
27. Janet Staiger. "Announcing wares, winning patrons, voicing ideals: Thinking about the history and theory of film advertising." *Cinema Journal* 29 (no. 3, Spring 1990): 12.
28. "Play to foster thrift." *New York Times*, March 29, 1914, p. 37.
29. "Advertising for Universal." *Variety*, June 28, 1919, p. 46.
30. "Screen advertising." *Variety*, August 22, 1919, p. 82.
31 "Against advertising films." *Variety*, December 5, 1919, p. 65.
32. Advertisement. *Variety*, December 26, 1919, p. 194.
33. "Inside stuff—on pictures." *Variety*, January 9, 1920, p. 56.
34. "Neilan on advertising films." *Variety*, January 23, 1920, p. 65.
35. "Publicity versus advertising in the movies." *The Outlook* 128 (June 8, 1921): 234.

36. "Advertising by film." *Times* (London), November 9, 1921, p. 10.

37. "English commercial firms in advertising pictures." *Variety*, May 26, 1922, p. 1.

38. Frank A. Tichenor, *op. cit.*, pp. 84–87.

39. "Advertising in movies." *Printers' Ink* 172 (August 15, 1935): 40.

40. "Collecting on picture names." *Variety*, February 14, 1919, p. 56.

41. "Inside stuff—on pictures." *Variety*, September 22, 1922, p. 43.

42. Janet Staiger, *op. cit.*, p. 12.

## Chapter 2

1. "Nat'l ad men for talkers." *Variety*, February 15, 1928, p. 9.

2. "Educational talkers." *Variety*, June 27, 1928, p. 3.

3. "Commercial talking shorts may soon be offered free for showings in theatres." *Variety*, May 8, 1929, p. 5.

4. "Hays calls movies big aid to business." *New York Times*, November 14, 1929, p. 24.

5. "Hays lauds movies as a trade stimulus." *New York Times*, March 30, 1930, p. 6.

6. "Tiring of advertising tie-up screen stars and studios refuse commercial offers." *Variety*, November 14, 1928, p. 4.

7. "Names in pictures are restricted from recommending commercial product by Hays' office resolve." *Variety*, October 6, 1931, p. 3.

8. "Stars' ad coin walloping Hays ban." *Variety*, January 19, 1932, p. 3.

9. "Auto exploitation talking film free show with names, stars and Follies beauts." *Variety*, January 23, 1929, p. 11.

10. Paul G. Hoffman. "Will the talkies talk their way into mass selling?" *Magazine of Business* 56 (August 1929): 149–150, 194.

11. "Commercial talking shorts may soon be offered free for showings in theatres." *Variety*, May 8, 1929, p. 5.

12. "Talkies to aid sales." *New York Times*, May 28, 1931, p. 30.

13. "2 new advantageous tie-ups as exploitation for films, theatres, stores and Publix." *Variety*, August 7, 1929, p. 189.

14. *Ibid.*

15. *Ibid.*

16. "Buy now campaign planned through Philadelphia movies." *New York Times*, July 30, 1932, p. 1.

17. "Lobbies as billboards for commercial firms' publicity." *Variety*, June 4, 1930, p. 61.

18. "Dynamite seen in newly offered free commercialized newsreels." *Variety*, April 8, 1931, p. 2; "Indies in N.W. raise defense fund." *Variety*, April 8, 1931, p. 23; "Rocky Mountain indies in meeting condemn double features, etc." *Variety*, May 20, 1931, p. 29.

19. "Allied news minus advertisers, so footage free." *Variety*, September 1, 1931, p. 3.

20. "Publix in with commercial film for revenue with own trailers." *Variety*, May 7, 1930, p. 35.

21. "Chi. exhibs cancel advertising shorts as direct source of grief." *Variety*, September 10, 1930, p. 32.

22. "Screen ads are satisfying to Publix." *Variety*, February 11, 1931, p. 11.

23. "Publix ad reels in minor spots first, loophole in Hays ban on screen plugs." *Variety*, September 20, 1932, pp. 12, 44.

24. *Ibid.*

25. Henry W. Hough. "Putting it over with movies." *Scientific American* 140 (May 1929): 428–429.

26. "Selling—with sound effects." *Business Week*, October 26, 1929, p. 37.

27. "The film world." *Times* (London), February 12, 1930, p. 12.

28. "Chains playing ad shorts." *Variety*, February 26, 1930, p. 9.

29. Peter B. B. Andrews. "The sponsored movie." *Advertising & Selling* 16 (December 10, 1930): 36, 38.

30. "Chains playing ad shorts." *Variety*, February 26, 1930, p. 9.

31. "See commercial advertising as vast amusement income source apply radio idea to theatre." *Variety*, May 28, 1930, pp. 2, 33.

32. "Talkies adopt radio methods in new sponsored programs." *Business Week*, July 30, 1930, p. 8.

33. "Commercial shorts slow showing; now in Par. houses to decide." *Variety*, November 12, 1930, p. 28.

34. "Ad reel rate—attendance." *Variety*, January 28, 1931, pp. 3, 21.

35. *Ibid.*

36. "Names for WB advertising shorts; five million circulation stated." *Variety*, February 4, 1931, p. 15.

37. "Screen advertising going to showdown." *Variety*, April 1, 1931, p. 4.

38. S. H. Walker and Paul Sklar. "Business finds its voice." *Harper's Monthly Magazine* 176 (February 1938): 318.

39. W. D. Canaday. "How Lehn & Fink

are using talking picture shorts." *Printers'
Ink* 154 (March 19, 1931): 17–18.
40. *Ibid.*, pp. 17–19.
41. *Ibid.*, pp. 19–20.
42. "Six advertising talkies get talked
about." *Printers' Ink* 154 (March 26, 1931):
75.
43. "Business anxiously watches reaction to sponsored shorts." *Business Week*,
April 8, 1931, p. 14.
44. Marsh K. Powers. "How far can
commercial sponsorship be extended?"
*Printers' Ink* 155 (April 30, 1931): 49–50.
45. "Ads on 50% of U.S. screens." *Variety*, May 13, 1931, p. 7.
46. Darwin Teilhet. "Propaganda stealing the movies." *Outlook and Independent*
158 (May 27, 1931): 112.
47. *Ibid.*
48. *Ibid.*, pp. 113, 126.
49. *Ibid.*, p. 126.
50. *Ibid.*, pp. 126–127.
51. "Fox off all ad shorts." *Variety*, February 25, 1931, p. 7.
52. "Screen advertising occupying attention of industry's solons: general protection of industry." *Variety*, February 25,
1931, p. 7.
53. "Double barrage for advertising on
screen by dailies and Laemmle." *Variety*,
March 4, 1931, p. 7
54. "Advertising shorts divide men in
both ends of picture trade." *Variety*, March
18, 1931, p. 5.
55. "All screen ads discontinued." *Variety*, April 15, 1931, p. 5.
56. "Rocky Mountain indies in meeting
condemn double features, etc." *Variety*,
May 20, 1931, p. 29.
57. "Loew circuit bans film advertising." *New York Times*, May 18, 1931, p.
19.
58. "Newspapermen and Publix agree
that public will decide screen ad future."
*Variety*, April 29, 1931, p. 4; "Publix ad reels
in minor spots first, loophole in Hays ban
on screen plugs." *Variety*, September 20,
1932, p. 12.
59. "Fox off all ad shorts." *Variety*, February 25, 1931, p. 7; "Screen advertising
occupying attention of industry's solons:
general protection of industry." *Variety*,
February 25, 1931, p. 7.
60. "Exhibs ask about ads in features."
*Variety*, March 25, 1931, p. 35.
61. "Dynamite seen in newly offered
free commercialized newsreels." *Variety*,
April 8, 1931, p. 2.
62. "Full length ad features." *Variety*,
May 6, 1931, p. 5.

63. "Refunding on comm. shorts." *Variety*, June 9, 1931, p. 7.
64. "Newspapers put an end to advertising movies." *Business Week*, July 8, 1931,
p. 22.
65. "Publix ad reels in minor spots first,
loophole in Hays ban on screen plugs." *Variety*, September 20, 1932, p. 44.
66. "Breaking into the movies." *New
York Times*, August 23, 1929, p. 20.
67. Donald Crafton. *History of the American Cinema: 4 The Talkies: American Cinema's Transition to Sound, 1926–1931.* New
York: Charles Scribner's Sons, 1997, pp.
191, 193.
68. "7 national ads in one talker." *Variety*, February 11, 1931, p. 7.
69. "Screen advertising going to showdown." *Variety*, April 1, 1931, p. 4.
70. "Advertising in features violation."
*Variety*, April 8, 1931, p. 23.
71. "Studios on coast receive newspaper blasts." *Variety*, June 9, 1931, p. 5.
72. "Camouflaged ads in features tempt
large studios as grosses dwindle." *Variety*,
June 23, 1931, p. 3.
73. "National advertisers' free prop service for films is a crash idea." *Variety*, July
28, 1931, p. 5.

## Chapter 3

1. "Open war on free shows." *Variety*,
December 4, 1934, pp. 1–2.
2. "Newspapers, theatre men resentful
of cuffo Standard Oil vaudeshow." *Variety*,
December 4, 1934, p. 2.
3. "S. O. free shows called off; theatres
to assume salaries." *Variety*, December 11,
1934, pp. 1–2.
4. "Booking confusion and commercial
plugs from stage mark route of Esso show
adopted by circuits." *Variety*, December 18,
1934, p. 2.
5. "Free show menace bobs up again
with dozen firms talking stunts." *Variety*,
September 25, 1935, pp. 1, 17.
6. "Chesterfield cigs' free shows draw
many who've never been in theatres before." *Variety*, September 25, 1940, pp. 5, 17.
7. "Free shows slough Balto." *Variety*,
September 25, 1940, p. 5.
8. "Merchants hypo—films." *Variety*,
June 19, 1935, p. 11.
9. "Movies." *News-Week* 6 (July 20,
1935): 33.
10. "Newsreels' commercial plugs nixed
by exhibs." *Variety*, May 15, 1940, p. 24.
11. "Studio gold rush tie-up." *Variety*,
May 29, 1935, p. 3.

12. "Screen players bally a brewery." *Variety*, August 14, 1940, p. 2.

13. "Cashing in on *Gone with the Wind*." *Business Week*, December 30, 1939, pp. 14, 16.

14. "Par's commercial dept., with 63 licenses, close behind Disney's." *Variety*, February 7, 1940, p. 20.

15. Harry Chapin Plummer. "Stars sell cars." *Automotive Industries* 78 (January 29, 1938): 142, 144.

16. *Ibid.*, p. 145.

17. "100% rise in commercial film prod. in N.Y. indicates gen'l biz upswing." *Variety*, October 23, 1935, p. 2.

18. William J. Ganz. "You ought to be in pictures." *Advertising & Selling* 25 (October 24, 1935): 28, 66.

19. S. H. Walker and Paul Sklar. "Business finds its voice." *Harper's Monthly Magazine* 176 (February 1938): 317.

20. William Bird. "Enterprise and meaning: sponsored film, 1939–1949." *History Today* 39 (December 1989): 24.

21. *Ibid.*, pp. 24–25.

22. *Ibid.*, p. 26.

23. *Ibid.*, pp. 26–27.

24. *Ibid.*, p. 27.

25. *Ibid.*, pp. 27–29.

26. *Ibid.*, pp. 29–30.

27. "Coast theatres using radio program trailers in return for ether plugs." *Variety*, July 15, 1936, p. 57.

28. "1-minute commercial pix." *Variety*, September 16, 1936, p. 3.

29. "Luckies may use screen shorts." *Variety*, June 16, 1937, p. 1.

30. "Industrial movies come of age." *Business Week*, October 9, 1937, pp. 36, 39.

31. "Commercial pix." *Variety*, January 5, 1938, p. 48.

32. "Admen ogling screens." *Variety*, March 9, 1938, pp. 7, 21.

33. Thomas M. Pryor. "Blow, ye trade winds." *New York Times*, March 27, 1938, sec. 10, p. 4.

34. "Camera! Action! Sales!" *Business Week*, May 27, 1939, pp. 39, 42–43.

35. *Ibid.*, p. 43.

36. *Ibid.*, pp. 43–44.

37. Fred H. Fidler. "Today's commercial movies." *Advertising & Selling* 33 (October 1940): 21.

38. *Ibid.*, pp. 21–22.

39. "Commercial movies." *Advertising & Selling* 34 (February 13, 1941): 209–210.

40. Dwight L. Wardell. "The business movie industry." *Dun's Review* 49 (October 1941): 29.

41. "Ad movie splurge." *Business Week*, December 13, 1941, pp. 66–67.

42. "Boo ads on the screen." *New York Times*, August 5, 1937, p. 19.

43. "Court silences booing of Georgia movie ads." *New York Times*, August 31, 1937, p. 12; "Advocate of screen adv. has ideas." *Variety*, September 8, 1937, p. 2; "Theatre drops booing suit." *New York Times*, September 3, 1937, p. 13.

44. Bruce A. Austin. "Cinema screen advertising." *Boxoffice* 121 (April 1985): 29.

45. "Screen ads as life saver." *Variety*, February 28, 1933, p. 7.

46. "Screen ads returning with 2,600 secondary houses now listed." *Variety*, July 4, 1933, p. 4.

47. "The film in business." *Times* (London), March 14, 1934, p. 10.

48. "Ad films go over in Britain." *Times* (London), April 8, 1939, p. 24.

49. "Movie merchandising." *Business Week*, June 15, 1935, p. 18.

50. *Ibid.*, pp. 19–20.

51. "Commercial pix." *Variety*, January 5, 1938, p. 48.

52. "Elaborate comm'l short." *Variety*, March 9, 1938, p. 7.

53. "Animated color film for Ipana." *Printers' Ink* 182 (March 10, 1938): 23.

54. Thomas M. Pryor, *op. cit.*

55. "News and notes of the advertising field." *New York Times*, August 15, 1938, p. 22.

56. "Commersh pix increase in scope." *Variety*, March 22, 1939, p. 6.

57. "Comm'l short gave him (10G) heart pain." *Variety*, May 15, 1940, pp. 1, 24.

58. Fred H. Fidler. *op. cit.*, p. 23.

59. "Movies are guilty of escapism, can be proud of it, Hays finds." *New York Times*, March 29, 1938, p. 23.

60. "Showdown seen between major film companies and sponsored pictures." *Variety*, April 27, 1938, p. 6.

61. "Advertising movies banned by Warner." *New York Times*, May 12, 1938, p. 27.

62. "News and notes of the advertising field." *New York Times*, February 1, 1939, p. 28.

63. "Stahlman urges free press fight." *New York Times*, April 27, 1938, p. 21.

64. "News and notes of the advertising world." *New York Times*, April 27, 1938, p. 30.

65. "Commercial films' break." *Variety*, May 11, 1938, pp. 1, 6.

66. "Industrial movies come of age." *Business Week*, October 9, 1937, p. 36.

67. Thomas M. Pryor, *op. cit.*
68. "Industrial films' serious inroads has Hollywood mulling comm'l prod." *Variety*, March 30, 1938, p. 6.
69. "Brand conscious movies." *Printers' Ink* 172 (August 1, 1935): 21.
70. *Ibid.*, pp. 21, 24.
71. *Ibid.*, p. 24.
72. "Advertising in movies." *Printers' Ink* 172 (August 15, 1935): 40.
73. "Brand conscious movies." *Printers' Ink* 172 (August 22, 1935): 46.
74. "Alleged advertising in pix irks exhibs; 20th–Fox issues a denial." *Variety*, May 5, 1937, p. 5.
75. "Expose free commercials in films." *Variety*, January 19, 1938, p. 1.
76. Harry Chapin Plummer, *op. cit.*, p. 146.
77. Thomas M. Pryor, *op. cit.*
78. W. Adolphe Roberts. "Trade follows the film." *Dun's Review* 47 (February 1939): 20–22.
79. *Ibid.*, p. 22.
80. *Ibid.*, pp. 22, 46.
81. "Firms get free ads in movies." *Business Week*, September 2, 1939, p. 26.
82. *Ibid.*
83. *Ibid.*, pp. 26–27.
84. *Ibid.*, p. 26.
85. "Indirect film commercials always hypo sales, a Hooper report avers." *Variety*, November 15, 1939, p. 7.
86. Michael Schudson. *Advertising, the Uneasy Persuasion*. New York: Basic, 1984, pp. 101–102.

## Chapter 4

1. "Everything follows the film." *Variety*, January 9, 1946, p. 3.
2. *Ibid.*, p. 38.
3. "You can sell almost anything but politics or religion via pix—Zanuck." *Variety*, March 20, 1946, p. 3.
4. "Industrial comm'l pix key stimulants to production, employment—Golden." *Variety*, September 5, 1945, p. 3.
5. "Biz's propaganda pix pitch." *Variety*, October 10, 1945, p. 5.
6. William Bird. "Enterprise and meaning: sponsored film, 1939–1949." *History Today* (December 1989): 30.
7. "1945–1948 boxoffice take." *Variety*, December 22, 1948, p. 3.
8. "Royal Crown opens biggest movie tie-up, featuring Bing Crosby." *Printers' Ink* 214 (January 25, 1946): 124.
9. Beatrice de Baltazar. "How movies provide free promotion for products."

*Printers' Ink* 217 (October 11, 1946): 42–43.
10. "Telecast's news-and-commercials new ad-screen wrinkle on B'way." *Variety*, October 17, 1945, pp. 1, 50.
11. "Commercial films used to big advantage in foreign countries." *Variety*, February 6, 1946, p. 13.
12. "Ad agency exec says commercial pix biz too picayune to interest majors." *Variety*, March 13, 1946, p. 27.
13. "Advertising news and notes." *New York Times*, March 14, 1946, p. 43.
14. "Commercial films' '46 jackpot." *Variety*, December 18, 1946, pp. 5, 29.
15. "16 mm pix ramifications running deep with dept. store circuit latest quirk." *Variety*, November 28, 1945, p. 3.
16. "See time buys on comm'l films." *Variety*, January 2, 1946, pp. 3, 28.
17. *Ibid.*, p. 28.
18. "Commercial pix over the video whets yen for regular theatre showings." *Variety*, May 22, 1946, p. 18.
19. "Advertising news and notes." *New York Times*, July 17, 1946, p. 36.
20. "RKO-Pathe's Ullman decries idea of ad-pix spreading into theatres." *Variety*, April 9, 1947, pp. 7, 20.
21. "Chas. Skouras envisions more ad pix on major screens if palatable." *Variety*, April 21, 1948, p. 3.
22. "Ad label on commercial films a blow to that upcoming biz." *Variety*, April 28, 1948, pp. 9, 22.
23. "Koret adds new twist to Hollywood fashion tie-ins." *Sales Management* 58 (April 15, 1947): 76.
24. *Ibid.*, p. 80.
25. *Ibid.*, pp. 76, 80.
26. "Rank plans utilizing his pictures to push British industrial goods." *Variety*, March 27, 1946, p. 4.
27. Susan Spillman. "Marketers race to leave their brand on film." *Advertising Age* 56 (July 1, 1985): 3; Beatrice de Baltazar. "How movies provide free promotion for products." *Printers' Ink* 217 (October 11, 1946): 42.
28. Corbin Patrick. "Indies warn against overuse of commercial plugs in features." *Variety*, July 24, 1946, p. 11.
29. "Indiana indies frothing against beer plugs in 5 recent features." *Variety*, December 22, 1948, p. 3.
30. "Exhibs take a peek at *Look* plug and beef; 20th derides charges." *Variety*, September 14, 1949, p. 18.
31. Mike Connolly. "National advertisers cut in Hollywood for millions in for-

free exploitation." *Variety*, July 30, 1947, pp. 1, 16.
32. Kay Campbell. "Hollywood, more than ever, going for those ad tieups." *Variety*, January 7, 1948, p. 22.
33. *Ibid.*
34. Stephen Prince. *History of the American Cinema: 10 A New Pot of Gold: Hollywood Under the Electronic Rainbow, 1980–1989.* New York: Charles Scribner's Sons, 2000, p. 138.

## Chapter 5

1. "Glamour in $250,000,000 payoff." *Variety*, April 12, 1950, pp. 1, 18.
2. "The painless plug." *Time* 69 (May 6, 1957): 104.
3. "More theatres playing ad pictures, TV softens up auds into acceptance." *Variety*, June 7, 1950, p. 20.
4. "NBC, Century chain in video tie for newsreels on large screen." *Variety*, November 8, 1950, pp. 1, 69.
5. "Local sponsors of newsreels." *Variety*, October 28, 1953, p. 11.
6. "How 60-second theater screen ads sell our products abroad." *Sales Management* 70 (March 15, 1953): 132.
7. *Ibid.*, pp. 132, 134.
8. "Sponsors shy away from plug pix, blame TV, COMPO's downbeat note." *Variety*, July 22, 1953, p. 5.
9. "15,000 theatres now reap record $5,000,000 from screen commercials." *Variety*, August 5, 1953, p. 5.
10. Robert J. Landry. "Films' role in nation's ad boom." *Variety*, October 21, 1953, p. 5.
11. "On-screen advertising boom." *Variety*, December 1, 1954, p. 24.
12. "Wide-screen selling." *Business Week*, March 6, 1954, pp. 110–111.
13. "Sindlinger test hints public reacts better to screen ads because of video conditioning." *Variety*, March 2, 1955, pp. 5, 70.
14. "Ad films in 16,000 theatres." *Variety*, August 15, 1956, pp. 7, 22.
15. "How to sell a captive audience." *Printers' Ink* 258 (January 25, 1957): 81.
16. "Invisible ads tested." *Printers' Ink* 260 (September 20, 1957): 44.
17. "Notes and comments." *New Yorker* 33 (September 21, 1957): 33.
18. "Ads you'll never see." *Business Week*, September 21, 1957, pp. 30–31.
19. "The invisible invader." *Newsweek* 50 (September 23, 1957): 70.
20. "The subliminal fight gets hotter." *Printers' Ink* 261 (October 4, 1957): 17.

21. *Ibid.*
22. Mark Crispin Miller. "Hollywood the ad." *The Atlantic Monthly* 265 (April 1990): 42.
23. Alexander R. Hammer. "Advertising: the message they pay to see." *New York Times*, March 9, 1958, sec. 3, p. 8.
24. *Ibid.*
25. *Ibid.*
26. Bruce A. Austin. "Cinema screen advertising." *Boxoffice* 121 (April 1985): 29.
27. "Theater-screen ad business holds own as TV educates viewers to accept ads." *Advertising Age* 29 (July 7, 1958): 74.
28. "Advertising in the movies: an old medium with new services, new strength." *Printers' Ink* 264 (August 1, 1958): 51.
29. "French highbrows like movie screen ads—they're more creative: Sarrut." *Advertising Age* 29 (December 1, 1958): 3, 79.
30. Ellen Conn. "Ading it up." *Village Voice* 34 (July 25, 1989): 68; Bruce A. Austin, *op. cit.*, pp. 30–31.
31. "Product payolas loading airwaves down; pluggers trip over each other." *Variety*, February 7, 1951, p. 1.
32. "Product plug chiseling on web airers now a big payola operation." *Variety*, April 11, 1951, p. 1.
33. "The plug lobby." *Time* 57 (May 14, 1951): 110.
34. Jack Hellman. "Feds eyeing free plugs for taxes, but it's the recipient who pays." *Variety*, November 7, 1951, p. 1.
35. J. D. Reed. "Plugging away in Hollywood." *Time* 33 (January 2, 1989): 103; Mary Gabriel. "Marketing in movies no longer plays hide and seek." *Vancouver Sun*, April 21, 2000, p. D1; John McGuire. "Lights, camera, Bud." *The Daily News* (Halifax), June 10, 1995, p. 25.
36. "Plots sneak in advertising." *Variety*, August 7, 1957, p. 3.
37. *Ibid.*, pp. 3, 22.
38. "Script doctor." *Printers' Ink* 269 (November 6, 1959): 31.

## Chapter 6

1. "Set up 20th–Fox licensing corp; further evidence of film distribs esteem for commercial by-products." *Variety*, June 15, 1966, pp. 3, 22.
2. Leonard Sloane. "The subtle sell." *New York Times*, April 25, 1971, sec. 3, pp. 1, 13.
3. *Ibid.*, p. 13.
4. Judy R. Goldsmith. "Public relations on film." *Public Relations Journal* 34 (September 1978): 2.

5. "Movie ad boom abroad while commercial television lags." *Printers' Ink* 271 (June 3, 1930): 13.

6. "Major advertisers take to movie screens." *Printers' Ink* 270 (January 21, 1960): 46.

7. Philip Shabecoff. "Advertising: messages on the movie screen." *New York Times*, September 3, 1961, sec. 3, p. 10.

8. *Ibid.*

9. "Cherry to offer dealers TV ads for theater use." *Advertising Age* 36 (August 30, 1965): 32.

10. Philip H. Dougherty. "Advertising: spots at the movies." *New York Times*, September 20, 1971, p. 73.

11. A. D. Murphy. "Why ruin film theatres' fixed big appeal—no ads?" *Variety*, May 25, 1977, p. 13.

12. John Cocchi. "Cinemavision president discusses commercials for theatres concept." *Boxoffice* 111 (August 1, 1977): 4.

13. *Ibid.*

14. "Tests set for ads in 1,000 film theaters." *Advertising Age* 48 (October 10, 1977): 1, 112.

15. "Tonight at the movies: the latest national ads." *Business Week*, October 24, 1977, p. 39.

16. "MPAA's ad-pub rap at revival of on-screen ads; mass trailers." *Variety*, November 16, 1977, p. 7.

17. "Start of comm'l sell spots on screen." *Variety*, November 16, 1977, p. 29.

18. "Patrons vote no on theater ads; FTC office orders a warning." *Advertising Age* 48 (November 21, 1977): 1.

19. "FTC sez cinemas must warn patrons if using comm'ls." *Variety*, November 16, 1977, pp. 1, 95.

20. James P. Forkan and John Revett. "Patrons are buying in-theater ad idea, sellers maintain." *Advertising Age* 48 (November 28, 1977): 2.

21. *Ibid.*, pp. 2, 71.

22. "Film ads find cold reception in Penna." *Boxoffice* 112 (November 28, 1977): E3.

23. "On-screen ads divide Boston." *Variety*, November 30, 1977, p. 30.

24. "Ads begin to appear at Colorado theatres." *Boxoffice* 112 (December 12, 1977): W4.

25. "Next a word." *Time* 110 (December 5, 1977): 89.

26. "Prod U.S. Justice to curb distribs war on pic ads." *Variety*, December 28, 1977, p. 4.

27. "UA chain signs under protest on share-of-screen-ads coin." *Variety*, January 18, 1978, p. 30.

28. "WB re on-screen ads: strict if a big pic, indulgent if routine." *Variety*, January 25, 1978, p. 5.

29. Aljean Harmetz. "Ads in film houses resisted." *New York Times*, March 8, 1978, p. C17.

30. Avery Mason. "Some see on-screen ads as boon but circuits object strenuously." *Boxoffice* 113 (July 17, 1978): NE1.

31. Sam Lasoff. "Big screen commercials: faster relief for exhibitors." *Film Comment* 15 (January/February 1979): 67–68.

32. James P. Forkan. "Screenvision luring supporting ad cast." *Advertising Age* 50 (April 16, 1979): 41.

33. "No more screen ads in N.J." *Boxoffice* 115 (July 2, 1979): 18.

34. James P. Forkan. "Yamaha, Sony spots burst onto the big screen." *Advertising Age* 50 (November 26, 1979): 20.

35. James P. Forkan. "L-M ready for sequel Screenvision ads." *Advertising Age* 51 (June 23, 1980): 12.

36. David Bergmann. "Coast aversion to screen ads spares blurbs of *L.A. Times*." *Variety*, May 5, 1982, p. 6.

37. "Planted commercial products not payola-a-la-TV if in features." *Variety*, October 19, 1960, p. 15.

38. Kay Campbell. "Commercial tieups back after slumps." *Variety*, December 27, 1961, p. 7.

39. Holly Selby. "A double-o sell job; bonded brands." *The Edmonton Journal*, December 18, 1997, p. C1; Benjamin Mark Cole. "Madison Avenue meets Hollywood and Vine." *California Business Magazine* 21 (August 1986): 65; Stuart Elliott. "The spot on the cutting-room floor." *New York Times*, February 7, 1997, p. D2.

40. "Sinatra, Lewis in tie-in derby." *Advertising Age* 34 (August 19, 1963): 3.

41. John M. Lee. "Advertising: tie-ins with movies increase." *New York Times*, January 12, 1964, sec. 3, p. 12.

42. *Ibid.*

43. Philip H. Dougherty. "Advertising' a mixed view of 4th quarter.' *New York Times*, September 21, 1970, p. 70.

44. Michael Schudson. *Advertising, the Uneasy Persuasion*. New York: Basic, 1984, p., 102.

45. Steven Mintz. "You oughta be in pictures." *Sales & Marketing Management* 127 (September 14, 1981): 38.

46. *Ibid.*, pp. 39–40.

47. David Linck. "Brand names go Hol-

lywood: props that sell." *Boxoffice* 118 (April 1982): 32.

48. *Ibid.*, pp. 32–33.

49. *Ibid.*, p. 33.

## Chapter 7

1. Frank Ratcliffe. "Brit survey sez blurbs more effective in cinema than on TV." *Variety*, August 11, 1982, p. 41.

2. "U.K. screen time nearly booked up." *Variety*, April 13, 1988, p. 38.

3. Martin Hedges. "Plenty of lobby in the cinema." *Times* (London), November 16, 1988, p. 32.

4. Alexandra Frean. "Advertising soon at a cinema near you." *Times* (London), March 26, 1997, p. 23.

5. Julian Lee. "It could be a blockbuster year for advertisers." *Times* (London), August 24, 2002, p. 47.

6. Bruce A. Austin. "Cinema screen advertising." *Boxoffice* 121 (April 1985): 30; Hazel Guild. "German advertising bounding forward: cinemas selling big." *Variety*, May 20, 1987, pp. 1, 110.

7. Wei-na Lee and Helen Katz. "New media, new messages." *Journal of Advertising Research* 33 (January/February 1993): 78.

8. "Trailer with a hitch." *American Film* 8 (April 1983): 13–14.

9. David Kalish. "The cinema sell." *Marketing & Media Decisions* 21 (August 1986): 24.

10. Richard W. Stevenson. "Ad phobia at movies easing up." *New York Times*, September 17, 1986, p. D18.

11. *Ibid.*

12. Cyndi Dale. "Mixed reviews on cinema advertising in U.S. marketplace." *Back Stage* 27 (November 28, 1986): 23.

13. Joe Agnew. "Big screen ads target young, upscale market." *Marketing News*, July 17, 1987, p. 4.

14. Michael Rottersman. "Close-up: cinema advertising." *Boxoffice* 123 (November 1987): 14–15.

15. Joyce Rutter. "At the movies." *Advertising Age* 59 (June 6, 1988): C15, C41.

16. Bernice Kanner. "Commercials at the movies." *New York* 22 (January 23, 1989): 24.

17. *Ibid.*, pp. 24–25.

18. "Big screen ads." *Marketing News* 23 (February 13, 1989): 26.

19. Ellen Conn. "Ading it up." *Village Voice* 34 (July 25, 1989): 68.

20. "Sex, lies and commercials." *New York Times*, August 26, 1989, p. 22.

21. Gerald Clarke. "Hoots and howls at ads." *Time* 134 (September 18, 1989): 70.

22. Marcy Magiera. "Advertisers crowd onto big screen." *Advertising Age* 60 (September 18, 1989): 14–15.

23. Kim Foltz. "Films and commercials are a growing double feature." *New York Times*, January 29, 1990, p. D12.

24. David Kalish. "On media's doorstep." *Marketing & Media Decisions* 23 (July 1988): 39.

25. *Ibid.*, pp. 40, 44.

26. Gerald Clarke, *op. cit.*

27. Wei-na Lee and Helen Katz, *op. cit.*, pp. 75, 80–81.

28. Kim Foltz. "Disney bars commercials at showing of its films." *New York Times*, February 10, 1990, pp. 33, 44.

29. Richard Gold. "Mixed reviews for Disney's ban on blurbs." *Variety*, February 14, 1990, p. 5.

30. *Ibid.*, p. 16.

31. Michael Lev. "Disney cites survey on theater ads." *New York Times*, April 11, 1990, p. D25.

32. Michael Lev. "Warner joins Walt Disney in banning ads at its films." *New York Times*, April 18, 1990, p. D17.

33. "Ruthless people." *The Economist* 315 (April 21, 1990): 72.

34. Scott Hume and Marcy Magiera. "What do moviegoers think of ads?" *Advertising Age* 61 (April 23, 1990): 4.

35. "Captive audiences." *New York Times*, April 25, 1990, p. A28.

36. Marcy Magiera. "Studio ad bans aid in-theater media." *Advertising Age* 61 (October 8, 1990): 72.

37. Richard Brunelli. "Tartikoff: no future for ads before movies." *Mediaweek* 1 (November 11, 1991): 2.

38. Mark Hudis. "Lights, camera, commercial!" *Mediaweek* 3 (November 1, 1993): 14.

39. Marcy Magiera. "On-screen ads unspool new tactics." *Advertising Age* 64 (December 13, 1993): 10.

40. Dade Hayes. "The preshow must go on ... and on." *Variety*, November 14, 1999, pp. 9–10.

41. Karen J. Bannan. "Advertising." *New York Times*, October 8, 2001, p. C10.

## Chapter 8

1. Michael Schudson. *Advertising, the Uneasy Persuasion.* New York: Basic, 1984, p. 102.

2. Janet Maslin. "Plugging products in

movies as an applied art." *New York Times*, November 15, 1982, p. C11.

3. *Ibid.*

4. *Ibid.*

5. "Free on a match." *American Film* 8 (November 1982): 16.

6. David T. Friendly. "Selling it at the movies." *Newsweek* 102 (July 4, 1983): 46.

7. *Ibid.*

8. *Ibid.*

9. Aljean Harmetz. "Fox to sell rights to plug goods in films." *New York Times*, December 21, 1983, p. C19.

10. *Ibid.*

11. *Ibid.*

12. *Ibid.*

13. *Ibid.*

14. Peter Hall. "Terms of endorsement." *Village Voice* 29 (February 7, 1984): 34.

15. Bob Smith. "Casting product for special effect." *Beverage World* 104 (March 1985): 83, 91.

16. "Looking ahead." *Television/Radio Age* 32 (April 29, 1985). 26.

17. Susan Spillman. "Marketers race to leave their brand on films." *Advertising Age* 56 (July 1, 1985). 3, 55.

18. *Ibid.*, p. 55.

19. *Ibid.*

20. Robert M. Fineout. "Products in a supporting role." *Public Relations Journal* 41 (August 1985): 32–33.

21. *Ibid.*, p. 33.

22. Hazel Guild. "Product plugs both a bane and a boon to German pic biz." *Variety*, August 14, 1985, pp. 2, 31.

23. Kevin T. Higgins. "There's gold in silver screen product plugs." *Marketing News* 19 (October 11, 1985): 6.

24. *Ibid.*

25. Jim Gluckson. "Casting products in films." *Boxoffice* 121 (December 1985): 34, 36.

26. Benjamin Mark Cole. "Madison Avenue meets Hollywood and Vine." *California Business Magazine* 21 (August 1986): 65.

27. *Ibid.*, pp. 65, 67.

28. Paul Harris. "Two health groups blast promotion of products in films." *Variety*, October 16, 1985, p. 6.

29. "Valenti dismisses beef about products in pics." *Variety*, October 30, 1985, pp. 5, 35.

30. Roma Felstein. "Star turns for brand names." *Times* (London), June 7, 1987, p. 63.

31. David Kalish. "Now showing: products!" *Marketing & Media Decisions* 23 (August 1988): 28–29.

32. Lenore Skenazy. "Brand names star in *Mac & Me.*" *Advertising Age* 59 (September 5, 1988): 58.

33. J. D. Reed. "Plugging away in Hollywood." *Time* 133 (January 2, 1989): 103.

34. Steven W. Colford. "Tobacco critic opens new front." *Advertising Age* 60 (March 27, 1989): 6.

35. *Ibid.*

36. "CSPI calls for movie subtitles identifying products." *Broadcasting* 116 (April 3, 1989): 57–58.

37. *Ibid.*, p. 58.

38. Douglas C. McGill. "Questions raised on product placements." *New York Times*, April 13, 1989, p. D18; Jon Silberg. "When screens become billboards." *American Film* 14 (May 1989): 12.

39. Ann Lallande. "The Capitol cutting room." *Marketing & Media Decisions* 24 (July 1989): 130.

40. "Behind film's warning on cigarettes." *New York Times*, July 13, 1989, p. D19.

41. Lois Sheinfeld. "Dangerous liaisons." *Film Comment* 25 (September/October 1989): 71–72.

42. Edmond M. Rosenthal. "Paid props enter CPM era." *Television/Radio Age* 37 (October 2, 1989). 42.

43. *Ibid.*, p. 43.

44. Laura Loro and Marcy Magiera. "Philly products angle for ringside in *Rocky V.*" *Advertising Age* 61 (February 5, 1990): 20.

45. Judann Dagnoll. "Disney still offers product plugs." *Advertising Age* 61 (February 26, 1990): 25.

46. Nancy A. Lang. "You oughta be in pictures." *Beverage World* 109 (April 1990): 34–36.

47. Michael Fleming. "Product plugola padding pic producers' budgets." *Variety*, May 9, 1990, pp. 1, 22.

48. James Bone. "Those obvious objects of desire." *Times* (London), May 16, 1990, p. 19.

49. "MasterCard makes the movies." *United States Banker* 100 (June 1990): 90.

50. "Media skeptic." *Rolling Stone*, July 12, 1990, p. 19.

51. Caroline Lees and Tim Rayment. "Shades wars: how big money goes riding on a film star's nose." *Sunday Times* (London), July 22, 1990, sec. 1, p. 5.

52. Anne Coulton. "Lodging goes Hollywood." *Lodging Hospitality* 46 (July 1990): 12.

53. Steven W. Colford. "Lawsuit drills Fox, Cato." *Advertising Age* 61 (December 3, 1990): 3.

54. *Ibid.*, pp. 3, 57.
55. "A jilted starlet sues." *Advertising Age* 61 (December 10, 1990): 30.
56. Greg Evans. "Lawsuits tarnish appeal of product placement." *Variety*, December 17, 1990, p. 73.
57. Anita Busch. "Killers doesn't go better with Coke." *Variety*, August 29, 1994, p. 8.
58. Steven W. Colford. "Tobacco group ends paid placement." *Advertising Age* 61 (December 17, 1990): 31.
59. Randall Rothenberg. "Critics seek F.T.C. action on products as movie stars." *New York Times*, May 31, 1991, pp. D1, D5.
60. Dennis Wharton and Jennifer Pendleton. "D.C. group brands product placement as plugola." *Variety*, June 3, 1991, p. 18.
61. "Product placement." *New York Times*, December 16, 1992, p. D17.
62. Marcy Magiera. "Product placement group is formed." *Advertising Age* 62 (September 16, 1991): 46.
63. Marcy Magiera. "Social messages urged in product placement." *Advertising Age* 62 (November 25, 1991): 28.
64. Stuart Elliott. "Advertising." *New York Times*, January 9, 1992, p. D22.
65. Sid Bernstein. "A world overrun by ads?" *Advertising Age* 63 (January 27, 1992): 20.
66. Marcy Magiera and Alison Fahey. "Coke makes movies." *Advertising Age* 63 (March 16, 1992): 2.
67. Adam Bryant. "Advertising." *New York Times*, March 30, 1993, p. D23.
68. Christian Mork. "Product placement gets kick out of PG pix." *Variety*, May 24, 1993, p. 5.
69. Adrienne Ward Fawcett. "Free TV ad plugs are on the rise." *Advertising Age* 64 (July 21, 1993): 21.
70. Stuart Elliott. "Advertising." *New York Times*, October 8, 1993, p. D15.
71. Bernice Kanner. "All the right movies." *New York* 26 (November 29, 1993): 20, 22.
72. Michael McCarthy. "Studios place, show and win: product placement grows up." *Brandweek* 35 (March 28, 1994): 30.
73. Philip J. Holts. "Company spent $1 million to put cigarettes in movies, memos show." *New York Times*, May 20, 1994, p. A16.
74. *Ibid.*

75. Ron Glover. "In this shoot-'em-up, the car got plugged." *Business Week*, March 21, 1994, p. 8.
76. Joan Oleck. "That's Hollywood." *Restaurant Business* 94 (January 20, 1995): 28, 30.
77. John McGuire. "Lights, camera, Bud." *The Daily News* (Halifax), June 10, 1995, p. 25.
78. Damon Darlin. "Junior Mints, I'm gonna make you a star." *Forbes* 156 (November 6, 1995): 90–94.
79. Maryanna Lewyckyj. "Computers go Hollywood." *Toronto Sun*, November 8, 1995, p. 40.
80. "The power of a plug." *Management Today*, February 1996, p. 82.
81. David Leonhardt. "Cue the soda can." *Business Week*, June 24, 1996, pp. 64, 66.
82. Stuart Elliott. "The spot on the cutting-room floor." *New York Times*, February 7, 1997, p. D1.
83. *Ibid.*, p. D2.
84. *Ibid.*
85. "Scorecard." *Sports Illustrated* 86 (February 24, 1997): 25; "Reebok settles movie dispute." *New York Times*, October 6, 1997, p. D2.
86. Suna Chang. "Bond of gold." *Entertainment Weekly*, November 28, 1997, pp. 10–11.
87. Joshua Hammer and Corie Brown. "Licensed to shill." *Newsweek* 130 (December 15, 1997): 43.
88. Clifford Rothman. "Hollywood's up in smoke." *The Province* (Vancouver), August 27, 1997, p. B7.
89. Rick Lyman. "In the 80's: Lights! Camera! Cigarettes!" *New York Times*, March 12, 2002, p. E1.
90. *Ibid.*, pp. E1, E3.
91. Karen Hudes. "Independent film, but with a catch: a corporate logo." *New York Times*, November 15, 1998, sec. 2A, p. 43.
92. *Ibid.*
93. Jennifer Tanaka. "The Apples of their eyes." *Newsweek* 132 (November 30, 1998): 58.
94. Brian Palmer. "When product placement goes horribly, horribly wrong." *Fortune* 138 (December 21, 1998): 48.
95. Christopher Goodwin. "American excess." *Times* (London): June 28, 2002, sec. TT2, p. 19.

# Bibliography

"Ad agency exec says commercial pix biz too picayune to interest majors." *Variety*, March 13, 1946, p. 27.

"Ad films go over in Britain." *Times* (London), April 8, 1939, p. 24.

"Ad films in 16,000 theatres." *Variety*, August 15, 1956, pp. 7, 22.

"Ad label on commercial films a blow to that upcoming biz." *Variety*, April 28, 1948, pp. 9, 22.

"Ad movie splurge." *Business Week*, December 13, 1941, pp. 66–67.

"Ad reel rate—attendance." *Variety*, January 28, 1931, pp. 3, 21.

"Admen ogling screens." *Variety*, March 9, 1938, pp. 7, 21.

"Ads begin to appear at Colorado theatres." *Boxoffice* 112 (December 12, 1977): W4.

"Ads on 50% of U.S. screens." *Variety*, May 13, 1931, p. 7.

"Ads you'll never see." *Business Week*, September 21, 1957, pp. 30–31.

Advertisement. *Variety*, December 26, 1919, p. 194.

"Advertising by film." *Times* (London), November 9, 1921, p. 10.

"Advertising for Universal." *Variety*, June 28, 1918, p. 46.

"Advertising in features violation." *Variety*, April 8, 1931, p. 23.

"Advertising in movies." *Printers' Ink* 172 (August 15, 1935): 40.

"Advertising in the movies: an old medium with new services, new strength." *Printers' Ink* 264 (August 1, 1958): 50–51.

"Advertising movies banned by Warner." *New York Times*, May 12, 1938, p. 27.

"Advertising news and notes." *New York Times*, March 14, 1946, p. 43.

"Advertising news and notes." *New York Times*, July 17, 1946, p. 36.

"Advertising shorts divide men in both ends of picture trade." *Variety*, March 18, 1931, p. 5.

"Advocate of screen adv. has ideas." *Variety*, September 8, 1937, p. 2.

"Against advertising films." *Variety*, December 5, 1919, p. 65.

Agnew, Joe. "Big screen ads target young, upscale market." *Marketing News*, July 17, 1987, p. 4.

"All screen ads discontinued." *Variety*, April 15, 1931, p. 5.

"Alleged advertising in pix irks exhibs; 20th–Fox issues a denial." *Variety*, May 5, 1937, p. 5.

"Allied news minus advertisers, so footage free." *Variety*, September 1, 1931, p. 3.

Andrews, Peter B. B. "The sponsored movie." *Advertising & Selling* 16 (December 10, 1930): 36, 38.

"Animated color film for Ipana." *Printers' Ink* 182 (March 10, 1938): 23.

Austin, Bruce A. "Cinema screen advertising." *Boxoffice* 121 (April, 1985): 29–32.

"Auto exploitation talking film free show with names, stars and Follies beauts." *Variety*, January 23, 1929, p. 11.

de Baltazar, Beatrice. "How movies provide free promotion for products." *Printers' Ink* 217 (October 11, 1946): 42–43.

Bannan, Karen J. "Advertising." *New York Times*, October 8, 2001, p. C10.

"Behind film's warning on cigarettes." *New York Times*, July 13, 1989, p. D19.

Bergmann, David. "Coast aversion to screen ads spares blurbs of *L.A. Times.*" *Variety*, May 5, 1982, p. 6.

Bernstein, Sid. "A world overrun by ads?" *Advertising Age* 63 (January 27, 1992): 20.

"Big screen ads." *Marketing News* 23 (February 13, 1989): 16, 26.

Bird, William. "Enterprise and meaning: sponsored film, 1939–1949." *History Today* 39 (December, 1989): 24–30.

"Biz's propaganda pix pitch." *Variety*, October 10, 1945, p. 5.

Bone, James. "Those obvious objects of desire." *Times* (London), May 16, 1990, p. 19.

"Boo ads on the screen." *New York Times*, August 5, 1937, p. 19.

"Booking confusion and commercial plugs from stage mark route of Esso show adopted by circuits." *Variety*, December 18, 1934, p. 2.

"Brand conscious movies." *Printers' Ink* 172 (August 1, 1935): 21, 24.

"Brand conscious movies." *Printers' Ink* 172 (August 22, 1935): 46.

"Breaking into the movies." *New York Times*, August 23, 1929, p. 20.

Brunelli, Richard. "Tartikoff: no future for ads before movies." *Mediaweek* 1 (November 11, 1991): 2.

Bryant, Adam. "Advertising." *New York Times*, March 30, 1993, p. D23.

Busch, Anita M. "Killers doesn't go better with Coke." *Variety*, August 29, 1994, pp. 7–8.

"Business anxiously watches reaction to sponsored shorts." *Business Week*, April 8, 1931, p. 14.

"Buy now campaign planned through Philadelphia movies." *New York Times*, July 30, 1932, p. 1.

"Camera! Action! Sales!" *Business Week*, May 27, 1939, pp. 37–47.

"Camouflaged ads in features tempt large studios as grosses dwindle." *Variety*, June 23, 1931, p. 5.

Campbell, Kay. "Commercial tieups back after slumps." *Variety*, December 27, 1961, p. 7.

_____. "Hollywood more than ever, going for those ad tieups." *Variety*, January 7, 1948, p. 22.

Canady, W. D. "How Lehn & Fink are using talking picture shorts." *Printers' Ink* 154 (March 19, 1931): 17–20.

"Captive audiences." *New York Times*, April 25, 1990, p. A28.

"Cashing in on *Gone With the Wind.*" *Business Week*, December 30, 1939, pp. 14, 16.

"Chains playing ad shorts." *Variety*, February 26, 1930, p. 9.

Chang, Suna. "Bond of gold." *Entertainment Weekly*, November 28, 1997, pp. 10–11.

"Chas. Skouras envisions ad pix on major screens—if palatable." *Variety*, April 21, 1948, p. 3.

"Chesterfield cigs' free shows draw many who've never been in theatres before." *Variety*, September 25, 1940, pp. 5, 17.

"Chevy to offer dealers TV ads for theater use." *Advertising Age* 36 (August 30, 1965): 32.

"Chi. exhibs cancel advertising shorts as direct source of grief." *Variety*, September 10, 1930, p. 32.

Clarke, Gerald. "Hoots and howls at ads." *Time* 134 (September 18, 1989): 70.

"Coast theatres using radio program trailers in return for ether plugs." *Variety*, July 15, 1936, p. 57.

Cocchi, John. "Cinemavision president discusses commercials-for-theatres concept." *Boxoffice* 111 (August 1, 1977): 4.

Cole Benjamin Mark. "Madison Avenue meets Hollywood and Vine." *California Business Magazine* 21 (August, 1986): 65, 67.

Colford, Steven W. "Lawsuit drills Fox, Cato." *Advertising Age*. 61 (December 3, 1990): 3, 57.

_____. "Tobacco critic opens new front." *Advertising Age* 60 (March 27, 1989): 6.

_____. "Tobacco group ends paid placements." *Advertising Age* 61 (December 17, 1990): 31.

"Collecting on picture names." *Variety*, February 14, 1919, p. 56.

"Commercial films' break." *Variety*, May 11, 1938, pp. 1, 6.

"Commercial films' '46 jackpot." *Variety*, December 18, 1946, pp. 5, 29.

"Commercial films used to big advantage in foreign countries." *Variety*, February 6, 1946, p. 13.

"Commercial movies." *Advertising & Selling* 34 (February 13, 1941): 209–212.

"Commercial pix." *Variety*, January 5, 1938, p. 48.

"Commercial pix over the video whets yen for regular theatre showings." *Variety*, May 22, 1946, p. 18.

"Commercial shorts slow showing; now in Par houses to decide." *Variety*, November 12, 1930, p. 28.

"Commercial talking shorts may soon be offered free for showings in theatres." *Variety*, May 8, 1929, p. 5.

"Commersch pix increase in scope." *Variety*, March 22, 1939, p. 6.

"Comm'l short gave him (10G) heart pain." *Variety*, May 15, 1940, pp. 1, 24.

Conn, Ellen. "Ading it up." *Village Voice* 34 (July 25, 1989): 68.

Connolly, Mike. "National advertisers cut in Hollywood for millions in foi-free exploitation." *Variety*, July 30, 1947, pp. 1, 16.

Coulton, Anne. "Lodging goes Hollywood." *Lodging Hospitality* 46 (July, 1990): 12.

"Court silences booing of Georgia movie ads." *New York Times*, August 31, 1937, p. 12.

Crafton, Donald. *History of the American Cinema: 4 The Talkies: American Cinema's Transition to Sound, 1926–1931*. New York: Charles Scribner's Sons, 1997.

"CSPI calls for movie subtitles identifying paid products." *Broadcasting* 116 (April 3, 1989): 57–58.

Dagnoli, Judann. "Disney still offers product plugs." *Advertising Age* 61 (February 26, 1990): 25.

Dale, Cyndi. "Mixed reviews on cinema advertising in U.S. marketplace." *Back Stage* 27 (November 28, 1986): 1, 23.

Darlin, Damon. "Junior Mints, I'm gonna make you a star." *Forbes* 156 (November 6, 1995): 90–91+.

"Double barrage for advertising on screen by dailies and Laemmle." *Variety*, March 4, 1931, p. 7.

Dougherty, Philip H. "Advertising: a mixed view of 4th quarter." *New York Times*, September 21, 1970, p. 70.

_____. "Advertising: spots at the movies." *New York Times*, September 20, 1972, p. 73.

"Dynamite seen in newly offered free commercialized newsreels." *Variety*, April 8, 1931, p. 2.

"Educational talkers." *Variety*, June 27, 1928, p. 3.

"Elaborate comm'l short." *Variety*, March 9, 1938, p. 7.

Elliott, Stuart. "Advertising." *New York Times*, January 9, 1992, p. D22.

_____. "Advertising." *New York Times*, October 8, 1993, p. D15.

_____. "The spot on the cutting-room floor." *New York Times*, February 7, 1997, pp. D1–D2.

"English commercial firms in advertising pictures." *Variety*, May 26, 1922, p. 1.

Evans, Greg. "Lawsuits tarnish appeal of product placement." *Variety*, December 17, 1990, p. 73.

"Everything follows the films." *Variety*, January 9, 1946, pp. 3, 38.

"Exhibs ask about ads in features." *Variety*, March 25, 1931, p. 35.

"Exhibs take a peek at *Look* plug and beef; 20th derides charges." *Variety*, September 14, 1949, p. 18.

"Expose free commercials in films." *Variety*, January 19, 1938, p. 1.

Fawcett, Adrienne Ward. "Free TV ad plugs are on the rise." *Advertising Age* 64 (July 21, 1993): 21.

Fleming, Michael. "Product pluggola padding pic producers' budgets." *Variety*, May 9, 1990, pp. 1, 22, 24.

Felstein, Roma. "Star turns for brand names." *Times* (London), June 7, 1987, p. 63.

Fidler, Fred H. "Today's commercial movies." *Advertising & Selling* 33 (October, 1940): 21–23, 86.

"15,000 theatres now reap record $5,000,000 from screen commercials." *Variety*, August 5, 1953, p. 5.

"Film ads find cold reception in Penna." *Boxoffice* 112 (November 28, 1977): E3

"The film in business." *Times* (London), March 14, 1934, p. 10.

"Film producers raise wages." *New York Times*, February 9, 1913, sec. 3, p. 13.

"Film service for stores." *New York Times*, May 8, 1921, sec. 2, p. 11.

"The film world." *Times* (London), February 12, 1930, p. 12.

"Films in business." *Times* (London), September 5, 1921, p. 6.

Finehout, Robert M. "Products in a supporting role." *Public Relations Journal* 41 (August, 1985): 32–33.

"Firms get free ads in movies." *Business Week*, September 2, 1939, pp. 26–27.

Foltz, Kim. "Disney bans commercials at showings of its films." *New York Times*, February 10, 1990, pp. 33, 44.

_____. "Film and commercials are a growing double feature." *New York Times*, January 29, 1990, p. D12.

"Food investigators to report Monday." *New York Times*, August 29, 1914, p. 14.

Forkan, James P. "L-M ready for sequel Screenvision ads." *Advertising Age* 51 (June 23, 1980): 12.

_____. "Screenvision luring supporting ad cast." *Advertising Age* 50 (April 16, 1979): 41.

_____. "Yamaha, Sony spots burst onto the big screen." *Advertising Age* 50 (November 26, 1979): 20.

_____, and John Revett. "Patrons are buying in-theater ad idea, sellers maintain." *Advertising Age* 48 (November 28, 1977): 2, 71.

"Fox off all ad shorts." *Variety*, February 25, 1931, p. 7.

Frean, Alexandra. "Advertising soon at a cinema near you." *Times* (London), March 26, 1977, p. 23.

"Free industrial films." *New York Times*, June 25, 1923, p. 16.

"Free on a match." *American Film* 8 (November, 1982): 16.

"Free show menace bobs up again with dozen firms talking stunts." *Variety*, September 25, 1935, pp. 1, 17.

"Free shows slough Balto." *Variety*, September 25, 1940, p. 5.

Freeman, Lewis R. "Movie signboards." *Saturday Evening Post* 192 (January 17, 1920): 12–13+.

"French highbrows like movie screen ads—they're more creative: Sarrut." *Advertising Age* 29 (December 1, 1958): 3, 79.

Friendly, David T. "Selling it at the movies." *Newsweek* 102 (July 4, 1983): 46.

"FTC sez cinemas must warn patrons if using comm'ls." *Variety*, November 16, 1977, pp. 1, 75.

"Full length ad features." *Variety*, May 6, 1931, p. 5.

Gabriel, Mary. "Marketing in movies no longer plays hide and seek." *Vancouver Sun*, April 21, 2000, p. D1.

Ganz, William J. "You ought to be in pictures." *Advertising & Selling* 25 (October 24, 1935): 28, 66–67.
"Glamour in $250,000,000 payoff." *Variety*, April 12, 1950, pp. 1, 18.
Gluckson, Jim. "Casting products in films." *Boxoffice* 121 (December, 1985): 34, 36.
Gold, Richard. "Mixed reviews for Disney's ban on blurbs." *Variety*, February 14, 1990, pp. 5, 16.
Goldsmith, Judy R. "Public relations on film." *Public Relations Journal* 34 (September, 1978): 2, 61.
Goodwin, Christopher. "American excess." *Times* (London), June 28, 2002, sec. TT2, p. 19.
Grover, Ron. "In this shoot-'em-up, the car got plugged." *Business Week*, March 21, 1994, p. 8.
Guild, Hazel. "German advertising bounding forward: cinemas selling big." *Variety*, May 20, 1987, pp. 1, 110.
_____. "Product plugs both a bane and a boom to German pic biz." *Variety*, August 14, 1985, pp. 2, 31.
Hall, Peter. "Terms of endorsement." *Village Voice* 29 (February 7, 1984): 34.
Hammer, Alexander R. "Advertising: the message they pay to see." *New York Times*, March 9, 1958, Sec. 3, p. 8.
Hammer, Joshua and Corie Brown. "Licensed to shill." *Newsweek* 130 (December 15, 1997): 43.
Harmetz, Aljean. "Ads in film houses resisted." *New York Times*, March 8, 1978, p. C17.
_____. "Fox to sell rights to plug goods in films." *New York Times*, December 21, 1983, p. C19.
Harris, Paul. "Two health groups blast promotion of products in films." *Variety*, October 16, 1985, p. 6.
"Hays calls movies big aid to business." *New York Times*, November 14, 1929, p. 24.
Hayes, Dade. "The preshow must go on ... and on." *Variety*, November 14, 1999, pp. 9–10.
"Hays lauds movies as a trade stimulus." *New York Times*, March 30, 1930, p. 6.
Hedges, Martin. "Plenty of lobby in the cinema." *Times* (London), November 16, 1988, p. 32.
Hellman, Jack. "Feds eyeing free plugs for taxes but it's the recipient who pays." *Variety*, November 7, 1951, pp. 1, 63.
Higgins, Kevin T. "There's gold in silver screen product plugs." *Marketing News* 19 (October 11, 1985): 6.
Hilts, Philip J. "Company spent $1 million to put cigarettes in movies, memos show." *New York Times*, May 20, 1994, p. A16.
Hoffman, Paul G. "Will the talkies talk their way into mass selling?" *Magazine of Business* 56 (August, 1929): 149–150, 194.
Hough, Henry W. "Putting it over with movies." *Scientific American* 140 (May, 1929): 428–429.
"How 60-second theater screen ads sell our products abroad." *Sales Management* 70 (March 15, 1953): 132, 134.
"How to sell a captive audience." *Printers' Ink* 258 (January 25, 1957): 81.
Hudes, Karen. "Independent film, but with a catch: a corporate logo." *New York Times*, November 15, 1998, sec 2A, p. 43.
Hudis, Mark. "Lights, camera, commercial!" *Mediaweek* 3 (November 1, 1993): 14.
Hume, Scott and Marcy Magiera. "What do moviegoers think of ads?" *Advertising Age* 61 (April 23, 1990): 4.
"Indiana indies frothing against beer plugs in 5 recent features." *Variety*, December 22, 1948, p. 3.
"Indies in N.W. raise defense fund." *Variety*, April 8, 1931, p. 23.

"Indirect film commercials always hypo sales, a Hooper report avers." *Variety*, November 15, 1939, p. 7.

"Industrial comm'l pix key stimulants to production, employment—Golden." *Variety*, September 5, 1945, p. 3.

"Industrial films' serious inroads has Hollywood mulling comm'l prod." *Variety*, March 30, 1938, p. 6.

"Industrial movies come of age." *Business Week*, October 9, 1937, pp. 35–36+.

"Inside stuff—on pictures." *Variety*, January 9, 1920, p. 56.

"Inside stuff—on pictures." *Variety*, September 22, 1922, p. 43.

"Invisible ads tested." *Printers' Ink* 260 (September 20, 1957): 44.

"The invisible invader." *Newsweek* 50 (September 23, 1957): 70.

"A jilted starlet sues." *Advertising Age* 61 (December 10, 1990): 30.

Kalish, David. "On media's doorstep." *Marketing & Media Decisions* 23 (July, 1988): 39+.

_____. "The cinema sell." *Marketing & Media Decisions* 21 (August, 1986): 24–25.

Kanner, Bernice. "All the right movies." *New York* 26 (November 29, 1993): 20, 22.

_____. "Commercials at the movies." *New York* 22 (January 23, 1989): 24–25.

Klein, Julius. "What are the motion pictures doing for industry?" *Annals of the American Academy of Political and Social Science* 128 (November, 1926): 79–83.

"Koret adds new twist to Hollywood fashion tie-ins." *Sales Management* 58 (April 15, 1947): 76, 80.

Lallande, Ann. "The Capitol cutting room." *Marketing & Media Decisions* 24 (July, 1989): 130.

Landry, Robert J. "Films' role in nation's ad boom." *Variety*, October 21, 1953, pp. 5, 66.

Lang, Nancy A. "You oughta be in pictures." *Beverage World* 109 (April, 1990): 34–6, 86–87.

Lasoff, Sam. "Big screen commercials: faster relief for exhibitors." *Film Comment* 15 (January/February, 1979): 66–68.

Lee, John M. "Advertising: tie-ins with movies increase." *New York Times*, January 12, 1964, Sec. 3, p. 12.

Lee, Julian. "It could be a blockbuster year for advertisers." *Times* (London), August 24, 2002, p. 47.

Lee, Wei-na and Helen Katz. "New media, new messages." *Journal of Advertising Research* 33 (January/February, 1993): 74–85.

Lees, Caroline and Tim Rayment. "Shades wars: how big money goes riding on a film star's nose." *Sunday Times* (London), July 22, 1990, sec. 1, p. 5.

Leonhardt, David. "Cue the soda can." *Business Week*, June 24, 1996, pp. 64, 66.

Lev, Michael. "Disney cites survey on theater ads." *New York Times*, April 11, 1990, p. D25.

_____. "Warner joins Walt Disney in banning ads at its films." *New York Times*, April 18, 1990, p. D17.

Lewyckyj, Maryanna. "Computers go Hollywood." *Toronto Sun*, November 8, 1995, p. 40.

Linck, David. "Brand names go Hollywood: props that sell." *Boxoffice* 118 (April, 1982): 32–33.

"Lobbies as billboards for commercial firms' publicity." *Variety*, June 4, 1930, pp. 27, 61.

"Local sponsors of newsreels." *Variety*, October 28, 1953, p. 11.

"Loew circuit bans film advertising." *New York Times*, May 18, 1931, p. 19.

"Looking ahead." *Television/Radio Age* 32 (April 29, 1985): 26.

Loro, Laura and Marcy Magiera. "Philly products angle for ringside in *Rocky V*." *Advertising Age* 61 (February 5, 1990): 20.

"Luckies may use screen shorts." *Variety*, June 16, 1937, p. 1.

Lyman, Rick. "In the 80's: Lights! Camera! Cigarettes!" *New York Times*, March 12, 2002, pp. E1, E3.

Magiera, Marcy. "Advertisers crowd onto big screen." *Advertising Age* 60 (September 18, 1989): 14–15.

_____. "On-screen ads unspool new tactics." *Advertising Age* 64 (December 13, 1993): 10.

_____. "Product placement group is formed." *Advertising Age* 62 (September 16, 1991): 46.

_____. "Social messages urged in product placements " *Advertising Age* 62 (November 25, 1991): 28.

_____. "Studio ad bans aid in-theater media." *Advertising Age* 61 (October 8, 1990): 72.

_____, and Alison Fahey. "Coke makes movies." *Advertising Age* 63 (March 16, 1992): 2.

"Major advertisers take to movie screens." *Printers' Ink* 270 (January 21, 1960): 46, 48.

Maslin, Janet. "Plugging products in movies is an applied art." *New York Times*, November 15, 1982, p. C11.

Mason, Avery. "Some see on-screen ads as boon but circuits object strenuously." *Boxoffice* 113 (July 17, 1978): NE1.

"MasterCard makes the movies." *United States Banker* 100 (June, 1990): 90.

McCarthy, Michael. "Studios place, show and win: product placement grows up." *Brandweek* 35 (March 28, 1994): 30, 32.

McFall, David. "The friendly war after the war." *Scientific American* 120 (June 21, 1919): 652, 657.

McGill, Douglas C. "Questions raised on product placement." *New York Times*, April 13, 1989, p. D18.

McGuire, John. "Lights, camera, Bud." *The Daily News* (Halifax), June 10, 1995, p. 25.

"Media skeptic." *Rolling Stone*, July 12–26, 1990, p. 19.

Meekins, Lynn W. "World markets for American manufacturers." *Scientific American* 119 (December 7, 1918): 456.

"Merchants hypo—films." *Variety*, June 19, 1935, p. 11.

Miller, Mark Crispin. "Hollywood the ad." *The Atlantic Monthly* 265 (April, 1990): 41–45+.

Mintz, Steven. "You oughta be in pictures." *Sales & Marketing Management* 127 (September 14, 1981): 38–40.

"More theatres playing ad pictures, TV softens up auds into acceptance." *Variety*, June 7, 1950, p. 20.

Mork, Christian. "Product placement gets kick out of PG pix." *Variety*, May 24, 1993, pp. 5, 18.

"Motion-pictures as business boosters." *Literary Digest* 65 (April 3, 1920): 92–97.

"Movie ads boom abroad while commercial television lags." *Printers' Ink* 271 (June 3, 1960): 13.

"Movie merchandising." *Business Week*, June 15, 1935, pp. 18–20.

"Movies." *News-week* 6 (July 20, 1935): 33.

"Movies aid foreign trade." *New York Times*, April 12, 1922, p. 4.

"Movies are guilty of escapism, can be proud of it, Hays finds." *New York Times*, March 29, 1938, p. 23.

"MPAA's ad-pub rap at revival of on-screen ads; mass trailers." *Variety*, November 16, 1977, p. 7.

Murray, Patricia. "When advertisers tried films." *Printers' Ink* 205 (November 19, 1943): 25–26.

Murphy, A. D. "Why ruin film theatres' fixed big appeal—no ads?" *Variety*, May 25, 1977, p. 13.

Musser, Charles. *History of the American Cinema: 1 The Emergence of Cinema: The American Screen to 1907.* New York: Charles Scribner's Sons, 1990.

"Names for WB advertising shorts; five million circulation stated." *Variety,* February 4, 1931, p. 15.

"Names in pictures are restricted from recommending commercial products by Hays' office resolve." *Variety,* October 6, 1931, p. 3.

"National advertisers' free prop service for films is a crash idea." *Variety,* July 28, 1931, p. 5.

"Nat'l ad men for talkers." *Variety,* February 15, 1928, p. 9.

"NBC, Century chain in video tie for newsreels on large screen." *Variety,* November 8, 1950, pp. 1, 69.

"Neilan on advertising films." *Variety,* January 23, 1920, p. 65.

"News and notes of the advertising field." *New York Times,* August 15, 1938, p. 22.

"News and notes of the advertising field." *New York Times,* February 1, 1939, p. 28.

"News and notes of the advertising world." *New York Times,* April 27, 1938, p. 30.

"Newspapermen and Publix agree that public will decide screen ad future." *Variety,* April 29, 1931, p. 4.

"Newspapers put an end to advertising movies." *Business Week,* July 8, 1931, p. 22.

"Newspapers, theatre men resentful of cuffo Standard Oil vaudeshow." *Variety,* December 4, 1934, p. 2.

"Newsreels' commercial plugs nixed by exhibs." *Variety,* May 15, 1940, p. 24.

"Next a word." *Time* 110 (December 5, 1977): 89.

"1945–1948 boxoffice take." *Variety,* December 22, 1948, p. 3.

"No more screen ads in N.J." *Boxoffice* 115 (July 2, 1979): 18.

"Notes and comments." *New Yorker* 33 (September 21, 1957): 33.

Oleck, Joan. "That's Hollywood." *Restaurant Business* 94 (January 20, 1995): 23+.

"100% rise in commercial film prod. in N.Y. indicates gen'l biz upswing." *Variety,* October 23, 1935, p. 7.

"1-minute commercial pix." *Variety,* September 16, 1936, p. 3.

"On-screen ads divide Boston." *Variety,* November 30, 1977, p. 30.

"On-screen advertising boom." *Variety,* December 1, 1954, p. 24.

"Open war on free shows." *Variety,* December 4, 1934, pp. 1–2.

"The painless plug." *Time* 69 (May 6, 1957): 104.

Palmer, Brian. "When product placement goes horribly, horribly wrong." *Fortune* 138 (December 21, 1998): 48.

"Par's commercial dept., with 63 licensees, close behind Disney's." *Variety,* February 7, 1940, p. 20.

Patrick, Corbin. "Indies warn against overuse of commercial plugs in features." *Variety,* July 24, 1946, p. 11.

"Patrons vote no on theater ads; FTC office orders a warning." *Advertising Age* 48 (November 21, 1977): 1.

"Planted commercial products not payola—a-la-TV if in features." *Variety,* October 19, 1960, p. 15.

"Play to foster thrift." *New York Times,* March 29, 1914, p. 37.

"Plots sneak in advertising." *Variety,* August 7, 1957, pp. 3, 22.

"The plug lobby." Time 57 (May 14, 1951): 110.

Plummer, Harry Chapin. "Stars sell cars." *Automotive Industries* 78 (January 29, 1938): 142–146+.

"The power of a plug." *Management Today,* February, 196, pp. 81–82.

Powers, Marsh K. "How far can commercial sponsorship be extended.?" *Printers' Ink* 155 (April 30, 1931): 49–50, 52.

Prince, Stephen. *History of the American Cinema: 10 A New Pot of Gold: Hollywood Under the Electronic Rainbow, 1980–1989.* New York: Scribner's Sons, 2000.

"Prod U.S. Justice to curb distribs war on pic ads." *Variety,* December 28, 1977, p. 4.

"Product payolas loading airwaves down; pluggers trip over each other." *Variety*, February 7, 1951, p. 1.

"Product placement." *New York Times*, December 16, 1992, p. D17.

"Product plug chiseling on web airers now a big payola operation." *Variety*, April 11, 1951, p. 1.

Pryor, Thomas M. "Blow, ye trade winds." *New York Times*, March 27, 1938, sec. 10, p. 4.

"Publicity versus advertising in the movies." *The Outlook* 128 (June 8, 1921): 234–235.

"Publix ad reels in minor spots first, loophole in Hays ban on screen plugs." *Variety*, September 20, 1932, pp. 12, 44.

"Publix in with commercial film for revenue with own trailers." *Variety*, May 7, 1930, p. 35.

"Rank plans utilizing his pictures to push British industrial goods." *Variety*, March 27, 1946, p. 4.

Ratcliffe, Frank. "Brit survey sez blurbs more effective in cinema than on TV." *Variety*, August 11, 1982, pp. 41–42.

"Reebok settles movie dispute." *New York Times*, October 6, 1997, p. D2.

Reed, J. D. "Plugging away in Hollywood." *Time* 133 (January 2, 1989): 103.

"Refunding on comm. shorts." *Variety*, June 9, 1931, p. 7.

"RKO-Pathe's Ullman decries idea of ad-pix spreading into theatres." *Variety*, April 9, 1947, pp. 7, 20.

Roberts, W. Adolphe. "Trade follow the film." *Dun's Review* 47 (February, 1939): 20–22, 46–47.

"Rocky Mountain indies in meeting condemn double features, etc." *Variety*, May 20, 1931, p. 29.

Rosenthal, Edmond M. "Paid props enter CPM era." *Television/Radio Age* 37 (October 2, 1989): 42–44.

"Rothenberg, Randall. "Critics seek F.T.C. action on products as movie stars." *New York Times*, May 3, 1991, pp. D1, D5.

Rothman, Clifford. "Hollywood's up in smoke." *The Province* (Vancouver), August 27, 1997, p. B7.

Rottersman, Michael. "Close-up: cinema advertising." *Boxoffice* 123 (November, 1987): 14–15.

"Royal Crown opens biggest movie tie-up, featuring Bing Crosby." *Printers' Ink* 214 (January 25, 1946): 124.

"Ruthless people." *The Economist* 315 (April 21, 1990): 72.

Rutter, Joyce. "At the movies." *Advertising Age* 59 (June 6, 1988): C15, C41.

Schudson, Michael. *Advertising, the Uneasy Persuasion*. New York: Basic, 1984.

"Scorecard." *Sports Illustrated* 86 (February 24, 1997): 25.

"Screen ads are satisfying to Publix." *Variety*, February 11, 1931, p. 11.

"Screen ads as life saver." *Variety*, February 28, 1933, p. 7.

"Screen ads returning with 2,600 secondary houses now listed." *Variety*, July 4, 1933, p. 4.

"Screen advertising." *Variety*, August 22, 1919, p. 82.

"Screen advertising going to showdown." *Variety*, April 1, 1931, p. 4.

"Screen advertising occupying attention of industry's solons: general protection of industry." *Variety*, February 25, 1931, p. 7.

"Screen players bally a brewery." *Variety*, August 14, 1940, p. 2.

"Script doctor." *Printers' Ink* 269 (November 6, 1959): 31.

"Seats' backs for ads in theatres." *Variety*, January 23, 1929, p. 1.

"See commercial advertising as vast amusement income source apply radio idea to theatre." *Variety*, May 28, 1930, pp. 2, 33.

"See time buys on comm'l films." *Variety*, January 2, 1946, pp. 3, 28.

Selby, Holly. "A double sell job; bonded brands." *The Edmonton Journal,* December 18, 1997, p. C1.

"Selling—with sound effects." *Business Week,* October 26, 1929, p. 37.

"Set up 20th–Fox licensing corp; further evidence of film distribs esteem for commercial by-products." *Variety,* June 15, 1966, pp. 3, 22.

"7 national ads in one talker." *Variety,* February 11, 1931, p. 7.

"Sex, lies and commercials." *New York Times,* August 26, 1989, p. 22.

Shabecoff, Philip. "Advertising: messages on the movie screen." *New York Times,* September 3, 1961, sec. 3, p. 10.

Sheinfeld, Lois. "Dangerous liaisons." *Film Comment* 25 (September/October, 1989): 70–72.

"Shoes advertised in movies." *New York Times,* October 13, 1913, p. 13.

"Showdown seen between major film companies and sponsored pictures." *Variety,* April 27, 1938, p. 6.

Silberg, Jon. "When screens become billboards." *American Film* 14 (May, 1989): 12.

"Sinatra, Lewis in tie-in derby." *Advertising Age* 34 (August 19, 1963): 3.

"Sindlinger test hints public reacts better to screen ads because of video conditioning." *Variety,* March 2, 1955, pp. 5, 70.

"Six advertising talkies get talked about." *Printers' Ink* 154 (March 26, 1931): 75.

"16 mm pix ramifications running deep with dept. store circuit latest quirk." *Variety,* November 28, 1945, pp. 3, 17.

Skenazy, Lenore. "Brand names star in *Mac & Me.*" *Advertising Age* 59 (September 5, 1988): 58.

Sloane, Leonard. "The subtle sell." *New York Times,* April 25, 1971, sec. 3, pp. 1, 13.

Smith, Bob. "Casting product for special effect." *Beverage World* 104 (March, 1985): 83, 91.

"S. O. free shows called off; theatres to assume salaries." *Variety,* December 11, 1934, pp. 1–2.

Spillman, Susan. "Marketers race to leave their brand on films." *Advertising Age* 56 (July 1, 1985): 3, 55.

"Sponsors shy away from plug pix, blame TV, COMPO's downbeat note." *Variety,* July 22, 1953, p. 5.

"Stahlman urges free press fight." *New York Times,* April 27, 1938, p. 21.

Staiger, Janet. "Announcing wares, winning patrons, voicing ideals: Thinking about the history and theory of film advertising." *Cinema Journal* 29 (no. 3, Spring, 1990): 3, 31.

"Stars' ad coin walloping Hays ban." *Variety,* January 19, 1932, p. 3.

"Start of comm'l sell sports on screen." *Variety,* November 16, 1977, p. 29.

Stevenson, Richard W. "Ad phobia at movies easing up." *New York Times,* September 17, 1986, p. D18.

"Studio gold rush tie-up." *Variety,* May 29, 1935, p. 3.

"Studios on coast receive newspaper blasts." *Variety,* June 9, 1931, p. 5.

"The subliminal fights gets hotter." *Printers' Ink* 261 (October 4, 1957): 17.

"Talkies adopt radio methods in new sponsored programs." *Business Week,* July 30, 1930, p. 8.

"Talkies to aid sales." *New York Times,* May 28, 1931, p. 30.

Tanaka, Jennifer. "The Apples of their eyes." *Newsweek* 132 (November 30, 1998): 58.

Teilhet, Darwin. "Propaganda stealing the movies." *Outlook and Independent* 158 (May 27, 1931): 112–113+.

"Telecast's news-and-commercials new ad-screen wrinkle on B'way." *Variety,* October 17, 1945, pp. 1, 50.

"Tests set for ads in 1,000 film theaters." *Advertising Age* 48 (October 10, 1977): 1, 112.

"Theater-screen ad business holds own as TV educates viewers to accept ads." *Advertising Age* 29 (July 7, 1958): 74.

"Theatre drops booing suit." *New York Times*, September 3, 1937, p. 13.

Tichenor, Frank A. "Motion pictures as trade getters." *Annals of the American Academy of Political and Social Science* 128 (November, 1926): 84–93.

"Tiring of advertising tie-up screen stars and studios refuse commercial offers." *Variety*, November 14, 1928, p. 4.

"Tonight at the movies: the latest national ads." *Business Week*, October 24, 1977, p. 39.

"Trailer with a hitch." *American Film* 8 (April, 1983): 13–14.

"2 new advantageous tie-ups as exploitation for films, theatres, stores and Publix." *Variety*, August 7, 1929, p. 189.

"UA chain signs under protest on share-of-screen-ads coin." *Variety*, January 18, 1978, p. 30.

"U.K. screen time nearly booked up." *Variety*, April 13, 1988, p. 38.

"Valenti dismisses beef about products in pics." *Variety*, October 30, 1985, pp. 5, 35.

Walker, S. H. and Paul Sklar. "Business finds its voice." *Harper's Monthly Magazine* 176 (February, 1938): 317–329.

Wardell, Dwight L. "The business movie industry." *Dun's Review* 49 (October, 1941): 24–30.

"WB re on-screen ads: strict if a big pic, indulgent if routine." *Variety*, January 25, 1978, p. 5.

Wharton, Dennis, and Jennifer Pendleton. "D.C. group brands product placement as plugola." *Variety*, June 3, 1991, p. 18.

"Wide-screen selling." *Business Week*, March 6, 1954, pp. 110–111.

"You can sell almost anything but politics or religion via pix—Zanuck." *Variety*, March 20, 1946, pp. 3, 26.

# Index